A Programmed Course in

Anxiety Reduction and Courage Skills

Reducing Obsessions, Compulsions, Aversions, and Fears

Joseph M. Strayhorn, Jr., M.D.

Psychological Skills Press

Wexford, Pennsylvania

Published by Psychological Skills Press
www.psyskills.com

Author's email: joestrayhorn@gmail.com

ISBN: 978-1-931773-16-4

Cover art was drawn by Jillian Strayhorn around 2005.
(The words "Don't hunt us" are hidden in the markings of the larger duck on the front cover.)

Table of Contents

Chapter 1: Understanding Fears and Aversions, Part 1

1. This is a book about reducing fears and aversions. What do we mean by these words?

Most people know what the word fear means. It's the same as being frightened, scared, or anxious. It's almost the same as being worried. When we're scared, we tend to think things like "I'm in danger; I've got to protect myself!"

Sometimes people feel scared without knowing exactly what they're afraid of. This has been called "free-floating anxiety." But for most of us, there are certain situations that make us scared. And usually there are certain bad things that we think might happen in those situations. Those bad things are called the feared outcomes.

What's one of the ideas stated in this section?

A. Fear is connected with the thought of being in danger and needing to protect yourself,

Or

B. Learning relaxation is an important way to reduce unrealistic fear?

2. What is an aversion? It's like a fear, but an aversion can involve any bad feeling, not just fear. For example, someone has an aversion to a certain food. When he thinks of this food, he doesn't really feel scared, but rather disgusted. Or someone else might have an aversion to doing math. The idea of doing math doesn't make the person feel scared, but more frustrated and confused. Someone else has a strong aversion to criticism. The criticism tends to make the person feel angry rather than scared. An aversion is an association between a certain situation and a bad feeling.

The main idea of this section is that

A. We work to reduce aversions in the same ways we work to reduce fears, or

B. Aversions are like fears, only they can involve any bad feeling, not just fear?

3. The first step in dealing with fears and aversions is to figure out which ones we want to reduce, and which we want to hang onto. Some fears and aversions make us better off, and some make us worse off. We want to choose

carefully whether we would be better off with or without the fear or aversion.

A main point of this section is that

A. An example of an aversion is someone who hates doing homework, or
B. some fears or aversions are harmful, and some are useful, and it's important to tell the difference between the two?

The daily courage skills workout

4. Much of this book will be concerned with how we can reduce fears and aversions, when we want to. If we want to reduce fears and aversions, there are very good ways of doing this. Many researchers have studied how to reduce fears and aversions, and thousands of people have succeeded in making their lives much better by reducing these bad feelings.
    The best ways of reducing fears and aversions involve learning. They involve practicing certain things over and over, just as if you were learning math or learning to play a musical instrument.

One idea of this section is that

A. People really can learn to reduce fears and aversions, if they are willing to work and practice at it, or
B. Aversions are sometimes helpful, in reminding us to avoid situations we should avoid?

5. If you want to stay in very good physical condition, you have to keep exercising, pretty close to every day, for the rest of your life. That's not bad news, if you enjoy exercising!
    For people with very unpleasant anxiety symptoms or aversions, what if you could keep them from bothering you by doing a "workout" every day? And what if the courage skills workout involved some fairly pleasant things to do in your mind: imagining yourself handling situations well, consciously presenting other images to your mind, relaxing your body, perhaps doing some breathing training exercises, and getting exercise in the usual sense of moving your body? A few minutes of conscious practice each day in courage skills can make a vast difference in the quality of the remainder of life's moments!

In this section the main idea is that

A. it's important not to give in to self-pity or to let others pity you too much, even though that can be pleasant,
or
B. a few minutes of doing a "courage skills workout" each day, throughout your life, can make the rest of life much more pleasant?

6. It may be possible to get away with less than daily practice in courage skills. But, it may not. As you read this book, you will learn various techniques that can be practiced in a few minutes. My advice is to decide upon a practice routine for yourself, and to do it daily, whether or not you are feeling that you "need" it.

A great pianist, Paderewski, spoke about practicing the piano. He said, "If I miss one day of practice, I notice it. If I miss two days, the critics notice it. And if I miss three days, the audience notices it."

Most people who fail at reducing their anxiety or aversions do so because they do not know how to do a daily courage skills workout. Of those who do find out how to do so, most fail because they do not practice anywhere close to daily.

As you read this book, you will learn more and more about what to include in your daily workout; if you then have the self-discipline to actually do the daily workout, I feel very confident that you will benefit greatly.

The great pianist, Paderewski, felt that

A. it was best to take a few days off every now and then to keep from being burned out,
or
B. he needed to practice every day if he wanted to perform best?

Fear can be very useful

7. Is it a good idea to get rid of all fear? Not at all: fear is often a very useful emotion. Why is it useful? Because it makes us want to protect ourselves from danger.

Here's an example. Jack was hiking in the woods with some friends. They came to a huge gorge. There was a very flimsy, old, rickety rope bridge going across this gorge. If the bridge were to break, whoever was on it would probably fall a long way, to his death. One of Jack's friends said, "Hey Jack, let's see how much guts you have. I dare you to go across that bridge."

Jack looked at the bridge carefully. He saw that the rope was very frayed and rotten. He saw the rocks far down below. When he thought of walking across this rope bridge, he felt scared. He said to his friend, "No way. And don't even think about going across that bridge yourself."

This section gave an example wherein fear was

A. very useful, because it kept the person from a real danger,
or
B. something the person should be ashamed of?

8. Here's another example. Lisa is walking in the street. She hears and sees a truck coming her way, really fast. She is so scared that she runs and jumps off the road very fast, just before the truck whizzes past her.

 Her fear not only gave her the wish to protect herself. It also caused her body to get a lot of energy very quickly. Her body released, very quickly, the chemicals that helped her to run quickly.

One of the ideas in this section is that

A. Fear can be very harmful when it makes us avoid things that are good for us,
or
B. fear not only makes us want to avoid danger; it also can give us lots of energy to use in protecting ourselves?

Unrealistic or useless fear

9. But sometimes we have fear when we are not in danger, or in very little danger. We call this type of fear unrealistic or useless.

 For example, someone has studied for a science test very much. Still, when he goes in to take the test, he is so scared that he can hardly think. He does lots worse on the test than he would have, if he had been able to calm down. In this case the fear did not protect him from something dangerous. It got in the way of his doing something he wanted to do.

This section gave an example of a(n)

A. useful fear,
or
B. useless fear?

10. Here are some more examples of situations where unrealistic fears can get in the way:
 A man is very much afraid of giving speeches.
 A boy is afraid of all dogs, even little ones who have never bitten anyone.
 A woman is afraid to invite other people to get together with her.
 A girl is afraid of sleeping in her room by herself.

A teenager is afraid to go to school because he fears that he will throw up, or that someone else will throw up.

A woman is afraid to ride elevators.

A teenager is afraid of meeting and talking with new people.

These are all situations where you might expect that the person would

A. want the fear to stay the way it is, because it protects from danger,
or
B. want the fear to get less than it is, because it gets in the way of happy living?

11. Sometimes what people are afraid of is not as concrete or visible as a fear of snakes or a fear of driving a car or a fear of being in high places. Sometimes people are afraid of situations that people get into with each other. For example, a young woman gets into a relationship with a man. She finds herself getting more and more scared as she gets to know him better. She finally realizes that what she is afraid of is being left and rejected: that he will leave her and that she will feel heartbroken.

This is an example of a fear where

A. it was easy for anybody to see what the person was afraid of,
or
B. the person had to do some thinking, to figure out what she was afraid of?

12. Aversions can be useful or useless also. Suppose someone is on a camping trip, and he takes a taste of a wild plant. It tastes terrible, and he spits it out. Later he finds out that this plant would have been poisonous to him if he had eaten it.

The aversion that the person had to the taste of the plant was

A. useless,
or
B. useful, because it protected him from real danger?

13. Someone else has an aversion to hearing people's fingertips or fingernails rubbing against paper. It's not a fear, exactly, but just a very unpleasant feeling, the type that some people also get when they scrape their nails against a chalkboard. Suppose that this person's aversion to hearing fingers rub against paper is so strong that he has a very hard time getting his work done and paying attention at school.

This aversion is

A. useful, because it protects against a real danger,

or

B. useless, because even though there is no danger, the bad feelings cause lots of discomfort?

14. To sum up: when you deal with fears and aversions, a first step is to figure out whether the fear or aversion is useful or useless.

     This often isn't as easy as it seems. It's seldom that there is absolutely zero danger. What's more often true is that we have fear or an aversion that is too large for the danger. For example: someone has a huge aversion to needles and getting shots. In this situation there certainly is the danger of physical pain. It's just that the pain is not so bad that it's worthwhile to feel terrified; the fear makes getting stuck a lot more unpleasant than it should be.

The point made here is that

A. you don't have to have absolutely no danger for a fear or aversion to be useless,

or

B. nightmares often bother people who have lots of fears?

15. Here's another example. Someone is totally afraid to fly on airplanes. The person realizes that there is a certain chance that the plane will crash, and that's danger. However, it's very unlikely that the plane will crash. The fear is too large in proportion to the danger, and the person would be better off without the fear.

This section gave an example where

A. the fear was useless because there was absolutely zero danger,

or

B. the fear was useless because the person would be better off without it?

16. Sometimes a high level of fear is useless even when the danger is severe. Imagine a pilot whose plane is plunging downward. The pilot realizes that he and his passengers are in great danger. But he purposely turns down his fear level so that he can stay cool enough to figure out what to do. He thinks calmly, and figures out how to pull his plane out of its nose dive, giving a happy ending to our story. If he had wasted his time screaming, trembling, crying, and acting out great fear, the story would not have ended so happily! The moral of the story is that sometimes fear is useless even when it is very realistic and the danger is very great. The question you will want to ask yourself is: "How much fear or aversion will most help me handle this situation the best I can?" If the fear or aversion interferes with

handling the situation well, you'll want to turn it down.

The main point of this section is that

A. figuring out how much danger you are in helps you decide whether a fear is useful or useless,
or
B. sometimes fear is useless even when you are in very great danger?

Physical danger, economic danger, social danger, and danger of failure

17. When we are figuring out whether a fear is useful or useless, and whether or not we are really in danger, it's good to think about four types of danger. These are based on four types of things that people need.

First, we need to have our physical health and safety. We need not to be hurt; we need to be warm enough but not too hot; we need air; we need not to have things hit or cut our bodies. We need not to be shot or otherwise hurt by other people. Things that threaten to hurt us cause physical danger.

When a person is realistically scared to climb a steep cliff, the person is probably worried about

A. economic danger,

or
B. physical danger?

18. The second type of need is to own certain things that money can buy. We have to have food and water, shelter from the weather, and clothing. We often need medical care. And there are many other things that we like to have, that we can buy with money, even if they are not absolutely necessary. Situations where we stand to lose a lot of money put us in economic danger.

Someone is at a casino, and he gets the urge to bet almost all his money in a gambling game. He feels great fear. This fear is useful, for he is in danger.

What kind of danger is this person in?

A. economic danger,
or
B. social danger?

19. A third type of need is to have friends, to be liked, to be accepted, to feel a sense of belonging to a group. This need appears to be strongly built into almost all people's brains. Situations where we might be rejected, lose friends, or lose our reputations are called social danger.

A person goes to a party, but fears that when she speaks to people, the people will think she's stupid or awkward and won't like her.

The danger that makes her scared is

A. physical danger,
or
B. social danger?

20. Once we are physically safe, have our economic needs secure, and have a secure group of friends, we form all sorts of other goals; some are minor, and some are major. Someone plays a chess game against the computer, and he wants to win; he feels nervous when he discovers that one of his main pieces is threatened. Or, someone forms a goal of successfully teaching a student to read; the person feels nervous when it looks as though the student might get so demoralized as to give up. Someone wants his children to be good people, and feels afraid that people might lead them into bad habits.

Someone is trying to help the managers of a company get along with the workers. When the workers and the managers get so mad that they will no longer speak to each other, the person feels nervous.

The person feels nervous because he is in

A. physical danger
or
B. danger of failure?

21. Here's something interesting about how our brains work: people often feel just as great fear from the danger of failure when the goal is very minor, as when the goal is very important. For example, someone goes dancing with people whom the person doesn't know and likely will not see again. But the person has the goal of dancing well, and feels great anxiety about failing at this goal. Meanwhile, the person does not have a job. He is spending his savings every day. The goal of keeping in good economic health doesn't cause such a great feeling of fear in this person.

The fear of failure evolved so as to motivate us to work to succeed. It's good to thoughtfully decide, "What are the most important goals?" and "What do I do to increase my chances of succeeding at them?" When we have really good answers to these questions, we can work on the things that are really important. We will need less fear of failure, because we are more likely to use our efforts well.

One of the points made by this section is that

A. sometimes we feel great fear from the danger of failure, even when the goal is unimportant,
or

B. sometimes people avoid the danger of failure by not setting goals, but this strategy comes with a great price?

22. We can be in more than one type of danger at once. For example, a doctor is doing an operation. The patient's condition gets lots worse. The doctor senses three dangers: he may not achieve his goal of helping the person; his reputation may suffer; and he may get sued and lose most of his money.

The doctor is aware of

A. social danger, economic danger, and danger of failure,
or
B. physical danger, moral danger, and lateral danger?

23. Why is it good to be aware of the different types of danger? Because whenever we feel scared, or whenever we feel an aversion, it's good to be able to figure out exactly how much danger we're in. If we think of these four types of danger, we can often think more clearly about what the dangers are and are not.

The point of this section is that

A. physical danger usually takes priority over the danger of failure,
or

B. thinking systematically about the different types of danger helps us figure out more clearly how much danger we are in?

Probability, and utility: how likely it is, and how good or bad it is

24. When we are figuring out how dangerous a situation is, and how realistic or unrealistic a fear is, two words are very helpful to use: probability and utility. Probability is the answer to the question, "How likely is it that something will happen?" If the probability is 100%, that means that the thing is sure to happen. If the probability is 0%, that means that the thing is sure not to happen. If the probability is 50%, that means the thing has the same chance of happening as heads' coming up when you flip a coin. If the probability is 10%, that means the thing has the same chance of happening as drawing a red poker chip out of a box that has 1 red chip and 9 white chips – it means it would happen about 10 out of every 100 trials.

The main purpose of this section is

A. to tell what is meant by probability,
or
B. to tell what is mean by utility?

25. The utility of something is how good or bad it is. We use the word "disutility" to mean how bad something is. If I should accidentally set off a bunch of bombs that destroy the whole earth and every living thing on it, that would be bad about 100 on a scale of 100 – it would have a disutility rating of 100. If my mailbox comes loose from its post, which means that I have to spend half an hour fixing it, that's bad maybe 3 on a scale of 100. If I lose all the money I have, but my family members and I remain in good health, that's bad maybe 50 on a scale of 100. And so forth. Different people will have different ratings for how bad different events are.

The main purpose of this section is

A. to explain and give examples of what disutility is,
or
B. to show a foolproof way of figuring out exactly how bad something is?

26. When people have unrealistic fears, sometimes the probabilities or disutilities that they estimate are very high. For example: someone is about to take an airplane trip and is very scared that the plane will crash. When someone asks, "How likely do you think it is that the plane will crash," the person says, "About 50%." This means that the person thinks it's just as likely that the plane will crash, as that it won't crash. But how realistic is this probability? Thousands of planes have already taken off and landed in just the last few days, and not one of those has crashed. If the chances were really 50%, half the planes that took off would have crashed.

This section illustrates the sort of reasoning one uses to conclude that

A. the probability that a bad thing would happen is actually much lower than the person first thought,
or
B. the disutility of a certain bad thing is actually much lower than the person first thought it was?

27. At other times, people overestimate how bad something is: they guess too high on the disutility. For example, someone is afraid of going for a job interview, because he is afraid the interviewer won't like him, and he won't get the job. His friend asks, "And if that does happen, how bad would it be?" The person replies that it would be 90 on a scale of 100 bad.

"Really?" his friend replies. "Lots of people go for lots of interviews before they get offered a job. You'd get practice for the next interview. You wouldn't get the job, but you'd be no worse off than if you hadn't gone for the interview."

The friend is trying to convince the person that

A. the probability of not getting offered a job is not very high,
or
B. the disutility of not getting offered the job is not very high?

28. Figuring out probabilities and disutilities of bad outcomes helps us realize whether our fear is unrealistic or realistic. If our gut feeling about the probability or disutility of something bad is much higher than the evidence can support, our fear or aversion is probably unrealistic.

But thinking about probabilities and utilities sometimes does something else even more important. Sometimes this type of thought helps us to reduce unrealistic fears. Just lowering our probability or disutility estimates can sometimes help us realize that we're in lots less danger than we thought we were, and that can reduce our fear.

One point of this section is that

A. When we think about the evidence for probabilities and disutilities, that can help us to lower unrealistic fears and aversions,

or
B. fear is something that we do with our brains and the rest of our bodies?

Some of the problems people can solve with the methods taught by this book

29. The simplest sort of problem that people solve by using methods to get over unrealistic fears is called a phobia. The person feels terrified when in a certain situation: on elevators, near flying insects, crossing bridges, in airplanes, in a car, when lying in bed at night alone, when trying to go to school, and so forth. Or, the person feels terrified that an imagined outcome may occur: perhaps I'll get cancer, perhaps I'll throw up in front of people, and perhaps I'll fail a test. It's no secret why phobias are a problem: fearfulness is no fun. There's a second reason why phobias are a problem: they often cause us to avoid doing things we would be better off doing. For example, someone avoids public speaking because of a phobia, and loses out on many job opportunities for that reason.

One of the points made by this section is that

A. phobias cause problems because of unpleasantness and avoidance,
or
B. people can sometimes have fear without realizing what they're afraid of?

30. Other very common fears have different names, but they are still fears of certain types of situations or imagined situations. For example, the fear of being separated from a loved one or caretaker is called separation anxiety; the fear of being embarrassed in front of others is called social anxiety; fear of leaving home and going to certain places (for example, a crowded store) is called agoraphobia; fear of getting a serious or fatal illness is called hypochondriasis; and so forth. People tend to make up big words for fears that people come up with.

A major point of this section is that

A. There are lots of different labels for problems that are basically fears of certain sorts of situations,
or
B. fear of heights is called acrophobia?

31. Having great fear of being fat (and to avoid this, making oneself far too thin) is called anorexia nervosa. Unrealistically fearing that other people are plotting against you or out to get you is called paranoia. (Realistically fearing that people are out to get you is called normal life for far too many people in our world!) Having a huge fear that one looks ugly is called body dysmorphic disorder. When people have experienced something really horrible, they often have a great aversion to their own memories of what took place. This is called acute stress disorder or posttraumatic stress disorder. The methods described in this book can help with all these fears and aversions.

The purpose of this section is to

A. introduce a theory of how fears get started,
or
B. give more examples of problems that fear-reduction methods can help solve?

32. When we have unrealistic fears, usually there's at least a little bit of real danger. Often what unrealistic fears do is not to imagine danger when there is absolutely none, but to take a small danger and imagine it to be huge.

For example, whenever you touch something or someone, there's a small danger of picking up germs. Doctors in hospitals are taught to wash their hands often, to avoid spreading germs. Some people let the fear of getting germs on their hands interfere way too much with their lives, by feeling compelled to wash their hands over and over, dozens of times each day. We use the word "compulsion" to describe repeated behaviors like this.

The main point of this section is that

A. some people wash their hands too much,
or
B. when we have unrealistic fears, often there's at least a little bit of real danger that is being blown out of proportion?

33. Sometimes what we fear is not a situation outside us, but our own thoughts and urges. For example, a young mother gets the image in her mind of harming her own baby. This thought seems so scary, forbidden, and immoral to her that she tries very hard to get it out of her mind immediately. But trying very hard not to think it only tends to make it come back to mind more frequently. A thought like this that keeps coming back to mind, even though we wish it wouldn't, is called an obsession.

This section had to do with

A. the fear of our own thoughts,
or

B. the fear that other people will do bad things to us?

34. Sometimes aversions can seem to come out of nowhere for no particular reason. For example, a girl develops an aversion to drinking water out of a certain type of glass. Or a boy finds it very unpleasant to wear certain items of clothing. Or someone feels very upset if his socks are not pulled up to the same height. Or someone feels a great aversion to the objects on a desk not being lined up just right. Or suddenly someone fears that he may utter curse words at very inappropriate times. Or someone suddenly begins to fear throwing up or that other people will throw up.

This section gives examples of

A. fears that have very clear-cut reasons for starting up,
or
B. fears that seem to come out of nowhere?

35. Many therapists used to believe that the most important strategy with fears was to find out why they arose, to understand where they came from. Many people with fears feel that it is necessary to understand why the fear began, in order to reduce it.

However, it is very lucky that we have very good and effective ways of reducing fears that do NOT depend upon a full understanding of why the fear arose. This is lucky, because sometimes no matter how much we probe and talk and think, we can't figure out why one person would get a certain fear and another person would not. Often the best explanation we can come up with is that some people are born with brains that are much more disposed to develop fears than others!

The point made by this section is that

A. it's very helpful to understand how fears got started, when you are trying to get over them,
or
B. fears fortunately can be reduced even if we never understand why they got started?

36. Sometimes, though, it is very helpful to do lots of thinking to figure out just what you are afraid of and what you are avoiding.
      For example: a child finds that he has a mounting sense of tension and anxiety when he is called upon to do group learning activities with other kids at school. At first he can't understand why he gets this feeling. But when he talks and thinks about the situation enough, he figures out that he is really afraid of losing in a competition. He imagines that the people in the group are competing

with each other to see who can do the best job. The idea of his not coming out on top produces painful feelings. By learning to reduce those aversions, he learns to relax and cooperate in group activities.

The purpose of this section was to

A. convince the reader that people can get over fears,
or
B. give an example of a situation where someone had to think to figure out exactly what he was afraid of?

37. Lots of times people aren't even aware what they are afraid of, when they fear a certain abstract type of interpersonal situation. Here's an example where the person fears sticking up for his own way, which is called assertion or assertiveness.
      One boy goes over to another boy's house to play. They are doing an activity that the first boy doesn't enjoy at all. But that boy is afraid to say, "Let's do something else." for fear that the friend will not like him or disapprove of him or feel upset. Because he is afraid of sticking up for his own way, he doesn't have as much fun, and it turns out the friend doesn't have as much fun either. But when he learns to get rid of this aversion and tell people what he wants and what he doesn't want, he ends up having lots

more fun with people and they have more fun with him.

The type of interpersonal situation the person was afraid of in this story was

A. the situation where it's good to stick up for your own way or use assertion skills,
or
B. the sort of situation where it's good to get help from someone and depend on someone?

38. Here's another example of an interpersonal situation that someone can be afraid of.

A person values being tough, strong, and self-reliant. It turns out that things go wrong in the person's life, and much unhappiness comes to the person. The person could really use a lot of support from someone else, and could use someone to talk to in figuring out how to make his life happier. But the very idea of asking someone for help or talking to someone about his problems makes this person feel guilty, ashamed, and scared. Things get so bad that the person has a big tantrum and breaks expensive things. The result is that other people insist on his getting some help. People who can't get help sometimes act out the need for help by doing something that makes other people say "You need help."

The person in this example had a strong aversion to

A. being alone,
or
B. getting help?

39. Here's yet another example of someone's having a fear without realizing exactly what she is afraid of. A young woman has to write a long article to get a degree in school. But she finds that she is blocked – she just can't get her work done on this article. She doesn't complain of fearing anything – she just complains of being unable to work.

When she thinks and talks about things a lot more, though, she figures out that she's very afraid of the disapproval that people might give her when they read what she's written. More importantly, she's also afraid of what she says to herself about what she writes. She's afraid she'll say to herself, "This is stupid. How can you be such a bad writer?" The fear of criticism from others and from herself has been stopping her.

Before doing lots of thinking and talking, the woman in this story didn't realize that

A. fear of criticism was the real key to her work block,

or

B. she wasn't working as much as she should?

40. Sometimes we are afraid of two things, and we have to choose between one and the other. This is very painful situation called conflict. For example, someone is at a party. He is very much afraid of simply standing or sitting by himself, without talking with somebody, because he thinks that people will look at him and brand him a social outcast. On the other hand, he feels quite nervous about approaching other people and saying something to them. He's afraid that he will say the wrong thing or come off as looking awkward. So no matter what he does, he feels very uncomfortable. The fear of talking with people and the fear of standing alone *conflict* with one another. By reducing both his fear of being alone and his fear of starting social conversations, he learns to enjoy social gatherings rather than to dread them.

The person in this example

A. feared getting help from other people,
or
B. feared both standing alone and having social conversations at parties?

41. Another person finds that she gets episodes in which she feels her heart pounding and her hands trembling and sweating. During these episodes she also feels great fear that something horrible will happen, such as that she will die. She also fears that she will not get enough air and suffocate. These episodes have been referred to as panic attacks. Some people with panic attacks fear going out into public, not wanting the embarrassment of having a panic attack around others.

Many people with panic attacks fear that they are about to die, and this of course makes the panic even worse. Yet there are ways of learning to handle panic attacks that can turn them from a horrible experience into a minor annoyance, or even get rid of them altogether! We will discuss these techniques later.

A panic attack consists of

A. sadness, crying spells, feeling no energy, feeling hopeless,
or
B. trembling, sweating, heart pounding, feeling scared, and feeling that you can't get enough breath?

42. Others of us are in the habit of worrying about the outcome of just about anything that hasn't already happened yet. There is a social event – maybe I'll be embarrassed. There is a

contest – maybe I'll lose in a humiliating way. Something depends on good weather – oh no, the weather may be bad. I have a good, close friend – what if I lose that friend? I have a short vacation – but the vacation will end. And so forth.

People who worry also about the future also tend to worry about the past. Did I say something that offended someone at the party I went to? Did everyone think bad things about me when I made a tiny mistake in my speech?

The habit of worrying about the past and the future is called generalized anxiety disorder. People can change these habits and come to enjoy what is going on now, learn from past mistakes, and make reasonable plans for the future.

This section told about the problem of

A. worrying too much,
or
B. avoiding work, because of an aversion to the work experience?

43. There are still more problems that good fear-reduction skills can help solve. Another one is nightmares. Here we are frightened by the scary images that pop into our minds while dreaming. People can learn to change their dreams, and to drastically reduce the frequency of nightmares.

One of the points made in this section was that

A. you can learn to change what goes on in your mind while you're sleeping,
or
B. dreams have been a source of fascination for fiction writers over a course of centuries?

44. Speaking of sleep: Many people approach the hour of going to bed with a feeling of dread, that they will not be able to get to sleep and that they will lie and toss and turn and worry. The fear of sleeplessness causes them not to be able to get to sleep. This and other fears contribute greatly to trouble sleeping, or insomnia, which is a very common problem. Using good fear-reduction skills can help people sleep much better.

The major point of this section is that

A. exposure to the scary situation is one of the most important ways people get over fears,
or
B. another big problem fears cause is trouble sleeping?

45. Another form of aversion is low frustration tolerance, or low fortitude skills. In this type of problem, the person seems to feel very great pain

whenever he fails to get what he wants. If he asks somebody for something and the answer is no, he has a tantrum rather than taking it in stride. If he loses a game, it feels like the end of the world. If someone doesn't seem to like him, that feels like a major tragedy. In this type of problem, the aversions that all of us seem to have to some degree get magnified to such proportions that they cause great unhappiness.

The task of the person with this type of problem is to reduce the aversion to frustration in general. Fortunately, we can learn fortitude skills.

The point made by this section is

A. another aversion problem is feeling too bad when we don't get whatever we want,
or
B. another aversion problem is getting into the habit of using alcohol or other drugs to reduce bad feelings?

46. Sometimes people with low frustration tolerance are also unable to tolerate other people's mistakes and failures. This aversion can produce anger control problems. When people have power over other people – for example when they are the bosses at workplaces – sometimes they become extremely upset and lash out angrily when someone else does something imperfectly. Much unhappiness is caused by powerful people who have aversions to any mistakes made by the people under them. People can reduce their aversion to other people's mistakes, using methods very similar to those someone uses in getting over a fear of elevators.

This section has to do with

A. the aversion some people have to other people's mistakes or failures, or
B. the aversion some people have to their own mistakes and failures?

47. The list of problems that good fear-reduction and aversion-reduction skills can help continues!

Now we can add to the list bunches of things that people do to try to reduce the pain they feel from fears and aversions. Using drugs to try to reduce pain is an extremely common strategy. Alcohol is the number one drug used for this purpose. The narcotic drugs, such as heroin, morphine, or oxycodone are pain-killers that addict lots of people.

People can make themselves less likely to get addictions -- and more likely to get over them if they have them—by learning good aversion-reduction techniques to help themselves enjoy life more.

The problems that were discussed in this section

A. are fears or aversions,
or
B. are problems that come from the ways people try to escape the pain of fears and aversions?

48. When life is painful because of fears and aversions, sometimes people use overeating as a way of getting some pleasure. And overcoming aversions to exercise, using the methods this book details, can aid greatly in weight control. Also, if one can reduce the aversion to the deprived feeling that comes from stopping eating before being really full, weight control is much easier.

This section names

A. aversions, the reduction of which can help with weight control,
or
B. reasons why it is good to weigh not too much, not too little, but a just right amount?

49. Another way that people try to escape fears and aversions is to try to get other people to make sure that they never have to experience the situation they don't like. Someone with low frustration tolerance, for example, might become very bossy to try to get other people to do what he wants. This bossy and controlling behavior can cause someone to lose friends, and to find himself alone in the world. Reducing the aversion to frustration can result in much better relationships with people.

The point made by this section is that

A. fears and aversions can cause physical problems,
or
B. reducing aversions can help with the quality of relationships?

50. Good fear-reduction and aversion-reduction skills can also be very helpful for our bodies. Learning to reduce fears and aversions can help us get over headaches, stomachaches, and a wide variety of other physical problems. Our brains are highly connected to the rest of our bodies, and when our brains are feeling safe and secure, the rest of our bodies tend to do better.

The point of this section is that

A. reducing fears and aversions can prevent or relieve physical problems,
or
B. the process of reducing fears and aversions can result in higher work performance?

51. Another problem that aversion-reduction methods can help solve is depression. When someone suffers too much from fears or aversions, and especially when the person develops the thought of, "Things are bad and there's nothing I can do about it," sometimes the person gives up hope and feels helpless; this feeling has been called depression. One of the central ideas that cause depression is, "What's the point of trying? Nothing that I do will have any effect." But becoming expert at aversion-reduction techniques gives us a bunch of things to do that do have a good chance of making things better.

The point made by this section is that

A. fears and aversions are easy to reduce,
or
B. reducing fears and aversions helps people not to feel depressed?

52. The good news is that we can do something to reduce fears and aversions. It takes work, but if we are willing to work hard enough, we can almost certainly reduce our fears and aversions.

Research has gone on without ceasing for the last several decades on how to reduce fears and aversions. Very much useful information has accumulated. If you have fears and aversions that bother you, you do not need to re-invent the wheel! You can take advantage of the knowledge that other people have worked very hard to gather. We can be very hopeful that anybody willing to put in time and effort can learn how to reduce fears and aversions.

The author implies that

A. reducing fears and aversions is quick, easy, and effortless!
or
B. reducing fears and aversions is a lot of work, but very possible?

53. If you have fears or aversions that you need to reduce, you are most definitely not alone. Hundreds of millions of people on this planet have anxiety disorders. In a very big survey, anxiety disorders were the most common sort of psychological disorder found. But the task of reducing unrealistic or useless fears and aversions is not just for people with diagnosed anxiety disorders – it is a task that everyone grapples with! It is hard to imagine a person who cannot benefit from reducing at least some fears or aversions. As human beings, we are not born or manufactured with our emotional responses to situations rigged in exactly the way that is best for us. To

be human is to need to readjust our emotional responses to situations.

The point of this section is that

A. people who need to reduce fears and aversions form a small and isolated group,
or
B. almost every human being needs to reduce at least some fears and aversions?

54. Most people have conquered the fear of more situations than we can even remember. For example, someone was afraid to ride a bicycle at first, but then got used to it, and doesn't even remember the scary part. Or someone felt a yucky or scary feeling about a certain food, but then learned to like that food, and forgot the aversion that was there at first. Or someone was nervous about separating from a parent to go to school, but then started to feel safe, and forgot about how it felt at first.

The point the author is making is that

A. we all need to get over fears and aversions, even if we forget that we've done so,
or
B. the process of getting over fears and aversions is something that should be taught in school?

55. Some people who have problems with fears or aversions may develop an aversion to thinking about their own fears and aversions! For example, someone has anxiety about meeting new people and talking to new people. This is bad enough. But then the person develops a great sense of shame about the fact that she has more problems with this than other people do. She has developed an aversion to her own aversion!

Or for another example, someone feels scared of going to school because he is afraid of the disapproval he might get from not doing the work right. Then he starts feeling very resentful that he has to have been picked to have such a problem instead of someone else. He spends lots of time thinking, "Why did this have to happen to me?" He feels very resentful that fate has given him this problem to deal with, and that resentment leads him to act sullen with lots of people who are not to blame in the slightest! Again, he has developed an aversion to his own aversion.

The problem this section identifies is

A. getting rewarded by other people for having an aversion, when they take care of you "too well,"
or

B. getting an aversion to your own aversion?

56. For some people, the whole topic of anxiety and fear and aversions is one they would rather avoid altogether. The whole topic feels scary. But this avoidance keeps the problem from being solved.

One of the ways we learn to handle scary situations is by "prolonged exposure" to them: by dealing with them for long enough that we can get used to them. People who have an aversion to thinking about anxiety problems can sometimes do themselves a lot of good by "prolonged exposure" to thinking or reading about the subject of anxiety. One way to do that is to read this book! If you find yourself getting more and more comfortable thinking about the topic the more you do it, prolonged exposure is working!

What's a major point of this section?

A. Reading this book can overcome aversions to the topic of anxiety, by "prolonged exposure."
or
B. Being able to think of lots of options is very helpful when you are trying to solve a problem.

57. If you have any of the problems that come from too much fear or too much aversion, of course the best thing to do is to put as little energy as you can into feeling ashamed of or resentful about these problems. You'll need to put all the energy you can into working to improve things.

The purpose of this book is to tell you how to use your energy in the ways most likely to pay off for you.

The proverb that best paraphrases the message of this section is

A. "An ounce of prevention is worth a pound of cure,"
or
B. "It's better to light a candle than to curse the darkness?"

Chapter 2: How Fears and Aversions Are Created, Increased, and Sustained

Why do we get fears and aversions? part 1: genes

58. If fears and aversions cause so many problems, then why do so many people have so many of them? Why haven't people evolved, over centuries of natural selection, to be totally fearless, and to have no aversions?

The question this section poses is

A. Why do we have fears?
or
B. How do we get over fears?

59. The answer to why we evolved with fears and aversions built into our brains is that most of them are good for us! They help us stay alive. We usually pay little attention to the realistic fears that keep us alive. But, for example, suppose someone had absolutely no fear of heights. Suppose he found it fun to climb up high cliffs or tall trees and then try to fly like a bird. That person would not live long!

This section suggests that

A. fears and aversions come from something bad that parents do to children,
or
B. fears and aversions are built into our brains because most of them help us stay alive?

60. Researchers have experimented with infants who are just old enough to crawl. They have rigged up a floor called a "visual cliff": at a certain point, the floor is made out of glass, with another floor several feet below, so that it looks to the infant as if there is a cliff. Even when the infants have had no experience with crawling over cliffs and hurting themselves, they avoid crawling over the "visual cliff." The conclusion is that we don't have to learn a fear or aversion to going over cliffs – we are born that way!

The experiment described in this section concludes that

A. we're born with a fear of going over cliffs,
or

B. we have to learn to fear going over cliffs by trying it a few times and getting hurt?

61. There are lots more fears that are built into our brains because they help us survive. Or more accurately, we have the fears because they helped our ancestors survive. Why do so many people find snakes frightening? Our ancestors lived their lives around poisonous snakes for thousands of generations. Those with an instinct to avoid them (rather than go and pet them) were more likely to survive.

The best summary of this section is that

A. Not all snakes are poisonous, but enough of them are that it's good to avoid them,
or
B. We have many more fears built into our brains because at one time those fears helped in survival; the fear of snakes is an example.

62. Some of our inborn fears are not so concrete as the fear of snakes or of falling off cliffs. One of these is the fear of being disliked and rejected by other people.

Throughout history and prehistory, people who have had no aversion to having other people dislike them and exclude them have had a disadvantage when it has been necessary for people to band together and protect each other. In addition, those who are disliked and rejected have more trouble finding mates. So the wish to be liked, and the fear of being disliked, is to some degree built into the brains of almost all humans.

The main point of this section is that

A. Another built-in fear is the fear of being disliked,
or
B. People vary greatly, and some people have much more fear of being disliked than others do.

63. Many of our most troubling fears have had survival value at some point. Why do children so frequently fear sleeping in bedrooms by themselves? In a safe house, this fear does not help much with survival. But in a world filled with predators, such as the world our prehistoric ancestors lived in, those children who feared sleeping alone probably survived much more often than those who fearlessly wandered off and slept by themselves.

This section tries to explain

A. why plants that aren't good for us taste bad,
or

B. why children so often want to sleep with their parents?

64. We could go on for a good while in understanding how some of the fears that cause the most unnecessary suffering have been somewhat realistic at some point in human history. Why do young children fear separating from parents? Why are bees and spiders scary? Why do most plants that are not good for us taste terrible? Why is the sensation of vomiting so aversive? In each case, the answer is the same: to help with survival.

The best summary of this section is that

A. vomiting is very aversive,
or
B. lots of fears got built into the brain because of their survival value?

65. Why do people avoid painful medical procedures, such as getting shots, even sometimes when they can be life-saving? Because throughout human history, avoiding injury (and pain is the signal of injury) has been key to survival.

This section has most to do with

A. a person who has a phobia of getting blood drawn,

or
B. a person who has a fear of having someone else be more powerful than he is?

66. Another very common aversion (it usually isn't experienced as a fear) is aversion to doing work – also known as laziness. How could this possibly have survival value? Throughout human history, energy and labor have been scarce resources. Those people who have been lazy enough to figure out how to do something with less effort, have had more effort left over for other things. For example, those who learned how to train oxen to plow their fields probably enjoyed a higher yield of crops than those who did all the work themselves. Those who wanted to work purely for the sake of working, for example by moving big rocks from one place to another for no reason, probably used up their scarce energy that they could have used for their survival needs. Thus there is a certain survival advantage to finding the way to get by on the least amount of effort.

The point of this section is that

A. laziness is a big problem for human beings,
or

B. laziness probably exists to help people save their energy for what's most important for survival?

67. Of course, if people fail to put out any effort for anything, that's not good for survival either! So fortunately, our brains were built to want to do something, rather than to sit motionless. We weren't really built to be lazy in the sense of not doing anything. It's more accurate to say that people have evolved to want to save their energy for "the most important things" for survival. As any teacher can tell you, many people's brains appear not to have a built-in understanding of why reading, writing, or mathematics are important for survival. Overcoming "work-aversion," or laziness, often involves teaching our brains why a certain activity is important for our present-day survival, happiness, and well-being.

The point of this section is that

A. we are built not to be inactive, but to expend energy on the things we perceive as "most important,"
or
B. people with aversion to work usually benefit from "prolonged exposure" to work?

68. The main point of the last few sections is that fears and aversions are built into our genes. As is true with all inherited traits, some of us get more fears and aversions than other people get. Some people have more genes for fearfulness than others do. Some people from the very beginning of life tend to find disapproval and rejection much more unpleasant than other people do. How fearful or fearless you are partly depends on a process much like being dealt a random set of cards from a deck. You've been dealt a certain set of fear and aversion genes.

The point of this section is that

A. the exact location of fearfulness genes is not important for our purposes,
or
B. one reason some people are more fearful than others is that they simply have more fearfulness genes?

69. The fact that genes cause a lot of the variation in people's tendencies to fears and aversions does NOT mean that we're stuck with whatever fears and aversions we have! People can learn to be less fearful and to lower aversions.

Genes have a lot to do with how quickly and easily you can learn to do math, play piano, run a mile, dance, or play chess. But lots of work at learning any of these skills can often override genetic disadvantages that people might have started out with. The same is true with courage and fortitude skills.

The main point of this section is that

A. the fact that genes influence courage skills doesn't mean that you can't improve those skills by learning and working,
or
B. the fact that genes influence courage skills means there must be something physical in the brain that accounts for the differences between people?

70. If you happened to have gotten a lot of "carefulness genes" or "anxiety genes" or whatever we want to call them, should you envy the "born totally fearless" people? You shouldn't, because those people have even bigger problems! They tend to take risks without thinking. They tend to get themselves hurt more often and killed more often. They tend to suffer from their own impulsive acts, because there has not been a nagging fear that has told them, "Wait. Think before you do that. It could have bad consequences." These people can learn to use their heads to avoid taking unnecessary risks, just as people with

fears can learn to reduce their fears. Both have hard work to do.

This section tells us that

A. riding motorcycles is something that people with very low "carefulness genes" tend to do,
or
B. people with very low "carefulness genes" run into very big problems?

Why do we get fears and aversions? part 2: learning

71. Some people have more fears, not because they got more carefulness genes, but because they have had more experiences that have taught them to be fearful.

For example, a child is greatly afraid of dogs. We learn that when the child was a preschooler, a vicious dog attacked him and injured him severely. It's not hard to figure out that this person is afraid of dogs because his experience has taught him, "dogs are dangerous."

The point of this section is that

A. some fears come from experiences that teach us that something or other is dangerous,
or
B. sometimes social danger is just as scary as physical danger?

72. When a child has been attacked by one vicious dog, the fear often extends to all other dogs, most of which are not dangerous. But the brains of most of us are built on the assumption that "if one is dangerous, another in the same group is also dangerous." If one dog was very dangerous, the brain might guess that danger extends to all dogs, or maybe even all furry animals. When fears (or any other learned responses) spread to situations beyond the original one, the result is called *response generalization.*

This section explains why

A. people gradually reduce their fears when they are exposed for a long time to what they fear,
or
B. people have some bad experiences with one thing, and develop fears of many other things in the same group?

73. Response generalization often helps explain why some people fear trusting other people. They may be have been treated very badly by a close relative, as for example when a parent abuses a child. The child may then generalize the fear to other people with whom they might have a close relationship. The fear of getting close to other people is often a very confusing and difficult fear to deal with, much more harmful than the fear of heights or the fear of bees.

This section stated that

A. sometimes when people are treated badly by people they are close to, they come to fear closeness with all other people,
or
B. sometimes when people are stung by bees they come to fear all insects, including harmless ones?

74. Suppose we start with a child who finds science interesting. We put the child in a science class, and we give the child tests. This particular child is not good at recalling and giving back information, and the child gets back failing grade after failing grade on science tests, sometimes accompanied by disapproving comments. The school is repeatedly pairing a situation – doing science – with a consequence – being humiliated. The student gradually learns a large aversion to science.

This is the simple recipe whereby many fears and aversions are created. A situation occurs, and something very unpleasant follows. If this happens enough (and sometimes one time is enough), the situation starts to bring out very unpleasant emotions, as soon as the person sees it coming, before anything bad has even happened yet.

What's a summary of this section?

A. A simple recipe for creating fears and aversions is: repeatedly have a very unpleasant consequence follow a certain situation.
or
B. If you repeatedly sound a little tone, followed by a puff of air that leads people to blink their eyes, soon the tone starts to lead to the eyeblinks even without the puff of air.

75. People can learn that a certain situation is dangerous in ways other than by having something very unpleasant happen in that situation. One way is modeling. For example, when children saying good-by to a parent at a day care center see other children screaming and clinging to their parents, they may conclude that something dangerous is going on. Or when boys in a neighborhood avoid a certain house because they think it's haunted, they influence each other.

This section's point is that

A. learning to turn down your level of arousal helps you get over fears,
or
B. the models you see other people carrying out often teach you that a

certain situation is either dangerous or not?

76. Another major way that fears can be learned is by television, movies, and video games. If a child sees an image of another child being kidnapped while sleeping, or attacked by a monster while sleeping, one part of the brain may say, "it was just a story," but another part may more convincingly say, "I saw it, and seeing is believing." Going to sleep may suddenly seem to be a very dangerous activity.

This section tells us that

A. seeing scary movie images can create fears,
or
B. seeing images in movies of people being comfortable in certain situations can help us get over being scared of those situations?

77. People can also learn fears by getting instructions from other people about the danger of those things. For example: as Jack grows up, he constantly hears that the people of a different racial group who live in a nearby neighborhood are dangerous and that he should stay away from them. It's no surprise that Jack finds himself fearing people of this racial group.

The main point of this section is that

A. you shouldn't fear entire groups of people, because people are different within any group,
or
B. you can learn fears by having people tell you that certain things are dangerous?

How short exposures and escapes can increase fears and aversions

78. The word *exposure* is a very important one for our understanding fears. It means that you expose yourself to, or put yourself in, the situation that you fear, so that you can practice handling it. People get over fears of elevators by being in elevators; they get over aversions to work by doing work; and so forth.

Fantasy exposures, or imagining yourself in the scary situation, can also be effective.

Exposure to the situations one fears is one of the most necessary ingredients in getting over fears.

This section says that

A. getting into the scary situation, which is called exposure, is a very important way of getting over fears, or

B. exposure to scary situations takes so much self-discipline that lots of people fail at it?

79. If we are exposed to the same situation for a long enough time, we tend to "get used to it," or *habituate* to it. A funny scene in a movie may make you laugh out loud. But if you keep playing that scene over and over, the chances are that by the twentieth time you see it, it will no longer bring out the laughter it did at first. The same thing happens with fear and aversion. Habituation tends to occur in all animals, not just humans. Scientists have studied habituation even in a very small and simple sea animal: if you poke it with the end of a hair, it withdraws. But if you keep poking it, it "gets used to" the poking and after a while stops reacting to the touch of the hair. This principle of habituation is very important in learning to get over fears. By exposing yourself to the scary situation long enough, you have a chance to get used to it.

The purpose of this section was to

A. define the word *habituation*, and give some examples of how exposure leads to habituation, or
B. explain what happens in brain cells that allows habituation to take place?

80. But if pure exposure gets people over fears, why doesn't everybody get over every fear, automatically? If someone feels fear or aversion enough to complain about it, that person must be exposed to the scary situation fairly often, at least in fantasy. As the total time of exposure increases, why doesn't the fear just go away?

The question this section poses is

A. How, exactly, does exposure reduce fear?
or
B. If exposure reduces fear, why don't we gradually get over any fear that we often experience?

81. The answer to this question is that not all exposures reduce fear. In fact, some of them actually increase fear!

Let's imagine that a young child is taken to a preschool for the first time. As the parent starts to leave, the child screams, cries, and clings to her parent. After a few minutes of this, the parent decides to give up; the parent says, "OK, let's go home." The child, realizing that she won't be separated from the parent after all, experiences great relief.

What has the child "practiced" during the attempted separation? Not courage or calmness, but terror. Not deliberate exposure to the situation, but desperate attempts to escape it.

And the terror and efforts to escape have been rewarded by the great feeling of relief she got when she found out she didn't have to separate.

So if the parent takes her back to the preschool the next day, would you predict that she would be more scared, or less scared? Probably she will be even more scared, since she has practiced great efforts to escape and has been rewarded for them.

The story you just read gave an example of how

A. a long voluntary exposure reduces fears,
or
B. a short exposure, followed by escape, increases fears?

82. This story gives us a clue about how small fears can sometimes grow into larger ones. The more someone practices escaping the situation whenever it comes along, and the more those escapes are rewarded by relief from the fear or aversion, the more the fear grows.

Because this principle is so important, let's look at another example. Let's imagine a child who overhears someone talking about a car wreck reported on the news. This minor event is just disturbing enough that when the child goes to bed, he is a little fearful. He runs into his parent's room, where he sleeps the rest of the night. As soon as he gets to his parent's room, there is a nice feeling of relief. He feels much better than he felt when he was by himself.

The next night, his brain remembers the feeling of relief that came from escaping his room the previous night. Because of this, the urge to escape is even bigger. And the "urge to escape" is experienced as fear. Again the child escapes into his parent's room, and again he feels relief.

This story, so far, has illustrated that

A. staying in a scary situation for a long time can reduce fear,
or
B. escaping from a scary situation causes relief, which rewards the efforts for escape?

83. Now this child's parent tries to get him to stay in his own room. But now he works himself up into a frenzy of fear, and the parent thinks, "He's really scared. I don't want to be cruel to him." So again the child gets to sleep with the parent. Now the child has been rewarded, not for being just a little afraid, but for being very afraid.

As time goes by, and these experiences accumulate, the child always screams with terror when his parent tries to get him to sleep by himself.

This story is meant to illustrate that

A. a small fear can turn into a big one, as the person has brief exposures followed by escape,
or
B. if you are a parent, you should be ready to lose some sleep?

84. By the time the parent and the child decide to get serious about the boy's fear, everyone has forgotten about the car wreck reported in the news that got the fear started in the first place. And even if they could remember it, it wouldn't help anything. What is much more important to understand is how the little fear grew by being reinforced nearly every night with the pleasant relief of being able to sleep in the parent's room.

This section makes the point that

A. trying to remember exactly what got the fear started is often not very important, in comparison to what made the fear grow after that,
or
B. news shows should not emphasize accidents and violence as much as they do?

85. Here's one more example of how brief exposures followed by escape can make fears grow. Zelda is on an elevator. She starts feeling very uncomfortable and afraid that she will be trapped on the elevator. Just as the fear mounts to what seems like an unbearable level, the door opens, and she rushes off the elevator. As soon as she gets off, she experiences great relief. This feeling of relief rewards, or reinforces, the escape from the elevator. The next time Zelda gets on an elevator, her brain remembers the bad feeling while on the elevator and the relief upon getting off; this memory creates an even greater urge to get off the elevator than before. While on the elevator, she thinks "Oh I've got to get off, I can't stand this, this feels terrible, let me out of here." When the door opens, she bursts out the door, thinking "Thank goodness I'm off that thing!" Thus she experiences one more trial in which the elevator gets associated with bad feelings and escaping gets reinforced by relief. Over time, the urge to escape grows and grows. And what is fear, but the urge to escape?

With which of these statements would the author most likely agree?

A. Any kind of exposure to the situation you're afraid of will tend to reduce your fear,

or

B. "A very strong urge to escape a situation" and "a fear of a situation" are just about the same thing?

86. There's another way in which escape from scary situations prevents people from getting over fears. The escape from the feared situation makes it impossible for the brain to gather evidence that the feared situation is not dangerous and that the fear is unrealistic.

In experiments done in the twentieth century, researchers taught animals to be afraid and escape when certain signals were presented. They put a rat in a little chamber and turned on a light. A couple of seconds later, the rat got a shock from the wires on the bottom of the chamber. But the rat soon found that he could escape this shock by jumping over a little barrier into the other half of the chamber. When the light came on again, the rat would have to jump over the barrier if he wanted to escape the shock. It did not take very many or very severe shocks for these animals to learn to jump as soon as the light came on, so as to avoid all the shocks.

In this experiment so far, the rat's urge to escape when the light comes on, which the rat surely experienced as fear, would be called a(n)

A. unrealistic fear, because there is no danger,
or
B. realistic fear, because there's a danger of shock that the fear motivates the rat to escape?

87. Now suppose that the experimenters make the fear "unrealistic" by turning off the shock in the bottom of the cage permanently. Of course, the rat does not know that the shock is turned off. Suppose the experimenters keep turning on the warning light from time to time. How soon will the rat learn that it is safe to stay in the cage without jumping over the barrier?

The answer is that as long as the rat has the opportunity to escape as soon as the light signal comes on, the rat will probably *never* learn that there's no need to escape. The rat's jumping over the barrier just before the shock was scheduled to come on keeps the rat from finding out that the shock has been turned off. So the rat keeps jumping for hundreds more trials.

In the experiment described, the rat's escape from the scary situation

A. prevented the rat from finding out that the situation was now safe,
or

B. allowed the rat to get over the fear sooner?

88. Then the experimenters wondered: what would happen if they forced the rat to have prolonged exposure to the light, so that the rat could find out that the light no longer signaled shock? To find this out, they now raised the barrier so that the rat could not jump over it. Now when they turned the light on, the rat tried to escape, but couldn't. For a while, the rat looked very distressed. But as no shock occurred, and the light kept coming on and going off, the rat quickly became less and less distressed when the light came on. After a while, the rat seemed not to notice the light, and then, even when the barrier was lowered, the rat did not jump when the light came on. The fear that the rat had learned in the experiment was now "unlearned."

What is the point of this section?

A. By letting light be a signal that a shock was coming, the experimenters taught rats to escape when the light came on,
or
B. by preventing escape and exposing the rat to the light without the shock, the experimenters caused the rat to get over the fear that they had created in him?

89. I'm sorry that these animals, who had no choice about whether to be in this experiment, had to experience some pain and fear. I am not sure whether it was necessary to do these experiments to learn that escape allows fears to continue, and prolonged exposure can make fears go way. But these experiments did give dramatic evidence about how fears can be learned and unlearned. We can only hope that the animals were treated well after the experiments were over. They deserved long and pleasant lives because of their contributions to scientific progress.

This section

A. introduces a new principle about understanding fear,
or
B. digresses for a moment to reflect upon the rights and the welfare of the animals who participated in the experiments described above?

90. People are very different from rats, in that they can take conscious control over what they say to themselves, the images they visualize or hear, how relaxed or tense they are, and other behaviors that may make prolonged exposure to a scary situation less painful. Sometimes people can even make prolonged exposure a positive experience. This book will teach techniques of making prolonged exposure more pleasant.

But remember the important point: escape from a feared situation tends to reinforce fear, whereas prolonged exposure (especially with practice of handling the situation courageously) tends to reduce fear. This is one of the most important ideas about reducing fears and aversions.

A point made in this section is that

A. there are ways people can use to make prolonged exposure less painful, or
B. it's difficult to say exactly how long a time of exposure is "prolonged" enough?

Sometimes other people reinforce fears and aversions

91. Teresa, 8 years old, has a nightmare. She comes into her mom and dad's bedroom crying. Her mom and dad let her sleep with them for the rest of the night. (She is ordinarily not allowed to do this.) More nightmares occur, and the same thing happens again and again. The nightmares gradually get more and more frequent.

Being able to sleep with her parents is pleasant for Teresa. It's a reward that she doesn't usually get.

Could it be that her brain is figuring out that the way to get this nice reward is to have nightmares, and making them come more often, without Teresa's even realizing this? There is lots of evidence that indeed this can happen. Sometimes our brains increase fears in order to get the rewards that other people give us for being afraid, without our even realizing that this is going on.

The main idea of this section is that

A. if we get some reward for being afraid or having an aversion, our brains can increase the fear or aversion, without our even being aware of it,
or
B. it's good to decide whether a fear has to do with physical, economic, or social danger, or the danger of failure?

92. Ron's dad wants Ron to be a "real man," and is putting lots of pressure on Ron to go on a rock climbing trip with him. Ron doesn't like the idea of rock climbing at all, but does not want to simply refuse to go. He's in lots of conflict.

   Without knowing why, Ron develops a great aversion to eating almost all sorts of foods, and won't eat at all unless his mom makes food in a certain way. As a result of the aversion, his dad stops putting pressure on him to go rock climbing – this is a major reward. He also gets lots of attention from his mom, which is also rewarding. Is it possible that his brain could have figured out that the aversions might lead to the rewards they did lead to, without his even being aware of this? It's very possible. Our brains are designed to calculate how to get us what we find pleasant and how to avoid what we don't find pleasant.

This section

A. advises that you have a daily anti-aversion workout, with exercises selected from those described in this book,
or
B. gives another example of how an aversion might result from our brains' tendency to seek reinforcement or rewards?

93. Marcy gets sudden episodes in which she feels unloved by her family. She feels as if the world is about to end at these times, and it is very scary for her. She goes to her mom, who reassures her, tells her all the ways in which she is loved, rubs her back, gives her undivided attention, and appears willing to do almost anything to show Marcy that she is loved. (Marcy has recently felt that her younger brother was absorbing too

much of her parents' attention.) If the attentive and loving response from her mom occurs almost every time Marcy gets this sudden fear, it would not surprise us that the episodes will happen more and more often, because Marcy is getting a powerful reward for them.

This section presents

A. an explanation for why "self-talk" is important in overcoming fears and aversions,
or
B. an example of a fear or aversion that is increased by another person's reinforcement?

94. The idea that Marcy's fear of being unloved is being increased by reinforcement is NOT to say that Marcy is consciously calculating, "I will purposely do this in order to get my mom's attention and demonstrations of love." We can do things in order to get things, without even realizing that we are doing so.

When Marcy has this explained to her, and when her mom stops reinforcing Marcy's episodes of feeling unloved, the episodes steadily decrease, and then stop.

In this story, the reinforcer for the scary episodes was

A. getting the mom's pleasant and undivided attention,
or
B. being able to get out of going to school?

95. Would you like to hear an experiment that shows some evidence that we can do things in order to get rewards, without even realizing what we are doing? Some students were studying reinforcement. They had a professor who gave them lectures. Every once in a while the professor would use the phrase "i.e.," meaning "that is." ("I.e." stands for *ille est*, which is Latin for "that is.") The students decided they would do an experiment to see whether his saying "i.e." could be changed by reinforcement.

The first thing they did was to count how frequently the professor said "i.e." Then, they applied a reinforcer: each time he said this phrase, they would look interested, nod, give eye contact, or take notes.

What has happened in this true story so far?

A. The students in a course decided to see if they could change the rate at which a professor said a phrase, by manipulating the reinforcer of their own attentiveness.
or

B. The author is using this story to illustrate the fact that reinforcers can have their effects without our being aware of this.

96. When the students looked more attentive each time he said "i.e.," the professor started saying the phrase much more often.

Then they stopped applying the reinforcer. They did not look particularly attentive when he said the phrase. The frequency with which he said it went back down.

Then they looked attentive every time he said "i.e." again, and again the frequency went up.

They asked their professor whether he had noticed anything unusual. He had not! They showed him the graphs of his own behavior. He had been totally unaware of how he had changed his behavior to get the reward!

The main point of this true story is that

A. we can do things more or less often, in order to get a reward, without even being conscious of the fact that we are doing so,
or
B. the phrase, "i.e.," stands for "ille est," which is Latin for "that is"?

97. Sometimes getting help from other people is the key to getting over fears and aversions. Please do not interpret this section on reinforcement to mean that you have to deal with fears and aversions all by yourself. But as you get help, look for the sort of help that is not "contingent" on feeling bad. That is, look for the sort of help where you get rewarded for your success experiences and courage skill triumphs much more than you get rewarded for being afraid or avoidant.

What's the major point of this section?

A. The word "contingent" means "depending" – an arrangement where you get something depending on something else.
or
B. It's great to get help from others. You want to get the sort of help where you get rewarded for your courage skill triumphs much more than you get rewarded for having useless fears and aversions.

The vicious cycles of fear

98. Our goal in this chapter, and the previous one, is understanding the nature of fears and aversions. It's important to understand the idea of a vicious cycle, because there are several vicious cycles that make fears and aversions worse. In the vicious

45

cycles of fear, fear causes other things to happen more, which in turn cause the fear to get worse. A circular process gets going that tends to make things worse and worse.

The more you understand the vicious cycles that are involved in fears and aversions, the better you will be able to stay out of them. So as you read about these, don't let them worry you – you are helping yourself triumph over them by getting to know them better.

A vicious cycle occurs when

A. something bad makes something else happen, which then makes that bad thing happen even more,
or
B. people who are lost in the woods tend to walk around in circles?

99. We've already talked about one of these vicious cycles. This cycle goes as follows: fear → escape → relief → more fear. The more fearful someone gets, the more the person's exposures tend to be brief, frantic efforts to escape – the type of exposures that increase fear rather than decrease it. Thus the higher fear gets, the more the fear tends to be increased.

People's tendency to escape situations they greatly fear creates vicious cycles because

A. the greater the fear, the greater the tendency to escape, and escape during high fear makes fear even greater,
or
B. the greater the fear, the more the person wants to do something about it, which lessens the fear?

100. Here's another vicious cycle that gets going with fears and aversions. The pattern is that fear leads to avoidance, which leads to lower skill, which leads to more fear. For example, a student find math aversive. This leads the student to avoid doing math. When the student doesn't study and doesn't practice, the student falls farther and farther behind in math. The student is now even less competent in math relative to his classmates, he's even more afraid of tackling the math work, and so he avoids it more and more. The fear → avoidance → low skill → fear cycle is the cause of a huge amount of failure, misery, and unhappiness.

The main thing causing the vicious cycle this section talks about is that

A. people tend not to read their math books enough,
or
B. people tend to avoid practicing the skills they need for handling a

situation, when the situation itself causes them fear?

101. The cure for this vicious cycle is for the person to start practicing the skill very often, starting at the level at which he can be successful almost all the time. For example, the person works with a tutor and goes down to the level of math problems that he can already understand and do successfully. He gradually works his way up to a higher and higher level with a good deal of exposure and a good deal of reinforcement for success, until finally he is at the level where he can comfortably do the work that his classmates are doing.

Which strategy would the author recommend for someone with a fear of failure that interfered with reading skills?

A. Taking a long break from working on reading, so as to clear the mind and start over,
or
B. starting with reading tasks easy enough that the person could succeed almost all the time, and then working the way toward more difficult tasks?

102. A similar vicious cycle of fear is one in which fear leads to lower performance, which in turn leads to more fear. For example, a musician gets stage fright. The nervousness causes her to not be able to finger her instrument skillfully and the performance is embarrassing for her. When the next performance comes, she has the memory of the past failure and embarrassment; this makes her even more nervous than she was before.

The cure for this vicious cycle is lots of exposure to performance and lots of success experiences. She starts with low stakes performances, such as performances for her younger brother. She works her way up to performances for people at a nursing home, then to performances for groups of family members. Each time she can relax and perform well, she tries to reward herself in her own mind and greatly celebrate her success.

In this example, the person got over the fear by

A. starting with easy songs and working the way up to harder ones,
or
B. starting with non-scary audiences and working the way up to audiences where the stakes are higher?

103. Another vicious cycle is that where fear or aversion leads to procrastination, which leads to greater aversion. For example, someone has a paper due for school, but is just too

busy to finish it on time. After a few days, the person has forgotten a little bit of the subject matter for the paper; the person also feels guilty about the paper being late. Now the thought of working on the paper has become a little more aversive, because it is associated with some shame and guilt and feeling of failure. So the person avoids working on the paper, or procrastinates again, and feels some relief from this bad feeling. This reinforces avoidance, as we have discussed before. The more this cycle goes around, the less and less pleasant it gets to work on the paper.

The vicious cycle of procrastination is caused by

A. forgetting information necessary for the work, shame and guilt over putting it off, and being rewarded for putting it off by temporary relief from the bad feelings,
or
B. the fact that other people get angry when the work is not done?

104. The cure for the vicious cycle of procrastination involves trying not to feel bad about what is in the past. For example, the person tries not to feel too bad that the paper is late so far. Instead, the person tries to feel as good as possible about every single second of effort that can be put into working on the paper. This celebration of one's own work is crucial. It can counter the self-criticism that also contributes to the procrastination. Finally, prolonged exposure to working on the paper reduces the fear.

The cure for the vicious cycles of procrastination involves

A. rewarding oneself with food for doing work,
or
B. trying not to be stopped by shame and guilt, trying to celebrate every bit of work that is done, and trying to do prolonged exposure to the work?

105. Another vicious cycle occurs when someone who feels very fearful thinks, "Maybe I'm going crazy!" This thought increases the fear, and in turn makes it seem more likely to the person that he or she really is going crazy. The antidote to this vicious cycle is to stop and think, "This is fear, not craziness. It's unpleasant, but I'll get over it." For some people this is quite difficult to do.

In the vicious cycle described in this section,

A. fear keeps someone from going to sleep, which in turn makes the emotions more extreme,
or

B. fear leads someone to think, "Maybe I'm becoming crazy," which is a very scary thought.

106. The last vicious cycle of fear that we'll talk about now is a very important one for some people. We'll discuss it in greater detail in a later chapter. It's the vicious cycle of hyperventilation. Hyperventilation means breathing faster than we need to breathe. The vicious cycle comes about when fear increases hyperventilation, and hyperventilation increases fear.

When we breathe too fast, the reduced carbon dioxide in the blood causes a weird feeling. Sometimes the brain interprets this weird feeling as not being able to get enough air, as being about to suffocate. This then leads us to breathe even faster. Breathing even faster, of course, makes the weird feeling worse.

At the same time, when people realize that breathing faster is not getting rid of the unpleasant feeling, people often fear that something horrible will happen. "Maybe I'm having a heart attack," or "Maybe I'm about to die," are thoughts that often go through people's minds when they're having a hyperventilation episode. These thoughts create more fear, and the vicious cycle goes around and around.

The crucial thing that creates a vicious cycle of hyperventilation is that

A. the brain concludes, from the weird feeling caused by hyperventilation, that it needs to breathe faster,
or
B. the brain senses the weird feeling caused by hyperventilation and automatically breathes more slowly?

107. One part of the cure for this vicious cycle is to realize that the weird feeling caused by hyperventilation is unpleasant, but not dangerous or life-threatening. Once the person realizes that he is not about to die or have something really bad happen, the task becomes the lower stakes one of making things more pleasant and trying to get back to a normal feeling as soon as possible.

The second part of the cure for this vicious cycle is to learn to recognize the weird feeling as the one caused by breathing too fast, and to breathe more slowly. This enables the body to get back to its normal chemical balance and for the person to feel OK again.

The parts of the cure for hyperventilation that are mentioned in this section are

A. relaxing the muscles and going along a gradual hierarchy,

or
B. realizing that the attack is not dangerous, learning to recognize the feeling of having breathed too fast, and learning to breathe more slowly when that happens?

108. Once a hyperventilation attack has started, however, it is hard to breathe more slowly. Therefore, it is important to practice recognizing the feeling of having hyperventilated, and curing this feeling by breathing more slowly. In a later chapter I'll talk about how to practice this by hyperventilating just a little bit, on purpose.

In this section the author suggests

A. practicing breaking the vicious cycle of hyperventilation by hyperventilating a little on purpose, then slowing the breathing, or
B. starting to exercise as soon as a hyperventilation attack begins?

The flight or fight response

109. In understanding fears and aversions, a very important topic is the flight or fight response: the system that turns up the level of arousal and excitement in our bodies.

The flight or fight response is part of what is done by our autonomic nervous systems. The word autonomic sounds like automatic, and it has meant much the same thing.

The autonomic nervous system is not in charge of voluntary movements, for example those of the hands or feet or mouth or tongue. We have nerves going out from our brains that make our muscles move. These movements feel as though we are very much in control of them.

On the other hand, our brains also send out signals, by the autonomic nervous system, that cause our hearts to beat faster or slower, our skin to sweat more or less, our blood pressure to go up or down, our stomach and intestines to move faster or slower, and so forth. These functions are usually regulated without our paying conscious attention to them. Usually we are too busy figuring out what do to or say to have time to think about telling our hearts to beat faster or our sweat glands to sweat more or less.

The main contrast the author is making in this section is between

A. realistic fear and unrealistic fear, or
B. the autonomic nervous system versus voluntary muscle movements?

110. The fact that the autonomic nervous system usually makes its adjustments without our conscious attention does not mean that we have no control over this system. The autonomic nervous system makes its changes because we are aware of what is going on in our environment and we understand what sort of situation we are in. We can change the way we think about the situation we are in. When we do that, we can influence the activity of our autonomic nervous systems.

The main point of this section is that

A. the flight or fight response evolved in order to protect us from danger,
or
B. how we think about the situation we are in can greatly affect how our autonomic nervous systems respond to it?

111. Jane and Terri are hiking. Suddenly a snake crawls very close to both of their feet. Terri imagines that the snake may be deadly poisonous, and her autonomic nervous system responds so as to greatly increase her heart rate, rate of breathing, muscle tension, and sweating. Jane, however, recognizes the snake as a harmless garter snake, and her heart rate, rate of breathing, and so forth remain the same as they were before. What

accounts for the difference? They both experienced the same situation, but they gave it different meaning.

This section gives an example of how

A. our autonomic responses are influenced by what we think about the situation we're in,
or
B. by practicing changing our autonomic nervous system activity, we can learn to turn it up or down?

112. Why is the autonomic nervous system so important in understanding anxiety and aversions? It's because many of the symptoms that people have when they feel unpleasant anxiety are direct results of actions of the autonomic nervous system. Here are some of the symptoms of anxiety that people often feel:

1. Pounding heart
2. Faster heart rate
3. Sweating
4. Trembling or shaking
5. Rapid breathing
6. Feeling of choking
7. Tightness in the chest
8. Nausea or stomach pain
9. Feeling dizzy, unsteady, lightheaded or faint
10. Feeling unusually hot or cold
11. Muscle tension
12. Frequent urination

13. Diarrhea or constipation
14. Feeling of the mind racing

All of these body sensations and changes are affected by the autonomic nervous system.

The point of this section is that

A. what we think of as anxiety symptoms are mainly results of autonomic nervous system activity,
or
B. the autonomic nervous system has two main divisions?

113. The autonomic nervous system is divided into two parts. The part we're most concerned with is called the sympathetic nervous system. The word sympathetic doesn't have much to do with sympathy. The sympathetic nervous system is the part that gets activated the most in the flight or fight response. When we perceive that we are in great danger, our bodies automatically get ready to either fight an enemy or run away from the enemy. Our bodies are really getting ready for extreme exercise.

When we perceive that we need to either fight or run away, what happens?

A. The sympathetic nervous system increases its activity,

or
B. the sympathetic nervous system stops activity for a while?

114. Let's think about various things that go on when people get anxious, and think about how these bodily changes actually help if someone is going to do lots of exercise very quickly.
1. Pounding heart and faster heart rate: to carry oxygen to the muscles more quickly, and to carry carbon dioxide away from them more quickly.
2. Sweating: to cool us off when we generate heat from our muscle activity.
3. Increased muscle tension (leading to trembling): so our muscles are ready to respond with greater speed and strength.
4. Rapid breathing: to get oxygen in and carbon dioxide out more quickly.
5. Mind racing: so we can make quick decisions about how to stay alive.

The point of this section is that

A. the things the sympathetic nervous system does to our bodies when we are scared are meant to help us survive in dangerous situations,
or
B. the feeling of excitement can be pleasant or unpleasant depending upon whether we think we are safe or not?

115. What controls the fight or flight response? The perception of danger begins in our brains. From there, nerve impulses go primarily along the sympathetic nervous system. The nerve cells in the last parts of the sympathetic nervous system, the parts that are closest to the organs that it affects in the body, use a chemical called noradrenaline to move the signals from one nerve to another. In addition, the sympathetic nervous system sends signals to the adrenal glands (we have two of them, one on each side of our bellies). The adrenal glands then release a hormone called adrenaline. (Adrenaline is also known as epinephrine.) Adrenaline is carried by our blood to the organs that the sympathetic nerves go to, and stimulates the sympathetic nerves; adrenaline turns up the activity of the sympathetic nervous system. The release of adrenaline is a very important part of the flight or fight response.

The purpose of this section was to

A. teach you how to control your sympathetic nervous system,
or
B. describe the pathways along which action happens in the sympathetic nervous system when the flight or fight response occurs?

116. So, the flight or fight response evolved as a way of helping us be ready to fight enemies or run away from them. However, much of the danger that we face in the present day world does not make us fight enemies or run away from them. When we take a math test, when we go to a party, when we are about to invite someone to get together with us, or when we are about to give a speech or play the violin in front of other people, we may perceive ourselves in danger. Our flight or fight responses may get going at full speed. But if our sympathetic activity gets turned up too high, it interferes with our performance in these things rather than helping us. For example, the violin player wants to have steady hands, not hands that are trembling with fear.

The main idea of this section is that

A. the danger of failure occurs more frequently today than economic danger,
or
B. for many dangers we experience today, running or fighting doesn't help, and a big flight or fight response hurts our performance?

117. There are two ways of dealing with the flight or fight response. One of these is to learn to turn it down; the other is to learn to harness it and use

it. As an example of the first: someone is taking a test, and the person perceives herself as too excited for best performance. So she uses several relaxation techniques to actually turn down the flight or fight response, so as to do best on the test. As an example of the second strategy: a speaker feels the flight or fight response, but learns to harness it by speaking fast, loud, and forcefully, pacing back and forth across the stage, making very energetic gestures, and putting on an energizing performance for the listeners.

The two strategies for dealing with the flight or fight response that this section listed were

A. meditation and changing your thoughts,
or
B. turning down the flight or fight response, or finding a way to harness it and enjoy it?

118. Excitement, with all the signs of the flight or fight response, can be a very positive emotion. We know this partly because millions of people choose to spend money on roller coasters, scary movies, mountain climbing, motorcycle riding, sports contests, and other experiences that seem designed to bring out the flight or fight response.

Why is excitement sometimes very pleasant and sometimes very unpleasant? The experience of pleasure or pain largely depends on people's confidence in being able to make things turn out OK -- their belief that they are going to succeed in the situation. People who are very sure that things are going to come out OK interpret the flight or fight response as positive excitement. If the person is very sure that something horrible is going to happen, then the flight or fight response feels like unpleasant terror.

The main point of this section is that

A. whether the flight or fight response is pleasant or unpleasant depends on whether the person is predicting something good or bad to come out of the situation,
or
B. if someone is running a race, the flight or fight response is very useful?

The Yerkes-Dodson curve

119. Can you imagine the shape of a bell, or the shape of a mound of sand? If you were drawing it, you would have the line first go up, then come down. This is the shape of a graph called the Yerkes-Dodson curve. The picture below illustrates; the numbers

on the scales are imaginary units of how well you perform and how excited you are.

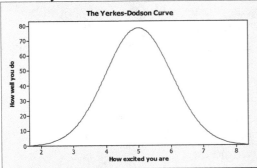

This curve is important in thinking about the best level of excitement for any given task.

The horizontal axis of the graph represents how excited or aroused you are. The farther you go to the right, the more excited you are. The vertical axis of the graph represents how well you perform on a certain task. The higher the graph goes up, the better is the performance. The graph shows how someone's performance rises and falls as excitement increases.

The purpose of the Yerkes-Dodson curve is to display

A. how someone's performance changes with changes in someone's level of excitement,
or

B. how many people have different levels of excitement?

120. Let's imagine that the curve represents someone's performance on a test. At the left side of the graph, there is very low excitement and very low performance. This means that if you are very, very unexcited, for example when you feel like you're about to go asleep, your performance is not very good. As you get more aroused and alert and awake, your performance gets better and reaches, at some point, the best performance you can give. For the example graph drawn above, the best performance comes when the excitement is about 5 (let's imagine that it means excited 5 on a scale of 10), and at that point, your performance is at the level of 80 (let's imagine that this score means 80 questions right).

This section was about the fact that

A. as you go from very low excitement to some middle region of excitement, your performance gets better,
Or
B. as you go from some middle level of excitement to a very high level of excitement, your performance gets worse?

121. Now let's look at the right side of the curve. If you keep getting more and more excited, to where the flight or fight response is in full play, the adrenaline begins to interfere with your performance. So this is why the curve starts sloping downward. If you get so nervous that you can hardly hold onto your pencil, your performance level is likely to sink very low.

A summary of what the Yerkes-Dodson curve shows is that

A. excitement is a result of greater adrenaline released into the bloodstream,
or
B. there's a level of excitement where you do your best performance, and performance goes down as you get either less or more excitement than this best level?

122. Different tasks require different levels of excitement for best performance. Thus there is not just one Yerkes-Dodson Curve, but lots of them for lots of different tasks. If you are running a sprint or playing football, peak performance will come with a very high level of excitement. You want to pump just about as much adrenaline as you can. On the other hand, if you're going to bed the night before the big athletic contest, and

your goal is to get a good night's sleep, you want to have just about as little excitement and arousal as you can muster while you're lying in bed. Your "performance" on the task of going to sleep is better the lower your level of excitement is.

The two situations this section mentions give examples where the peak of the Yerkes-Dodson curve would be

A. very high and very low,
or
B. in the middle?

123. On the other hand, if the task is taking a test, playing the violin, giving a speech, or trying to solve a problem with a family member, the peak of the curve is probably closer to the middle. For these sorts of tasks you want to be just excited enough to where you are thoroughly energized, but not so excited that your performance suffers.

In discussing and trying to solve a problem with a family member, suppose someone interrupts too much, yells at the family member, and jumps to a conclusion too quickly. This person is on the part of the Yerkes-Dodson curve where he or she is

A. too excited,
or

B. not excited enough?

124. The fact that the best level of excitement is different for different tasks is the reason why our bodies were designed to move our level of excitement up and down, rather than simply stay at one level. Our levels of excitement should go up or down depending on what we are trying to do, so as to bring out the best performance for the particular task.

     This, then, is one way to think about a goal we are working on: You want to get good enough at adjusting your level of excitement so that you get close to the best performance in whatever task you are doing. Whether the best performance comes from high, low, or medium levels of excitement, you can adjust the level to bring out your best performance. You are finding and achieving the level of excitement that gives you the best point on the Yerkes-Dodson Curve.

According to this section, a goal is

A. to stick to a medium range of excitement,
or
B. to adjust your level of excitement so as to bring out the best performance on whatever you are trying to do?

125. Of course, no one adjusts his or her level of excitement for best

performance with 100% success. Sometimes we will be more excited than we would like to be, or less excited than we would like to be, despite our best efforts. But if you have in your mind the goal of being able to turn up or down your level of excitement to perform the best on whatever task you have taken on, this will help you come as close to that goal as you can.

This section tells you that

A. if you follow a few quick and easy steps, your level of excitement will always be idea for every task you face, or
B. no one can always have the ideal level of excitement for every task, but if you have this goal, you'll probably come closer more often?

Chapter 3: Avoidance Versus Mastery

126. The purpose of realistic fear is to make us want to avoid dangerous situations. Fear of poisonous snakes makes us want to stay away from them. Fear of high-speed driving makes us want to avoid driving too fast. Fear of getting beat up makes us want to avoid making a hobby of insulting aggressive guys. Realistic fear of heights makes us want to avoid walking over cliffs.

This section

A. gives several examples of how the purpose of realistic fear is to make us avoid danger,
or
B. defines mastery as learning to handle a situation in an expert way?

127. With realistic fears, it's often very wise to keep avoiding the situation for as long as you live. This way the fear never goes away, but that's good! I don't want to get over my fears of picking up a king cobra or of driving 150 miles per hour down a back road!

And even with some unrealistic fears, permanent avoidance might be the best strategy. For example, Tom is very much afraid of all snakes, not just poisonous ones.

But he lives in a big city where he never has to encounter snakes. He decides to save his energy for more important things than getting over his fear of snakes.

The attitude expressed in this section is that

A. an unrealistic fear of doing useful work is something you must master,
or
B. with most realistic fears, and with some unrealistic fears, avoidance of the scary situation for the rest of your life is a good strategy?

128. If I decide that I really do want to get over an unrealistic fear, I am deciding I want not avoidance, but *mastery*. I want not to keep running away from the scary situation, but to face it and learn to handle it bravely. For example, someone with a fear of public speaking decides to work so hard and so long that he can be unafraid of giving speeches, and can enjoy them. For any unrealistic fears or aversions that you have, which do you choose: avoidance or mastery? This is an extremely important choice.

Which is the better summary of this section?

A. When a situation is scary for you, it's very important to choose whether you want to avoid it or master it.
or
B. It's easier to master a scary situation when you have learned to turn down your level of excitement?

129. Marla has such a large fear of vomiting and seeing other people vomit, that the fear makes her miserable. One day at school, someone in her class complains of feeling sick to his stomach. Marla thinks to herself, "I'm feeling the urge to escape from this situation, for example by running down to the nurse's office. But if I tough it out and stay here, I'll be doing an exposure that will help me get over my fear. Even if he does throw up, handling seeing that will be a big accomplishment."

In this example, Marla is aiming for

A. mastery,
or
B. avoidance?

130. A child is afraid of sleeping by himself. He finds that if he screams and resists strongly enough, his parents will give in and let him sleep with them. He feels great satisfaction and relief when he is able to sleep with his parents.

This child is aiming for

A. mastery,
or
B. avoidance?

131. Trini is afraid of writing – he fears embarrassing himself by having to turn in written work at school that someone may ridicule. If he were to choose courses in college so that they required multiple choice tests but not papers, he would be using one of these strategies.

Is it

A. mastery,
or
B. avoidance?

132. On the other hand, suppose that Trini takes an online writing course the summer before college. He writes something and turns it in almost every day, and gets feedback on his writing. He studies writing thoroughly. He purposely signs up for courses that will require him to write often and much. He uses this strategy to get much more comfortable with writing.

He is using the strategy of

A. mastery,
or
B. avoidance?

133. Daniel has aversions to lots of foods. There are only a few foods that he likes. He is invited to go to a friend's house for supper. He thinks, "It's very likely that they'll not have the things I like." So he turns down the invitation and stays home.

He is using the strategy of

A. mastery,
or
B. avoidance?

134. Suppose that later, Daniel gets another supper invitation. He thinks, "I'm going to go. Before I go, I'm going to practice eating some things I don't like very much, just to show myself I can do it. I'll have a good time talking with them and being with them, and I'll eat a good bit of what they give me, even if I don't like it. It will be an exposure that will help me get used to eating new foods. With enough exposure, maybe I'll start liking some more foods, or maybe I'll just learn to put up with eating stuff I don't like!"

He is aiming for

A. mastery,

or
B. avoidance?

135. I have seen people take only a couple of weeks to master fears that had bothered them for years. They spent years in avoidance before they finally decided on mastery. Why do people choose avoidance, when the mastery strategy ends the pain so much more completely?

One reason people avoid is that they aren't sure that aiming for mastery will work. People don't want to endure the suffering of exposing themselves to a scary situation unless they are absolutely sure that the fear will go away. For this reason, it's good to talk to people who have mastered their fears or read about other people's experiences of achieving mastery, to learn that this strategy really can work.

This section expresses the idea that

A. even though mastery usually results in much less suffering than avoidance does, people have a hard time working for mastery because they aren't sure that they will succeed,
or
B. if you hear or read about other people's experiences, you have a chance to practice empathizing with those people?

136. One way to learn that the strategies to achieve mastery of fears really work is to listen to and read about other people's experiences. Another way is to experience mastery yourself, with a small fear.

For example: John has a big fear that greatly affects his life: he is terrified of flying on airplanes. He could have a much better career if he could tolerate flying. He has another minor fear: looking out of windows of high buildings makes him somewhat uncomfortable.

He works on the easier fear first, and finds that he is able to get much more comfortable with high buildings. Once he has experienced firsthand that mastery strategies can work, he now is able to trust those strategies enough to tackle his fear of flying.

According to this section, one reason to tackle a smaller and less important fear first is

A. to gain the confidence that it is indeed possible to reduce fears,
or
B. to put off the really hard and uncomfortable work?

137. Once you have decided you want to go for mastery rather than avoidance, you will probably have to keep reminding yourself of this.

Avoidance is the natural thing to do when you feel fear or an aversion. You'll automatically drift toward avoidance unless you try hard not to.

For example: Jordan has decided that he wants to master his fear of social conversations with people. At a farmer's market, he sees someone that he knows and likes. He finds himself naturally looking away and walking the other direction. But then he reminds himself of his goal of mastery. He then decides to walk up to his friend, greet him, and have a friendly chat.

The main point of this section is that

A. if you want to overcome fears of socializing, you should get comfortable with "greeting rituals,"
or
B. once you've decided to go for mastery, you will probably have to remind yourself of this over and over?

138. Deciding to work for mastery of a fear or aversion can be one of the most dramatic turning points in someone's life. This decision can liberate one from a lifetime filled with fear and avoidance.

It's easier for people to make this courageous choice if they know more about the methods by which they can master scary situations. The next

two chapters will help you understand
what those methods are.

An idea expressed in this section is
that

A. eliminating certain fears and
aversions can lead to dramatically
better relationships with other people,
or
B. the decision to work toward
mastery rather than avoidance can be a
dramatic turning point in one's life;
it's easier to make if you know how
the work toward mastery is done.

Chapter 4: Ways to Reduce Fears and Aversions

You don't need to understand where they came from.

139. Many people think, "If I could only figure out where this fear came from!" One reason they think this, perhaps, is that many movies about psychological problems have a dramatic climax, in which someone finally remembers some scary event that created the problem, and after that the problem is solved. In real life, things very seldom happen that way.

Sometimes there are very obvious unpleasant events that make people fearful. Often, however, we're unable to figure out exactly where the fear came from. Often our best guess is that the fear started out small, and then a series of brief exposures and escapes increased the fear.

But the good news is that it's not necessary to go back into the past to figure out where fears and aversions came from, to learn to reduce or eliminate them!

The point of this section is that

A. thinking clearly about how bad the outcome could be, and how likely that bad outcome is, makes it easier to overcome the fear of that outcome, or
B. you can reduce or eliminate fears and aversions even without knowing how they got started?

Ways to reduce fears and aversions

140. In this chapter, we'll go through several ways to reduce or get rid of fears and aversions. As you read this list, don't worry if you don't know yet what I mean by these words. This chapter will explain them.

Objectives
Hierarchy
Attribution
Models
Practice
Reinforcement
Instruction and Information
Stimulus Control
Monitoring

(Mnemonic: Oh Am Prism)

The methods that are listed here are ways that you can

A. find out how fears and aversions got started,
or
B. reduce or eliminate fears and aversions?

Objectives

141. The first is *objective-formation* or *goal-setting*. If you very strongly wish to change in a certain way, you are more likely to do it. For example, someone who fears being in social situations with new people decides that it is a major goal to learn to handle those situations comfortably and competently. This person is much more likely to succeed than the person whose goal is to avoid such situations! Is your goal fear-reduction or avoidance? This is a key decision for everyone who is bothered by fears.

What's the major point of this section?

A. If you have a strong goal of reducing a fear or aversion, you're much more likely to succeed than if your goal is avoidance.
or

B. For realistic fears, usually the best goal is avoidance.

142. There are at least two ways of measuring how much someone wants something. One is to simply ask the person, for example, "On a scale of 0 to 10, how strongly do you desire to become confident and competent in social situations?" By this definition, someone who answers, "I want it 10 on a scale of 10," desires this goal at the maximum level.

The second way of measuring, however, is to observe the answer to the following question: once someone is taught the ways of working on the goal in question, how much time per day, on the average, does the person spend working toward the goal? Two people can both claim to desire a goal 10 on a scale of 10. But if one spends 0 minutes per day working on that goal, and the other spends 2 hours a day working on the goal, the second has a much stronger desire.

One major point of this section is that

A. a measure of how strongly you desire a goal is how much time per day you're willing to put into it,
or
B. because there are only a certain number of minutes in a day, goals are in competition with each other?

143. Once you have set a goal, it's useful to spell out to yourself very thoroughly why you want to achieve it. Suppose someone wants to get over a fear of going to school. Then someone asks, "Why do you want this?" If the person just shrugs, or says, "I don't know," it will probably be hard for that person to motivate himself to keep working toward his goal. But if the person can without hesitation rattle off several good reasons, we would bet much more heavily on his success.

The list of reasons why you want to succeed at the goal and what is in it for you to accomplish this goal is called the "internal sales pitch." You're trying to sell to yourself the idea of working hard on the goal.

What's the main point of this section?

A. When you set a goal, make a list of reasons why you want achieve it.
Or
B. When you set a goal, practice in your imagination the behaviors you need to do to accomplish the goal.

144. Here's an example of an internal sales pitch. It's a list of reasons why someone wants to get over the fear of going to school.

I want get over the fear of going to school so that:

1) I will be able to have fun with other kids at school.
2) People won't think I'm strange.
3) I won't get behind in my courses and have to take some of them over.
4) My family won't get into trouble with the law.
5) I can learn things that may be useful for me.
6) My parents won't be so upset.
7) I can make a school record that will help me get a better job.
8) I can have the pleasure of knowing I accomplished something that takes courage.
9) I can have an experience that will help me in getting over other fears.

Which of the following reasons did the person NOT list?

A. Not upsetting his parents,
Or
B. Getting to participate on sports teams?

145. Someone who is afraid of social conversation starts listing the reasons why he wants to get over this fear. His list starts out like this:

1) So that I can enjoy social situations more.

2) So that I can develop more friendships.
3) So that I can develop better relationships with the friends I already have.
4) So that I can have more fun in life in general.
5) So that I will feel more secure and supported, and less anxious.
6) So that I can function better at a job.

The purpose of writing down an internal sales pitch is to

A. increase your own motivation to achieve your goal,
or
B. allow you to give the list to someone so that you will lose face if you do not achieve your goal?

Probabilities and utilities

146. How do you decide which situations you really want to get used to, and not be afraid of, and which ones to avoid for the rest of your life? To review something we went over earlier: The words *probabilities and utilities*. are useful in figuring out whether a fear is realistic or unrealistic. A probability means how likely something is to happen. A probability of 100% means that

something is sure to happen, and a probability of 0% means it's sure not to happen. A probability of 50% means that the thing has the same chance of happening as a coin has of coming up heads.

Someone is afraid of going over a regular highway bridge, for fear that the bridge will fall while he is on it. Do you think that the probability of the bridge falling is

A. closer to 0%,
or
B. closer to 100%?

147. The word utility means how good or bad an event is. Some people use the word "disutility" to refer to how bad something is. If you are going to a party where there is a 25% probability that someone will mildly dislike you, a large fear would be unrealistic. If you are going to a party where there is a 25% probability that someone will shoot you, a large fear would be realistic! This is because the "disutility" of getting shot is a lot higher than that of being mildly disliked!

The event that the sun will explode and burn up the whole earth this year is

A. of very high disutility, but very low probability,

or

B. of very high probability, but very low disutility?

148. How do you use probabilities and disutilities in the process of setting your objectives for getting over fears? First, if the probability or the disutility of a bad outcome is low enough, the danger is low. This is how you decide that a fear or aversion is useless or unrealistic and your goal is mastery rather than avoidance.

      Second, if you have figured out that the danger is low, reminding yourself of this often can be a useful way to reducing your fear.

The purpose of this section was to

A. tell how to use fantasy rehearsal in getting over fears,

or

B. tell how to use your estimates of probability and disutility in deciding which fears to get over, and getting over them?

Allies

149. When you are setting your goals, you want to think about whether you want to try to get over the fear or aversion all by yourself, or whether you would like to get people to help

you in some ways. Many people make the mistake of trying to do the job all alone, when they could do it much more successfully with the help of other people, or "allies."

The author seems to say that

A. you need to solve your problems on your own;

or

B. many times, people are much more successful in their goals if they have helpers, which we can call allies.

150. Sometimes your most important allies are friends and family members. Lots of research has shown that having lots of "social support," meaning having a network of friends and family who are helpful and nice, is an important protector against anxiety. When we face stressful or possibly dangerous situations all by ourselves, it is much scarier than if we do it with lots of support from friends and relatives.

The main point of this section is that

A. having supportive people on your side is a very important protection against anxiety,

or

B. when you are in relationships, it's important to balance giving and taking, without doing only one or the other?

151. Here's an example of allies: Someone dreads school because he is being verbally harassed and picked on by another kid. But then he asks three friends for some help in ending this harassment. He finds that when he and his friends band together and all of them speak up to the bully to leave him alone, the bully feels outnumbered, and the harassment stops. If he had been afraid to use his allies, the situation would have turned out worse.

The author uses this incident as an example of how

A. getting support from your allies can reduce fear very effectively,
or
B. getting support from your allies can reinforce your fear if they are too nice and sympathetic and reward you too much for being afraid?

152. Sometimes friends and family members aren't expert enough to be the sorts of allies you need with certain types of problems. This is why experts sell their services. Sometimes people need doctors, lawyers, building inspectors, psychotherapists, financial counselors, dentists, and all sorts of other experts to help them out. Some people have a mental block against getting help, particularly when they feel as if they "should" be able to do the job themselves. If they can overcome their shame and consult an expert early, sometimes they can avoid a great deal of anxiety and other misery.

Which piece of advice does this section seem to agree with more?

A. Get expert help when you can use it, and save yourself a lot of pain,
or
B. if you want a job done well, do it yourself, and stand on your own two feet?

153. A special type of ally is a mental health professional. Many people with severe anxiety avoid using mental health professionals, for a variety of reasons. Hiring an ally who is an expert on the problem you are facing is often the most rational thing to do.

The advice of this section is

A. to use mental health professionals, without shame, if it helps,
or
B. to carefully check the qualifications of any mental health professional you think about getting help from?

154. Those who hesitate to get help from allies sometimes have a good reason. You want to avoid getting too much reinforcement for feeling bad. In other words, you want to avoid the setup where people give you what you want because you feel scared, and not when the fear goes away. The brain is programmed to figure out how to get what it wants. If being "sick" is the way to get what you want, the brain will be more likely to make you feel "sick." If the good feeling of being taken care of by someone who pities you is too pleasant, you can find yourself feeling bad in order to get that nice sympathy and caretaking. The best types of allies reward you, with their attention and kind words, for wanting to work on making things better, and for doing that work, not for feeling bad in and of itself.

In this section the author offers

A. a reason to be careful about support from allies,
or
B. a reason why you should get all the support you can without hesitation?

STEB and STEB revision

155. When you are setting goals, you want to be more specific than just thinking something like, "I want to get over my fear of social situations." You want to think in terms like this: "In _____ situation, I want to be able to think like this: _____; I want to have these emotions:_____; I want to behave in this way:_____." You want to make very clear the situations that are important, and the thoughts, emotions, and behaviors that you want to have in those situations. We can refer to a situation and the thoughts, emotions, and behaviors that go with it as a STEB.

STEB stands for

A. Situation, thoughts, emotions, and behavior,
or
B. Since Then, Even Better?

156. Suppose Felicia defines a goal as, "I want to get more comfortable in social situations." Rasheeda, who has a similar goal, defines it as follows:

"I want to be able to introduce myself to new people in any situation where people are standing around talking, and continue talking with them comfortably; to speak comfortably when called on in class; to get up in front of the class and make little presentations, and to talk on the phone – all with a level of discomfort of 2 or under on a scale of 10."

The more specific goals were set by

A. Felicia,
or
B. Rasheeda?

157. People tend to think of fear or anxiety as just an emotion. But the made-up word STEB can remind us that thoughts and behaviors greatly influence our emotions. Selecting and doing courageous thoughts and behaviors can help us enormously in feeling braver.

Our thoughts include the words you say to yourself, and the pictures and sounds you imagine. If you are walking over a bridge, thinking "Oh no, oh no, what if this bridge falls," and imagine yourself hurtling through the air immediately after the bridge falls, you're fairly likely to feel some fear. On the other hand, if you're thinking, "It's a lovely view from up here. I'm glad I got the chance to go hiking along this trail," and you imagine yourself showing your best friend the picture you're about to take, you're much less likely to feel afraid.

Here's a secret about thoughts: if you want to have the same emotions as nonanxious people, you think the same types of thoughts they think.

An important idea of the section above is that

A. you can influence your feelings by choosing which thoughts you want to think,
or
B. relaxing your body is a very important technique to use in reducing fear or aversion?

158. A very important type of thoughts is called self-reinforcement, also known as celebrating your own choices. Suppose that someone has a "work aversion" when it comes to doing math problems. This means that the person tends to feel more bored, tired, and restless the more problems he does, and these bad feelings increase rapidly. Suppose the person is saying to himself, as he does the problems, "This is such a drag. I've got so many to do. How can they expect me to do so much? I hate this." This sort of self-talk will surely increase the aversion.

This section gives an example of how

A. negative self-talk increases an aversion,
or
B. positive self-talk decreases an aversion?

159. But suppose the same person learns the art of self-reinforcing thoughts. Now as he does his work, he says things to himself like, "Hooray for me, I got started; that took self-discipline! I figured out how to do that one, good for me! I'm keeping my energy level up, I feel really good about doing that! I've been able to stay on task really well, that's cool! Wow, I'm done, I'm really pleased with the work I did!" The person is likely to feel much better about doing the work, and to reduce his work aversion.

An example of a sentence that is self-reinforcement or celebrating your own choice is

A. if I don't do this, bad things will happen,
or
B. I've been doing what I resolved to do, and I feel proud of myself for that!

160. When you are setting your goals for fear reduction, it's fine to speak of general goals such as "I want to get over my fear of social situations." But sooner or later, you will need to get specific. You will make a list of very specific situations, and decide how much distress each of these situations would give you if you were in it. You can rate the distress on a scale of 10, where 10 is most distress, and 0 is least. An example of a specific "social situation" is, "I go to a birthday party, at someone's house, and there are lots of people I don't know, and a few people I know just a little bit. I decide to try to chat with someone." If this situation would make someone very, very scared, then the person might rate the distress level as 8, 9, or 10 on a scale of 10. You will see such ratings referred to as the SUD level. SUD stands for "Subjective Units of Distress."

The advice in this section was that when you are setting your goals for fear-reduction, you should

A. imagine very specific situations that are scary, and give a rating to how scary they are,
or
B. learn skills of relaxing your muscles in order to bring down your fear?

161. When you are choosing the Behaviors you want to include in the STEBs you want to do more often, several are important. Perhaps most important is choosing to continue to stay in the situation, rather than to run away from it or otherwise try to escape it. This is called choosing "exposure" rather than "avoidance" or "escape." We'll talk more about this

when we speak of practice as a way of getting over fears.

A point made in this section is that

A. an important behavior to pay attention to is your facial expression,
or
B. an important behavior is staying in the scary situation rather than escaping it or avoiding it?

Tones of voice

162. When choosing your goals, another important behavior is your tones of voice. Even if you can't hear someone's words, you can usually tell how excited that person is by listening to how much the pitch of the voice goes up and down. This is partly because your feelings influence your tones of voice, but also because your tones of voice influence your feelings! If you speak to yourself and others in calm, relaxed tones of voice, you're less likely to feel very scared. On the other hand, if you're speaking in the same tones as people would use when they scream, "Help! The house is on fire!" you're more likely to feel afraid.

The main idea of this section is that

A. the mental pictures you have in your mind can make you scared or not scared,
or
B. you can change your feelings by purposely changing the tones of voice with which you speak to yourself and others?

163. Calm, relaxed, quiet tones of voice are not the only ones that people can use when they are purposely trying to be less afraid. Some people also very successfully use humorous tones, and say funny things, to keep themselves from being so scared. The tones of voice that go along with humor are quite varied.

The point made by this section is that

A. if you want to be less scared, speak in a tone that sounds like you're about to fall asleep,
or
B. saying funny things, in humorous tones of voice, can also reduce fear?

164. Here's an example. A person is very much afraid of vomiting in front of other people. To help reduce the fear, he spends some time thinking of funny lines to say if the dreaded situation comes. For example, he practices, bowing to the people who are all looking at him, and saying, "And that's the end of the first act.

The second act may be even more exciting!" He tries on a different line: He looks at his audience, shrugs, and says, "Guess I didn't need that breakfast all that much anyway!" Then he imagines looking at the audience and saying, "Well, that's the end of my performance for today's talent show; who wants to go next?" Then he imagines himself looking at the teacher and saying, "Sorry to have interrupted the class. I guess I should have raised my hand first." Even if he never gets the chance to use these lines, his practice with saying them in a relaxed and confident way makes him less fearful.

This section recommends making up ways of joking about scary situations

A. because humor tends to reduce fear,
or
B. because a career as a comedian is desirable for you?

165. Tones of voice are one of the ways in which people act the part of someone not suffering from fear or an aversion. The phrase "tones of voice" can also remind us of other ways of being a good actor: using the facial expressions and making the types of motions that communicate to others and to ourselves that we feel safe and secure and confident.

Why does this work? Because we feel the way we do partly because we notice what our bodies are doing, and if we act the part of a person who feels fearless well enough, our feelings can go along with our actions.

This section makes the point that

A. we should never hide our fear by trying to act unafraid,
or
B. by acting the part of an unafraid person, we can actually reduce our fears?

Breathing

166. Another important behavior to think about is your breathing. Particularly, anyone with anxiety should think about breathing more SLOWLY when in a scary situation. People can get into very unpleasant cycles where they breathe too fast; this makes them feel a strange feeling; sometimes the brain interprets this strange feeling as not having enough air; this makes them breathe even faster. A full-blown cycle of this is called hyperventilation, and hyperventilation contributes a lot to what are called panic attacks. But sometimes people can make themselves more anxious than they need to be by breathing too fast,

without having full-blown hyperventilation. How and when to slow your breathing is one of the great secrets everyone should know about.

With regard to breathing, this section advises that there are times when it's important to

A. breathe more slowly,
or
B. breathe more deeply?

Activation or arousal

167. Another important behavior to think about when you are setting goals is *arousal, or activation*, versus *relaxation*. How psyched up are you? How excited are you? How calm and peaceful do you feel? Later in this book, we'll discuss a variety of techniques for learning this crucially useful skill of turning down your excitement and relaxing. By relaxation, we're definitely not talking about someone's saying, "Just relax!" when you're feeling panicked. We're also talking about something more momentous than the word *relaxation* suggests. We're talking about gradually learning to take control of the excitement or arousal that your nervous system produces in you, and to be able to turn that excitement up or down at will! This means having a

way, or several ways, of directly making yourself more calm when you feel anxious. And since it's very difficult to feel anxious while at the same time feeling very calm, this technique can be extremely valuable in overcoming unrealistic fears.

The point of this section is that

A. If you sit down and relax a while when you feel nervous, you'll feel better.
or
B. If you gradually learn to raise and lower your level of excitement, you will have a tool that will be of major benefit in reducing any fears.

168. While we're talking about goal-setting and arousal or activation: sometimes the goal is not to reduce your excitement, but to change the excitement from unpleasant fear to positive, confident excitement.

For example, Leah is planning to sing before a lot of people. She is at first very nervous when she anticipates this. But her goal is not to turn down her arousal to the point where she's almost falling asleep when she steps on stage. Her goal is to have lots of excitement that she communicates to her audience, but to feel that excitement in a pleasurable way. She figures out that the difference is whether she thinks, "I can do it," or whether she thinks, "I'm going to fail." She works to the point where she feels very confident, and to have lots of fun singing. It takes her several performances before the excited fun outweighs the unpleasant fear, but she gets there.

The point of this section is that

A. in thinking about activation and arousal, lots of times our goal is not just to lower it, but to make it more pleasant,
or
B. activation and arousal often involve the action of adrenaline?

Doing, versus feeling, as the first marker of success

169. You will find it easier to succeed at fear-reduction if you define your success by what you do than by how you feel. You can remember this idea by the phrase *doing, versus feeling*, as the way of judging success. If you let feelings be your main guide as to whether you're succeeding, you're in danger of getting into a vicious cycle, that goes like this: "Oh no, I'm feeling scared. I didn't want to! I'm failing! That's so bad! Now I feel worse! Now I'm even more of a failure!" This is a vicious cycle to stay out of.

What's the point of this section?

A. When you wish strongly for fear-reduction, those wishes tend to be granted, because in the mind, wishing does tend to make things happen.
or
B. When you do something that causes unrealistic fear, count it as a success if you do a good job at it, whether or not you have anxiety while doing it.

170. Here's an example of "Doing versus feeling." Suppose that two people are giving a speech. Both of them are feeling very high anxiety. Both of them are doing a good job of giving the speech, so far. The first one is thinking, "Hurray for me! Despite the fact that I've got all this anxiety, I'm doing a great job! Feeling scared but performing well just teaches me that this anxiety will not defeat me!"

The second one is thinking, "Oh no! I'm feeling so scared! I need to get calmer, right now! Oh no, I can't get calmer!"

Which one of these will be more likely to enjoy the speech more, to have lower anxiety, and to avoid getting into a vicious cycle?

A. the first,
or
B. the second?

171. The phrase, "Doing versus feeling," is meant to remind you of this: Don't wait for your anxiety to go away before putting on a good performance. Go ahead and to start the good performance, even though you are feeling anxious. A good performance itself will be likely to reduce the anxiety. But even if it doesn't, you've still done what you need to do!

Which of these comes closest to the message of this section?

A. Do the right thing, and the right feeling will follow,
or
B. You must feel the right way before you can do the right thing?

172. When I use the word *performance*, I'm not just referring to public speaking or acting or singing. I'm talking about acting the same way a non-anxious person acts in whatever you are trying to do. For someone with a fear of intruders at bedtime, a good performance is relaxing with pleasant thoughts and staying in bed. For someone with a fear of school, a good performance may be showing up at school, paying attention in classes, doing the homework, taking the tests, and staying out of the nurse's office. For someone with a fear of bugs, a good performance may be sitting outside and watching a daddy-long-legs crawl along the ground. A good performance means doing whatever you wish you could do if you didn't have the unrealistic fear.

The author's purpose in this section was to

A. clarify what he meant by the word *performance* that was used in previous sections,
Or
B. emphasize the idea that learning to raise and lower your level of excitement helps greatly in getting over fears?

173. So far we've been talking about ways of reducing fear that are classifed under "objectives." We've talked about

Probabilities and utilities
Allies
STEBs
Tones of voice

Breathing
Activation versus relaxation
Doing versus feeling = success.

These can be remembered by the mnemonic PAST BAD.

The purpose of this section was to summarize

A. the reasons why people have fears or aversions,

or

B. several ways of reducing fears that we've made subtopics under "objectives," and a mnemonic for them?

Hierarchy – a list of situations in order of difficulty

174. The next technique to keep in mind is *hierarchy* as in "working your way up a hierarchy of difficulty." A hierarchy is a list of things in order. If you list scary situations in order of how scary they are, that's a hierarchy. In getting over fears or aversions, it's great to start exposing yourself to and practicing with the easier situations, and work your way up gradually to the harder ones.

The point of this section is that

A. When reducing fears, it's good to go straight to the scariest situation you can imagine, and do exposure to it,

or

B. When reducing fears, it's good to go gradually up a series of steps starting with not very scary situations and working your way up.

175. Suppose a person has a huge aversion to images of people's vomiting. This aversion causes avoidance of any situation where someone could get sick, and quite a bit of discomfort when there is a possibility of anyone's getting sick.

One of the ways of practicing handling the scary situation and doing exposure is to look at pictures representing vomiting. But rather than starting with the most graphic and disturbing pictures, it's good to start with mild ones. The first picture on a hierarchy I've used is a photo of white yarn. If you use your imagination, the yarn resembles someone vomiting. As you go up the hierarchy, the series of pictures includes photographs of pumpkins, pictures of statues, line drawings, cartoon characters, and so forth. The top of the hierarchy, as you might guess, is pictures of real people appearing to throw up.

The main principle this specific example is meant to illustrate is that

A. Pictures of yarn are a useful starting place in getting over an aversion to the image of vomiting,

or

B. Moving along a gradual hierarchy of scary situations often works better than going straight to the scariest situation?

176. Why is it usually a good idea to move through gradual steps rather than taking on the worst fears from the start? Because you can often get rid of a low fear without much pain and discomfort, and then (wonderful to behold) the fears above it on the list often seem to have become less scary also! Plus, having success experiences with low fears gives you the confidence and trust in the techniques, and the power to persist, that you will need for the higher fears.

Studies have found that exposure and practice seem to work, even if you go straight to the highest fear and start there. But going through a series of gradual steps seems much less painful for most people. Most people find it easier to get started and to stick with the fear-reduction project when it isn't so painful.

You don't necessarily have to go through the steps slowly. You can move along a hierarchy, but quickly, if you want to get over a fear in a hurry.

The author advises going through a series of hierarchical steps because

A. The fears only get reduced if you do it that way,
or
B. It's usually more pleasant to do it that way?

177. Hierarchy means that you both

1. figure out a series of small-enough steps that lead from where you are to where you want to go,
and
2. move up or down the hierarchy so that the level you are working on, at any time, is not too hard, not too easy, but at the right level of difficulty.

The expert use of hierarchy is one of the characteristics of excellent education. Excellent tutors move up and down the hierarchy of difficulty so as to maximize their students' success. They move down the hierarchy of difficulty as far as necessary for the student to have success experiences; they move up the hierarchy as their student becomes more and more expert. Getting over fears and aversions is a form of self-education, in which you are your own tutor.

The word *hierarchy* as we are using it here refers to

A. the way in organizations, some people are in charge of others, who are in charge of others, and so forth,
or
B. a set of steps to go through when you are learning things, arranged in order of difficulty?

178. Suppose that someone wants to get over a fear of bees and insects.

Here might be an example of a hierarchy for the person to go through.
1. I look at pictures of bees and other bugs.
2. I look at videos of bees and bugs flying and crawling around.
3. I watch a harmless bug crawl or fly around.
4. I let the bug be on my hand.
5. I go to a hornet's nest and watch the hornets from a closed car.
6. I get out of the car and look at the hornets' nest, from a safe distance.
The hierarchy can be broken down into even more steps if before each step there are two more steps: fantasy rehearsing that action, and observing someone else do it.

Although it would probably take longer for someone to go through all these steps than to go straight to the most difficult thing and do that first, it would also probably be

A. more pleasant,
or
B. more unpleasant?

Attribution

179. The next method is called *attribution*. The word attribution has to do with what sorts of labels you stick on yourself – what qualities, abilities, inabilities, or traits you think

of yourself as having. If someone thinks to himself, "I'm a very anxious person," or "I hate to work," he is *attributing* to himself the traits of anxiety or work-aversion. On the other hand, if the person thinks, "I can get over this fear, even though I haven't done it yet," or "I can gradually build my work capacity," then he is attributing to himself the ability to improve in these ways.

What's the main point of this section?

A. The word *attribution* comes from a word that has to do with giving; this word was also used in making the words *tribute* and *contribution*.
or
B. By the word *attribution*, the author refers to how we think of ourselves as having certain traits and characteristics?

180. Many people fail to improve because they make attributions about themselves that keep themselves stuck. They think, "This is just the way I am. I couldn't do that – it's just not me." Sometimes by learning to say things like, "It may take a lot of work, but I can change in this way," or "I haven't learned to do this yet, but I will feel really good when I have learned it," they help themselves to start logging in the time working. Sometimes the key to positive

attributions is to think, "Other people have learned to reduce this type of fear and aversion, and I can do it too." Sometimes it helps to read about studies in which people really did successfully get over fears and aversions in order to convince yourself that these are not permanent traits of people; they can be altered.

Attribution has to do with

A. how you think about what you're like,
or
B. what sorts of rewards you get for avoidance or exposure?

Modeling

181. A very important method is *modeling*. A model is something that you can imitate. When you are improving your behavior patterns, finding useful models to imitate can save people many hours of attempting to "reinvent the wheel." The more you can see real-life examples, or examples in movies or in written stories, or even in the stories that people tell you or that you make up for yourself, about people skillfully handling the situations, the easier it will be for you to handle them.

The author's attitude is that

A. you should strive to be a totally original person, and come up with your own ways of acting, independent of anything anyone else has done,
or
B. you should find the best models for imitation that you can, and run them through your mind often?

182. The principle of modeling implies that if you want to do something really well, it's good to have lots and lots of little stories in your memory bank, stories of someone (maybe even yourself) doing the thing really well. You'll probably notice that this book has scattered through it many brief stories of someone using a courage skills technique well. The more you keep these modeling stories in mind, the easier your task will be.

What's the message of this section?

A. You are more likely to imitate a model if you admire the character.
or
B. Lots of modeling stories regarding courage skills are interspersed through this book for you to use.

Practice (including fantasy rehearsal)

183. Perhaps the most important technique for fear-reduction is practice: you practice putting yourself in the scary situation and enacting the best and most reasonable thoughts, emotions, and behaviors that you can come up with.

If you want to practice handling a situation, you have to put yourself into the situation, in imagination or in reality. Putting yourself into a scary situation is called *exposure*, because you *expose* yourself to the scary thing. You put yourself in the situations you so much want to avoid. You do that so that you can get used to those situations, and so that you can practice handling them well.

You get over fears of high places by practicing being in high places. You get over fears of elevators by practicing being in elevators. You get over fears of the dark by practicing being in the dark. And so on. When you're in unrealistically feared situations long enough, you tend to get over the fear, especially if you're practicing handling the situation well during each exposure.

A way of summarizing the idea of exposure is that

A. if you want to handle a scary situation well, you need to practice with that situation,
or

B. being able to relax your muscles and turn down your level of arousal helps you handle exposures more successfully?

184. Here's a point that bears repeating many times. It's very important that your exposures last long enough. It's also important that you end your exposures when you've achieved your goal for that exposure, not because the fear got too bad for you to handle exposure any longer. The end of an exposure is usually a reward. For this reason, you want to have the ends of your exposures reward "goal attainment," or achieving something, rather than deciding "I can't take this any more."

This section advised you to end exposures when you have

A. accomplished what you set out to accomplish,
Or
B. stayed in the situation for as long as you can stand to?

185. If you have a brief exposure, then escape from the scary situation when the fear gets too bad, and feel great relief, your brain learns that relief shortly follows great fear. This probably makes you MORE afraid of the situation, not less. So end your exposure after a certain length of time,

or when the fear has gone down a certain amount. Be careful not to end your exposures in a way that rewards you for feeling fear!

Someone with a school phobia goes to walk around the school building after school. Which of the following plans is better?

A. Walk up and down the hallways for 25 minutes, and then celebrate a major achievement.
or
B. Walk around until you decide, "I've had enough; I can't take this any more," and then stop?

186. As we discussed in the previous chapter, a very important turning point comes when someone starts to view exposures as opportunities. This is the exact opposite of the attitude that most of us have toward a scary situation, which is "I want to get away from it and stay away from it!" The opposite of "deliberate exposure" is "avoidance." Once someone really makes up his mind that he wants to get used to the scary situation, to learn to handle it well, to confront it, to bring it on, rather than to avoid it, the battle is half won. This is what we have called the decision to "go for mastery."

The author feels that the battle is half won when a person

A. learns to relax effectively,
or
B. decides to deliberately deal with the scary or aversive situation rather than avoid it?

187. A very important method of practicing courageous STEBs is called *fantasy rehearsal*.
        Fantasy rehearsal means practicing a useful way of thinking, feeling, or behaving, in your fantasy, or your imagination. It is a wonderful fact about the human brain that when we imagine ourselves doing things well, we make it easier for ourselves to do those things well in real life.

The main point of this section is that

A. you can learn from practice in imagination, just as from real-life practice,
or
B. when you do fantasy rehearsals, you want to imagine handling the situation WELL.

188. It is very lucky that fantasy rehearsal works, because sometimes real-life practice isn't available, or else it's too difficult at the moment. Suppose that someone is playing in an important music concert. But just

thinking about playing on stage brings her great stage fright. Practicing handling the scary situation well is the key to getting over unrealistic fear. But how can she practice handling the scary situation well if it hasn't happened yet?

The answer is, she creates the scary situation in her imagination.

Our musician imagines sitting offstage, waiting for the performance to begin, hearing the audience file in and take their seats. Then she imagines the noise of the audience becoming silent, and the announcement. Then she visualizes herself walking onto the stage, looking confident, feeling pleasantly excited. Then, while imagining herself on the stage, she takes her real instrument and plays.

By using her imagination, the musician in this example has

A. gotten some practice in handling the concert situation well,
or
B. simply practiced playing the song one more time?

189. One of the great things about fantasy rehearsal is that you are limited only by the amount of time and energy you want to put into the work on reducing unrealistic fears. You can spend much time each day practicing handling the scary situation just as you'd like to handle it, if you want to. And you can be confident that this effort will get you closer and closer to the goal of reducing the unrealistic fear. It is wonderful that we have discovered the usefulness of fantasy rehearsal.

One of the points made by this section is that

A. It's great that by fantasy rehearsal, you can put time into working on reducing fears, in a way that really gets you somewhere!
or
B. Humorous ways of dealing with scary situations often relieve anxiety.

190. Pure exposure to scary situations, while simply waiting for the fear to go down, is often quite uncomfortable. In the past, prolonged painful exposure was thought to be the only way to get over unrealistic fears. But if you repeatedly imagine yourself handling the situation confidently, successfully, and with pleasure, you can sometimes reduce unrealistic fear without feeling much pain or discomfort. These sorts of pleasant fantasies are called "mastery fantasy rehearsals." This is another major breakthrough in reducing fear, and it is one of the big secrets of success in fear-reduction.

The main point of this section is that

A. "If there's no pain, there's no gain."
or
B. By imagining yourself handling scary situations confidently, successfully, and with pleasure, you can gain very much without much pain.

191. Anyone with anxiety problems should figure out a daily "courage skills workout." For example, once you learn techniques of getting yourself very relaxed and calm, it's good to practice those methods close to every single day, so that you become more and more expert at them. People who tend to start breathing too fast should practice every day with the exercise of purposefully breathing fast for a short time, feeling just a tiny bit of the strange feeling this brings on, and curing that feeling by breathing more slowly. Doing fantasy rehearsals of handling the situations most important for you also belongs on the daily workout. If it's possible to do real-life exposure and practice, this also should be done frequently.

A therapist often does well to act like a "personal trainer," working up lots of enthusiasm and motivation to do the daily exercises.

In this section, the author compares the person doing daily practice in courage skills to

A. a scientist making a discovery,
or
B. an athlete working out every day?

Reinforcement

192. Next on our list of methods of changing yourself for the better is *reinforcement*. Reinforcement means approximately the same thing as reward. The more you get rewarded for facing the feared situation and handling it successfully, the more confident you will feel about handling it in the future. Also, the more you are rewarded or reinforced for exposing yourself to the situation, the more you will tend to do more exposure in the future.

What's the point of this section?

A. Positive reinforcement means about the same thing as reward; when you get reinforced for doing something, you tend to do it more frequently.
or
B. It takes a great deal of self-discipline to withhold from yourself a reinforcer, and let yourself have it only when you have carried out a plan to earn it.

193. Reinforcement can come from someone else, or from within yourself. If you put on a public speech, or a public musical performance and the crowd applauds for you, the applause is reinforcement from someone else (called extrinsic reinforcement). On the other hand, suppose you practice for your speech or your performance and you say to yourself, "Hurray for me! I did a good practice!" Then the reinforcement is coming from what you say to yourself. (This is called intrinsic reinforcement.) Both reinforcement from outside you and from within you are important.

When someone is doing an exposure to a feared situation and thinks, "Hooray for me! I'm creating a courage triumph!" the person is delivering to himself

A. intrinsic reinforcement,
or
B. extrinsic reinforcement?

194. When you escape from a very unpleasant situation, the end of the unpleasantness is very rewarding; it is called negative reinforcement. Suppose you set out to do exposure and practice with a scary situation, and then lose your nerve because it's too distressing, and escape from it. The reduction of your distress reinforces escape, leaving you with an even stronger urge to escape next time. And the urge to escape is the same as fear. So losing the nerve and escaping tends to increase fear. I have explained this before, but it's so important that it bears repeating!

The idea repeated in this section is that

A. you should try to find people who will reinforce you for courage,
or
B. if you do exposure and then escape because it's too unpleasant for you, you probably increase your fear rather than decrease it?

195. One of the most important principles in the use of reinforcement is to avoid letting people reinforce you for having fears and aversions.

Lillian has been having lots of fears. Her parent is short on money, and is wanting to apply for disability so that the family can get sent a check each month as long as Lillian is having great fears. Lillian realizes that if they are successful, she would be rewarded for staying disabled and would be punished by the loss of money if she gets over her fears. She talks about this with her parent, and they decide not to apply for disability payments. They decide that she will put all her effort into getting better and not into getting something that can reinforce her for hanging on to unrealistic fears.

An idea behind this section is that

A. reinforcement for being scared can make us feel scared more often,
or
B. it is important not to use too much self-punishment in what we say to ourselves?

196. As we discussed in Chapter 2, reinforcement can increase fears and aversions without our even realizing that they are doing so. People do not need to think, "Hmm, here is what I want, and here is how I can get it. I'll just be scared more often, and that will let me get what I want." But our brains are constantly figuring out how to get what we want, even when we are not aware of it.

The main idea of this section is that

A. reinforcement can increase fears or aversions without our being at all conscious of trying to get the reinforcement,
or
B. the definition of reinforcement is something that comes after a behavior, that makes the behavior more likely to occur in the future?

197. Sean doesn't like to separate from his mom. He has a couple of panic attacks at school. The school personnel and his mom work out that when he has a panic attack, his mom will come over to the school and sit with him and comfort him and rub his back. The teachers notice that as soon as his mom shows up at school, he looks much calmer and stops looking panicked. They think, "This arrangement was a great idea." But then they notice that the panic attacks start happening more and more frequently. They finally are occurring several times a day. They figure out that his mom's visits are reinforcing the feelings of panic. They work out a different plan: that each time Sean goes for a few hours without having a panic attack, his mom will come over or talk with him on the phone to congratulate him. His panic attacks become much less frequent.

The main point of this story is that

A. getting something we want each time we get scared can make us get scared more often,
or
B. negative reinforcement occurs when something unpleasant stops happening?

198. Sandra is married to a man who is very critical and demanding. But

when she starts having anxiety symptoms, and fears leaving the house, he feels sorry for her and acts much kinder. (It turns out that he is afraid of losing her to some other man, and when she stays at home, he feels much less scared of that.) But his acting nicer to her when she is scared to go out reinforces her fear, and she gets more and more scared of leaving the house. For a long time neither of them is consciously aware of what is going on.

What's a major point of this little story?

A. We can rehearse brave actions in fantasy, and by doing so, we can make ourselves braver in real life.
or
B. When people are a lot kinder to us when we are scared, our brains can decide to make us scared more often, without our even realizing it?

199. On the other hand: imagine that Sandra manages to enlighten her husband about how he can really be helpful. She makes a list of courage skills triumphs that she wants to make – new places to go, new social situations to handle successfully, and so forth. Each time she does one of these, her husband now congratulates her, pats her on the back, celebrates with special meals, speaks about her

triumphs with pride, looks cheerful and happy, and does something fun with her that her increasing mastery has allowed her to enjoy. Her chances of success in her goals of mastery are vastly greater!

This section is meant to illustrate the point that

A. if someone close to you reinforces steps toward mastery rather than reinforcing avoidance, your success is more likely,
or
B. changing the way family members act toward you is unfortunately not so simple as just asking them to do so?

200. The ideal situation for getting over useless fears exists when people you care about are ready to celebrate your "courage skill triumphs." That is, each time you bravely expose yourself to a situation and practice the sort of thought, feeling, and behavior that you want to do more of, you get the congratulations, admiration, and joy of the important people around you, in a way that feels really good. You are reinforced for your steps toward mastery, and not for avoidance.

If your goal is to reduce unrealistic aversions or fears, you should strongly consider talking about reinforcement with your family or friends. If they can reinforce your courage skills triumphs and avoid reinforcing fear and aversion, you are much more likely to succeed!

But even if they can't change, you are always in control of your self-reinforcement. You can always say, "Hooray for me!" even when there is not someone else saying, "Hooray for you!"

The author's attitude is closer to which of these two?

A. If people around you can't reinforce you for steps toward mastery, you might as well give up.
or
B. If people around you can't change, and reinforce your aversion rather than mastery, at least you can redouble your efforts to reinforce yourself.

Instruction and information-seeking

201. Next is instruction and information-seeking. Lots of times, finding out the facts about the situation lets us handle the situation with less fear.

A few years ago a tick bit one of my daughters while we were on a hiking trip. We got the tick off quickly. But then I found myself in a state of high anxiety over whether my daughter would get Lyme Disease, a sometimes very troubling disease that is spread by ticks. As soon as we returned, however, I got onto the Internet and was able to find out that Lyme disease was almost never found in the ticks in the part of Virginia where we were, at least at that time. I also found out that if you get the tick off within a certain amount of time, the chance of getting Lyme Disease is small, even if the tick does have Lyme Disease. My fear went way down when I found this information, and it went down further when a phone call with my daughter's pediatrician gave further reassurance. If the information I had turned up had shown that she was in danger and needed to have further tests done or treatment, the information still would have been useful in helping us form a concrete plan.

The main point of this section is that

A. Western Virginia around the year 2000 was not a place where ticks spread Lyme disease very much,
or
B. finding the information and facts about the situation you're in helps you to deal with it better, and often reduces fear.

202. Here's an example of a different type of information seeking: A girl feels afraid that one of her friends

doesn't like her anymore. The friend has been acting less enthusiastic, and has been smiling at her less. So the girl decides to seek information by asking her friend about it. She says, "I notice you've been smiling less and being less enthusiastic for the last few days. Is there something wrong? Did I do something? Would you like to talk about it?" The friend replies that she's been worried about an illness that her grandmother has. The girl is then able to support her friend; she feels sympathetic instead of afraid. Because of her skillful information-seeking, she can strengthen the relationship rather than weaken it.

In this example

A. someone became less worried by moving gradually to more and more exposures,
or
B. someone became less worried by getting some information about what was going on in the situation she was in?

203. Instruction includes words or pictures that communicate to you how to do something or understand something. When you are learning not to fear a certain activity, it is good to take in as much good instruction as you can about how to do the situation well. If you are learning to get over a fear of public speaking, it helps to read books about how to do public speaking well. If you're learning to get over a fear of social conversation, it's good to read books on this subject.

This book, of course, is an example of a resource for instruction. The more you master the ideas in it, the better equipped you are to overcome fears and aversions. Even after you understand everything in it, the more time you spend reading to remind yourself of the ideas and methods, the better chance you have at succeeding at your goals.

In this section the author recommends

A. reading and re-reading instructions to keep yourself reminded of the important ideas,
or
B. doing anti-anxiety exercises at a routine time, the same time each day?

204. Instruction, combined with practice, often results in building the skills that help you to handle a situation comfortably, without fear.

Skill is often a huge antidote to fear. For example: if you are afraid of public speaking, skill-building means working to become an excellent public speaker. If you are afraid of being in social situations and having to make conversation with people, skill building means working to become an excellent social conversationalist. If you have test anxiety about math tests, skill building means working hard to become competent at the types of problems you'll face on the test. For a doctor who feels scared of making a mistake, lots of study and work in doing the job competently can be the best protection against anxiety.

The point of this section is that

A. getting able to handle a situation more expertly is often a great way to reduce your fear of that situation,
or
B. thinking more calming sentences tends to make us less scared?

Stimulus control

205. Our eighth general way of helping yourself change is *stimulus control*. The things that we see and hear, the things that we respond to, the situations we're in, are called stimuli. When someone tries to control the stimuli around him so as to bring out certain behaviors or thoughts or feelings, he is using stimulus control. For example, someone who wants to practice socializing more comfortably identifies certain people who, for whatever reason, seem to bring out more comfortable socializing in him.

The person purposely hangs out with these people more often.

As another example: a college student with an aversion to schoolwork finds that it is easier to work when sitting at a table at the college library, with hard-working students all around, than when sitting in the living room of a fraternity house. The student does well to put himself in the stimulus situations that bring out the desired way of acting.

The point of this section is that

A. when you are trying to do certain things, list your reasons for wanting to do them,
or
B. when you are trying to do certain things, try to put yourself in the situations that seem to stimulate those behaviors?

Monitoring

206. The ninth and final method of influence is *monitoring*. This means that you monitor, or measure and record, your progress as you go along. One way that people monitor their progress with fears or aversions is by rating their distress levels, or "SUD levels." (We mentioned earlier that SUD stands for *Subjective Units of Distress*.) If your SUD level is 10 on a

scale of 10, you feel just about as distressed as you can possibly get. On the other hand, if your SUD level is zero, you do not feel the slightest bit of distress. The distressed feeling that you are rating with a SUD level can be fear, discomfort, worry, anger, or any other unpleasant emotion. Very often, when people are working on fears and aversions, they will make a list of the situations that they want to get less scared of. They will rate how aversive each of those situations is to them. Over time, if their efforts are successful, the ratings of the SUD levels go down.

Having a list of your main fears and aversions, where you frequently write down the SUD level you would feel in each of those situations, is a way of carrying out

A. monitoring,
or
B. attribution?

207. Near the end of this book is a Fear and Aversion Rating Scale. This consists of a long list of situations that can cause fear or aversion, and 0 to 10 scale to rate your distress for each of them. It's good to come back to rate the situations again and again over time. That way you can track your progress, and celebrate when you see unrealistic distress going down.

The purpose of this section was to

A. talk about the theory of why monitoring causes improvement,
or
B. tell you about a questionnaire you can use to keep track of your progress in reducing fears and aversions?

208. Why is monitoring important? Because "what is measured, gets improved." The more you keep track of how you are doing, the more you will tend to do more of the things that increase your success. Putting numbers on how much we have accomplished is like keeping score in a game. It motivates us to achieve, and it helps us know when we are on the right track.

For example, if the graph of someone's SUD level while talking with people at breaks in school is coming down and down, the person knows to celebrate and to keep up the good work with whatever techniques she is using. If the graph is level or going up, the monitoring gives a signal that says, "Maybe you need to stay the course, but you should also consider trying something new."

One of the points of this section is that

A. monitoring helps you know whether to celebrate being on the right

track or to problem-solve in order to get on the right track,
or
B. moving down the hierarchy of difficulty is often a good response to a lack of progress?

209. Let's review the ways of reducing fears and aversions, and gaining courage skills, that we discussed in this chapter. There were 9 general methods. Under goal-setting or objective-formation, there were 7 aspects of goal-setting that help a lot with fear-reduction. Here are the methods we've discussed

1. Objective-formation, or goal-setting
   Probabilities and utilities
   Allies
   STEBs
   Tones of Voice
   Breathing
   Activation versus relaxation
   Doing rather than feeling

2. Hierarchy, or a series of steps of gradually increasing difficulty or complexity

3. Attribution, or thinking that you have the capacity to change

4. Modeling, or seeing positive examples of what you want to do

5. Practice, or rehearsal of what you want to do. To do this, you usually have to have *exposure* to the scary situation.

6. Reinforcement, or getting rewarded for good examples of what you want to do

7. Instruction, or hearing, reading, and learning about the situation or how to do what you want to do

8. Stimulus control, or putting yourself in the situations that bring out desirable behavior

9. Monitoring, or measuring and keeping track of how you are doing

Two mnemonics, for the 9 general methods and for the 7 methods classed under "objectives," are

A. A GOOD MAN and LONG LIFE, or
B. OH AM PRISM and PAST BAD?

210. Some people find it useful to memorize the list of methods you just read about. Memorizing them allows you to go through them one by one and think of ways to make things better, for any fear or aversion you develop. The lists in this chapter will also be helpful when you want to grow in any other psychological skills.

These methods give you a set of strategies that will enable you to take charge of your efforts to become a happier and more productive person.

The section you just read

A. states that the methods in this chapter are important enough to memorize,
or
B. emphasizes the point that you should practice daily?

Chapter 5: Listing Situations and Making Hierarchies

Deciding what you're really afraid of

211. An overnight school field trip is coming up, and four children are very much afraid of going on it. If someone were to ask, "What are they really afraid of," someone else might say, "Field trips, of course!"

But let's imagine that someone asks each of them, "What would be the worst or scariest thing about going on the field trip?" The first is very much afraid of riding on the bus, for fear that it doesn't have seat belts and there could be an accident. The second is afraid of wetting the bed and being humiliated when friends find out. The third is afraid of not being able to fall asleep in a new place and getting a bad headache (which she tends to get when very sleep deprived). The fourth is afraid of separating from his mom and not having her close at hand.

Thus what they were really afraid of was very different from one another.

The question that revealed what the four different kids were afraid of was

A. "When did you start feeling afraid of field trips?"

or

B. "What would be the worst thing about going on the field trip?"

212. Sometimes you have to ask the question, "What would be so bad about that," more than once. Imagine three kids who are afraid to go to school. When you ask, "What is bad about going to school," the answer for each of the three of them is the same: "I could catch a virus from someone, that causes me to throw up at school." But then, when you ask, "What is the worst thing about the idea of having the virus and throwing up," their answers are different.

The first says, "I would be so embarrassed to gross out the people I know." When you ask, "What would be so bad about that," the first says, "They would reject me and not want to be my friends."

The second says, "I couldn't handle the bad feeling of throwing up."

The third says, "I could get sicker and sicker and die."

What the three people in this example are really afraid of, respectively, is

A. school, separation from parents, and bullies,

or

B. rejection, pain, and death?

213. It's very useful to keep asking the "What's bad about that" question until you figure out what you're really most afraid of. The answer to the question very much affects how you go about getting over the fear.

Two people are afraid of going to bed at night. For the first, the answer to "What's the worst thing about that?" is, "I have images in my mind about monsters coming out from under my bed, to kill me." In this case, the person benefits from imagining these same monsters, transformed into helpful friends and allies. For the second person, the answer to "What's the worst thing about going to bed?" is, "I have the fear that while I'm sleeping, I'll stop breathing and die." For this person, getting some information about the drive to continue breathing, and how powerful it is, turns out to be very helpful.

This section

A. gives an example of how figuring out what you're really afraid of influences how you get rid of the fear,

or

B. gives an example of how learning to relax your muscles helps to get rid of fears?

214. Sometimes when you ask the question, "What is so bad about that," or "What's the worst that could happen with that," you find that what you're really afraid of is something you had not really realized before. For example, Jack gets periods of great anxiety, which in themselves are very scary. When Jack asks himself, "What is so bad about getting these episodes that I get," he answers himself, "The idea that I could lose control." When he asks himself, "What's so bad about losing control," he answers himself, "That I might do something that would hurt someone." When he thinks about the probability that he would hurt someone, given that he has never done so in the past, he immediately feels less afraid of his anxiety episodes.

The method the person in this example used to reduce his fear, once he figured out what he was really afraid of, was

A. thinking about probabilities,

or

B. prolonged exposure?

Making up specific situations to practice with

215. One of the major ways you get over fears is by fantasy rehearsals; this means that you practice, in your imagination, handling the situation well. When preparing to do this, you list a bunch of specific situations to practice with. The phrase *specific situation* means that if you described the situation to several movie makers, the movies they would make of the situation would be very similar to each other. The word *general* means that the movies could be very different.

The main purposes of this section are to

A. advise making up specific situations to practice with, and telling what specific means;
or
B. advise that when you make up situations, you take time to practice with them every single day?

216. Imagine that someone is preparing to get over a fear of heights. Suppose the person considers listing as a situation, "I'm in a high place." This is not very specific – there are all sorts of high places. There could be some high places that are very scary, and others that are much less scary. When the person lists more specific situations, he lists "I'm standing on the glass floor at the top of the CN Tower in Toronto, where I can look hundreds of meters straight down," he imagines that the distress or SUD level for this would be 10 on a scale of 10. He also lists, "I'm standing on the first of three steps of some stairs," and the SUD level for this is 1 on a scale of 10.

This section makes the point that when you make up lots of very specific situations,

A. they are easier to imagine vividly, or
B. they may fall at very different places on the hierarchy of difficulty?

Why make a hierarchy?

217. Let's review what the phrase *hierarchy of situations* means. It's a list, arranged in order of least scary to most scary. Suppose someone is afraid of dogs. Imagining a television program showing sleeping puppies is scary 0 on a scale of 10 – it's at the bottom of the hierarchy. Imagining actually being near a sleeping puppy is scary 2 on a scale of 10. Imagining petting a very friendly small dog, a cocker spaniel, is 5 on a scale of 10. Imagining petting a very friendly larger dog, a golden retriever, is 7 on a scale of 10. Imagining petting a

friendly large Rottweiler is 9 on a scale of 10. And imagining seeing a large Rottweiler barking ferociously is 10 on a scale of 10.

The purpose of this section is to

A. define the hierarchy of difficulty and give an example of it,
or
B. give an example of why a scale of 10 is better than a scale of only 3?

218. Suppose Gina has a major aversion to vomit, that causes a great deal of avoidance. Why not just start with the grossest image she can imagine, and work with that?

      One answer is that it's usually more pleasant to work your way up a hierarchy. This is because when you work with the images that cause the lower SUD levels and get used to them, something wonderful usually happens: the more difficult items also drop in difficulty. For example, as Gina practices dealing with pictures of stick figures throwing up, she finds that pictures of real people looking about to throw up become less scary.

The purpose of this section was to

A. explain why you should continue exposure for as long as you have planned, rather than escaping early if the going gets too rough,

or
B. explain why it's usually better to go up a hierarchy of situations than to start with the scariest of them?

219. Here's another reason to go up a hierarchy. Sometimes it takes a good bit of practice and exposure until the really high fears come down. If you don't have confidence that the fears really are going to come down, you're likely to give up in the middle of the job, and to think, "Other people get used to fears with prolonged exposure and practice – I don't." When you start with easier situations and reduce your fear of them to nearly nothing, you convince yourself that exposure and practice really do work for you. You give yourself the faith that it takes to do exposure and practice with the more difficult situations.

This section

A. gives another reason for making a hierarchy of situations,
or
B. explains how you make situations that are less scary, once you have scary situations?

How do you make up situations that are easier?

220. Lana was in a car wreck, where her car collided with another. She has a very scary memory of the wreck, rated 10 on a scale of 10. She would like to become less scared of this memory, by working her way up a hierarchy. How can she make up situations that are less scary?

One option is to change the outcome of the image. She imagines the two cars coming at each other, but each has a giant marshmallow strapped to the car; these absorb all the shock, and no one is hurt. This still stirs up fear at about 6 on a scale of 10.

Then she imagines the same marshmallow image, only now she is not in either of the cars, but someone else. This lowers the distress level to 5.

Then she imagines that the scene is taking place on an animated cartoon that she is seeing on television, with animals as drivers. This lowers the distress level to 3.

Finally, she imagines that she is standing at one end of a large auditorium, and the animated cartoon is playing at the other end, on a very small television set, and the scene is running backwards. This lowers the distress level to 1.

This section gives an example of

A. how to construct less scary situations, given a scary one,
or
B. why you should stick with an exposure long enough to reduce the fear?

221. If Lana is trying to get over her aversion to a memory of her own car wreck, why does it help to practice getting used to images of cartoon animal drivers bouncing off each other with marshmallow cushions? The fact that it does help is an example of a principle of the mind called *stimulus generalization*. This means that if you learn to respond in a certain way to a certain thing, you will probably respond in similar ways to a something that's just a little different. For example, a driver learns to stop the car in response to a stoplight of a certain shade of red; the driver also stops when she sees a stoplight that's much brighter red.

Which of the following is an example of stimulus generalization?

A. Someone has a fear of being in social conversations with kids at school. He finds that when he gets a lot more comfortable in conversations with family members, he becomes more comfortable with conversations at school.
or

B. Someone has a fear of social conversations at school. He finds that when the fear is so great that he stays home from school, the more times he skips school, the more afraid he gets.

222. So the strategy with making hierarchies is to pick situations, and change them around as necessary, so that you can do as much of the work as possible with not-very-painful situations. Here are some strategies making situations less scary:

1. Imagine someone else's experiencing them, rather than yourself. (For example, someone who is afraid of going to sleep in the dark imagines someone else going to sleep in the dark.)

2. Imagine that the scary thing you are facing is smaller or less intense. (For example, imagine that instead of giving a speech to an auditorium full of people, you are giving a speech in the auditorium with one supportive friend listening.)

3. Imagine that the situation turns out with a very happy ending. (For example, someone with a fear of taking tests at school imagines taking the test and knowing every question perfectly, and getting 100% correct.)

Suppose that someone with a fear of driving in traffic puts on their hierarchy the situation of driving around in a large, empty parking lot, very early in the morning with no one else there. Which strategy is the person using?

A. Having someone else be in the situation rather than yourself.
or
B. Making the scary situation less intense.

223. Here are some more ways of making situations less scary:

4. Imagine seeing the scary situation from a long way off.

5. Imagine cartoon characters in the scary situation rather than real people.

6. Imagine an intimidating person in a funny outfit or situation. (For example, someone has a fear of job interviews. She imagines the interviewer wearing a ballet dress and a top hat.)

7. Imagine yourself facing the scary situation with very powerful allies with you. (For example, someone who fears going to bed in the dark imagines lying in bed while Superman and a few other super-heroes sit watching over him in the room.)

8. Imagine that you are seeing the scene in a movie or on TV or reading it in a story rather than seeing it in real life. (For example, someone who is afraid of getting shots imagines reading a book about someone who learns to handle getting shots.)

Someone is afraid of getting dental work done. The person imagines looking through a telescope at someone else getting a filling in a tooth. The person is laughing and smiling and seeming to have a good time while this is going on. Which strategies is the person using?

A. happy ending, someone else rather than self, and far off?
or
B. powerful allies, cartoon characters, and less intense?

224. Here's a way that I do NOT recommend using, to make situations less scary, especially for real-life exposures: starting with very brief exposures and trying to work your way up to longer ones. (I hope that if you've read past chapters, this advice comes as no surprise!)

For example, suppose that Martina is afraid of lying in bed at night with the light off. She decides to turn the light off for only a couple of seconds, then a few more seconds, and gradually work the way up to longer periods of time with the light off.

Why isn't this the best way to make a hierarchy? Because of the principle that brief exposures followed by escape can increase fears. Especially if during the few seconds that the light is off, Martina is thinking, "Oh, I hate this, how many more seconds is it..." and then when the time is up, she is hugely relieved to turn the light back on, her brain is learning that darkness is bad – just the opposite of what she wants to teach it.

The author doesn't like brief exposures as a way of getting over fears because

A. the relief caused by the escape can reinforce escaping and increase the urge to escape the next time, which increases the fear,
or
B. if you relax your muscles, the exposure will probably be more pleasant?

225. What would be better ways for Martina to make a real-life hierarchy? She could get an adjustable night light, where she can gradually turn down the brightness. Over time, she does long exposures to dimmer and dimmer lights.

If she has very dark shades, or is willing to put up thick blankets over the windows, she can practice being in a dark bedroom during the daytime, which usually is much less scary than doing so at night. Or she can practice going into a dark closet during the daytime, and gradually closing the door to make it darker.

In this section the author advises

A. making a gradual hierarchy using the amount of darkness as what changes, rather than the amount of time in darkness,
or
B. making a gradual hierarchy by first having a supportive person in the room, then connected by phone, then not connected at all?

226. Have some people been successful at getting over fears by starting out with brief exposures and working their way up to longer ones? Yes. Does everyone who does long exposures feel a steady reduction of fear? No. There's something else very important, other than the length of the exposure.

What you *think* about the exposure is probably even more important than its length.

Let's suppose that someone is working on a fear of the dark, and she has a long exposure to a little dimmer light than usual. Suppose she is thinking, "Why am I doing this? I

don't like this. I want the light on brighter. This is stupid. If I get used to this, someone will expect me to make it even dimmer, and I don't want that at all." Suppose this person doesn't reduce her fear at all. Why does she fail? She's not motivated. She hasn't really made the decision to go for mastery rather than avoidance.

The point of this section is that

A. even long exposures may not work well, if your attitude is such that you are not really wishing for mastery,
or
B. although a "positive attitude" is good, it's important to be able to recognize the problems with situations and the drawbacks to plans?

227. On the other hand: suppose Martina, who is working on the fear of the dark, has a brief exposure to darkness and says to herself, "Yay! I did it! I'm so proud of myself! I will be even more proud if I can do it longer!" She feels great. She probably has reinforced herself for doing the exposure, more powerfully than her relief has reinforced her for escaping.

So what you think, your attitude, may be even more important than the length of exposure. But if you are wise, you will maximize your chances of winning the fear-reduction game by using both long exposures AND the right attitude!

What's the main point of this section?

A. It's good to think about the probability that anything bad will happen in the situation, and how bad it would be.
or
B. You will have the best chance of reducing fears if you have both a self-reinforcing attitude and long exposures.

After making a hierarchy, are you ready to start exposure and practice?

228. Someone might think that once you have a hierarchy of situations, you are ready to start practicing with exposure. But I think you're better off doing some more work first. That work is to figure out, and drill on, the thoughts, emotions, and behaviors that are best to do in the situations.

Remember STEB (situation, thought, emotion, behavior) and STEB revision? You want to practice, not just passively being in the situation, but handling the situation well.

This is why the next few chapters deal with types of thoughts and emotions and behaviors, before we get to doing exposure.

The main idea of this section is that

A. You want to decide not just what the scary situations are, but also what are the best thoughts, emotions, and behaviors to use in those situations.
or
B. In listing scary situations and making SUD ratings and hierarchies, you are doing the most important thing, which is to face your fears rather than avoid them.

Chapter 6: Thoughts, and the Four- and Twelve-Thought Exercises

The big idea of cognitive therapy

229. The word *cognition* is a fancy word for thought. Cognitive therapy, one of the most widely researched and useful methods for reduction of anxiety, is focused around one big idea. This idea is that by purposely choosing your thoughts about a situation, you can greatly influence how you feel and act in the situation. In other words: if you want to feel and act in a certain way about a situation, think the thoughts that lead to those feelings and actions.

What's the main point of this section?

A. We can influence how we feel and act by choosing our thoughts.
or
B. If you learn labels for different types of thoughts, you will be able to make better choices.

230. Often we are not aware of what we are saying to ourselves about a situation, because we aren't paying much attention to our thoughts. But when we pay attention to what we are thinking, the connection between thoughts and feelings becomes very clear.

For example: Sandra finds herself very uncomfortable and distressed in "social situations" – for example, going to a party or picnic. She's not really aware of what she says to herself in these situations. But then she imagines herself starting to get ready for a party, and pays attention to her "automatic thoughts." She finds the following automatic thoughts popping into her head: "Oh, no, how did I get myself into this? I'm going to look like a fool. People are going to wonder what's wrong with me. This is going to be terrible." With thoughts like these, it's no surprise that she dreads going to the party.

One of the points this section illustrates is that

A. it takes lots of practice to overcome habits of thought,
or
B. sometimes we're not aware of what we're saying to ourselves, until we pay conscious attention?

231. Sandra decides that she would feel better going to the party with a different set of thoughts, such as these: "I know how to act reasonably pleasant and polite, and if I do that, I'm not going to make any enemies. Even if some people don't like me, that won't be the end of the world. I'll smile and give people eye contact and greet them, and be a good listener if they talk to me. I'll give enthusiasm and approval in my tone of voice. I'll do an appropriate 'parting ritual' when I stop talking with them. If I can't think of brilliant things to say, that's OK. I'll just relax. I'm glad I've made these plans! It will be a real courage triumph for me to go and do this, no matter how it turns out."

Sandra finds, even while experimenting in her imagination, that when she talks to herself in this way, she feels much better.

This section

A. gives an example of someone's substituting less scary thoughts for more scary thoughts,
or
B. gives an example of someone's using biofeedback to help themselves relax?

Insight, redecision, and practice

232. If Sandra decides that a certain new thought pattern would make her feel and act better in "social situations," is her job over? No: there's a lot more work she has to do. She has probably practiced her old automatic thoughts thousands of times in her life. If she wants to get into a habit of a new thought pattern, she needs to practice the new pattern many, many times, so that it can compete with the old one. Fortunately, she does not have to go to another party each time she practices. She can practice in her imagination, using what we've called fantasy rehearsal. Each time she does a fantasy rehearsal of the new thought pattern, she is building up the strength of her new and more desirable thought habit.

The point of this section is that

A. it's good to go up a gradual hierarchy of situations, so that easier ones prepare you to face the harder ones,
or
B. once you've decided upon a new and more desirable thought pattern, it's good to practice it many times?

233. We can divide the process we just described with Sandra into three

steps: insight, redecision, and practice. Insight occurs when you become aware of your automatic thoughts about a situation. (You also become aware of what your habits of emotion and behavior are.) Redecision means coming up with thoughts (as well as emotions and behaviors) that you like better than those of your previous habit. And practice means that you use either fantasy or role-playing or real life to do the new pattern over and over, to build up its habit strength. Through insight, redecision, and practice, people can greatly improve their lives.

The purpose of this section was to

A. put names on three different steps people go through in improving their habits of thought, emotion, and behavior,
or
B. illustrate how reducing anxiety greatly increases the happiness of the person?

234. Sometimes the thoughts that we think about a situation are not yet put into words. Sometimes, when you ask someone, "What did you say to yourself in this situation," the truthful answer is, "I didn't say anything to myself." This doesn't mean that the person didn't think. It's possible to have thoughts of "Let me out of here!"

or "This is dangerous!" Or "Something horrible is going to happen," without actually having those words go through your mind.

The main point of this section is that

A. our thoughts about situations are not always expressed in words,
or
B. thoughts that are not put in words are often expressed in mental pictures?

235. If thoughts are not expressed in words, it's often good to put them into words. Language is an amazingly useful invention. When thoughts are expressed in words, you can examine them and see whether they are realistic and useful or whether they should be replaced by others. You can communicate them to other people. You can get feedback on them. This is why there is so much talking that goes on in the course of therapy for fears and aversions. The more you can get thoughts translated into words, the more control you have over them.

The author thinks that it's often good to translate thoughts into words because

A. this helps develop your overall verbal ability,
or

B. this helps you decide whether your thoughts are reasonable and desirable or not?

236. Here's another example of insight, redecision, and practice. Lucia finds it very unpleasant to go out into public places such as stores or crowded streets. Suppose she is asked to imagine being in the crowded place and to translate into words whatever thoughts pop into her head. The first words that come to mind are "I can't stand this! Let me out of here!" When she keeps imagining the situation and asking herself what is so bad about it, the thoughts that pop into her head are, "All these people are judging me and thinking that I don't look good." Now she has landed on a source of danger in the situation, and she can evaluate it.

So far, Lucia has worked on the stage of

A. insight
or
B. redecision?

237. Now Lucia considers the probabilities and utilities connected with her feeling that people are judging her. She decides that most of them don't care what she looks like, and that most of them don't give any evidence of noticing her at all. She also decides that if some of them look at her and think that she looks bad, this is their problem and she doesn't need to worry about it. She decides that some of them might think she looks good, but this too makes very little difference to her.

After such thought, she decides that in the situation, she would like to think to herself, "This situation is not dangerous. I don't need to worry about how strangers are judging me. If I hang in here long enough, I can get used to being here and eventually get rid of my unrealistic fear. That will be a major accomplishment; I will deserve to feel great about that!"

This section gives an example where Lucia does

A. practice
or
B. redecision?

238. Now Lucia repeatedly imagines herself in all sorts of different public places, and fantasy rehearses thinking in her new way. The more times she does this, the more a new habit builds up. After lots of this fantasy rehearsal, she purposely goes out into a store, and wanders around for a long time, rehearsing her new way of thinking about the situation. As she participates in this "prolonged exposure," she finds her SUD level going down and

down. She continues to go out to public places in real life, often.

In this section Lucia is described as going through the stage of

A. practice,
or
B. insight?

STEB and STEB revision

239. While going through the process of insight, redecision, and practice, it's good to keep straight whether you are dealing with the situation, your thoughts, your emotions, or your behaviors. The first letters of Situations, Thoughts, Emotions, and Behaviors form the word STEB. Improving your life largely consists in handling situations better: at coming up with better thoughts, emotions, and behaviors for given situations.

Let's spend just a little time practicing telling the difference between these.

How about these: "I've got to get out of here!" Or "This is unpleasant, but I can handle it." Or, "One option is that I could introduce myself to this person."

These are all examples of

A. situations,

or
B. thoughts?

240. The things that you say to yourself, as well as the visual or sound images you present to yourself, are thoughts. How about these: I'm sitting on a bus, and someone is staring at me. Or: I'm standing in line to sign in for a very important standardized test. Or: I've said an idea in class, and someone else criticizes it.

These are all examples of

A. situations,
or
B. emotions?

241. The circumstances we find ourselves in, which we react to with thoughts, emotions, and behaviors, are situations.

People have invented many one-word descriptions of emotions.

How about these words: anger, joy, determination, pride, confidence, compassion, fear, and guilt?

These are all examples of

A. situations,
or
B. emotions?

242. Behaviors often take more words to narrate.

How about the following: (In the situation where the person criticizes me) I say, "You have a point. I'll have to think about that." Or (in the situation where I am getting a shot) I smile at the nurse, relax my muscles, and look out the window. Or (in the situation where I'm at a party) I smile at people and give them eye contact, and when the person looks back, I say "Hi," and if the person says Hi back, I say "I haven't met you, my name is John McGee."

These are all examples of

A. behaviors,
or
B. emotions?

Twelve types of thoughts

243. When you are thinking about your own thoughts, and deciding which ones will serve you best, it's very useful to have labels for them. Below are twelve categories of thoughts, with examples of what they sound like. Let's start with the first six.

1. Awfulizing: This is bad; this is terrible; I can't stand this.
2. Getting down on yourself: I made a mistake; I did something wrong; I'm a bad person.

3. Blaming someone else: He made a mistake; he did something bad; he's a bad person.
4. Not awfulizing: This isn't the end of the world; I can take it.
5. Not getting down on yourself: I may have made a mistake, but I don't want to punish myself too much.
6. Not blaming someone else: I may not like what that person did, but I don't want to spend my energy blaming him.

Which type of thought do you think would be more associated with anxiety and aversion, of the following two?

A. Not blaming someone else,
or
B. Awfulizing?

244. Here are the second six of the twelve thoughts.

7. Goal-setting: Here is what I would like to accomplish in this situation: . . .
8. Listing options and choosing: I could do this, or that, or this other thing . . . I think this is the best one.
9. Learning from the experience: I learned something from this; here's what it is: . . .
10. Celebrating luck: I'm glad about this part of the situation, which is lucky for me.

11. Celebrating someone else's choice: I'm glad this person did this thing.

12. Celebrating your own choice: Hooray for me! I'm glad I made a good choice, and carried it out.

Which one do you think is most associated with feeling proud of yourself?

A. goal-setting,
or
B. celebrating your own choice?

245. Certain thoughts tend to lead to certain emotions. Blaming someone else tends to cause anger. Getting down on yourself tends to produce guilt.

The thought, "Oh no! Something terrible is about to happen! I can't stand this!" is an example of awfulizing. Do you think that this thought is more likely to produce

A. fear,
or
B. compassion?

246. Here's a very important idea: all of these types of thoughts are sometimes very useful, even awfulizing, getting down on yourself, and blaming someone else. *The goal is to be able to choose your thoughts according to what is most useful for the situation you are in.* Fear, guilt, and anger are sometimes useful emotions, also; we would not have evolved the capacity for them if they were not sometimes useful to us. However, many people get stuck in certain patterns, (most often awfulizing, getting down on themselves, or blaming other people) and continue to use these patterns, even when they are clearly not useful. They use these patterns by reflex and habit, not because they have consciously decided that these thoughts will work best. The goal is to stop thinking thoughts that are not useful to you, and to think the thoughts that make things come out better.

The point of this section is that

A. you should avoid awfulizing, getting down on yourself, or blaming someone else,
or
B. the goal is to select your own thoughts according to which are most useful to you?

247. When you choose to move from one thought to a second, because you think the second will be more useful, you have something big to celebrate. When this happens often, you have been liberated in a very important way. You are free from rigid habits of

thought, and you are free to choose what sort of thought serves you best.

What's an example of the type of mental process that the author likes, according to this section?

A. "I think I've done enough getting down on myself; I want to move to learning from the experience and listing options and choosing,"
or
B. "You're awfulizing; don't do that."

248. When you are training yourself to choose your thoughts according to what works best, one of the main goals is flexibility of thinking. By flexibility, I mean the ability to think in any of several different ways. The opposite of flexibility is rigidity. Rigidity occurs when you can only see one way of thinking about the situation you're in, and you can't change it, even if it isn't working well.

What's the main point of this section?

A. You want to be able to choose among various different types of thoughts, rather than to be stuck in one fixed pattern.
or
B. It's particularly important not to overgeneralize when you are thinking one of the first three types of thoughts.

249. Suppose that a man has a fear of insects. When even an harmless insect is around, the person thinks, "This is terrible! I've got to get away! I hate that thing!"

Later, he talks with someone about this incident. The person says, "Would you like to be able to think in a different way?"

The person replies, "Well, I just can't! And I don't even want to! Those bugs just gross me out! They make me feel so bad!" The man continues to believe that, because he is in the habit of awfulizing and feeling bad when around the bugs, there is no possible other way to think when in their presence.

The man in this little story is giving an example of

A. flexibility of thoughts,
or
B. rigidity of thoughts?

250. The Twelve-thought Exercise helps you make available to yourself all twelve thought patterns. To do this exercise, you pick any situation. (It can be a "courage choice point," meaning a situation that causes you unrealistic fear, or it can be anything else.) Then you practice making up an example of each of the twelve types of thoughts, about that situation.

Here's how the Twelve-thought Exercise would sound, as done by the person with an aversion to bugs. This section will give the first six.

1. (Awfulizing) This is really bad that a bug is around here!

2. (Getting down on yourself) Why do I have this reaction to bugs when other people don't? There's something wrong with me.

3. (Blaming someone else) That horrible little creature! I hate that bug!

4. (Not awfulizing) OK, so there's a bug. I'm not in danger. I have an aversion to bugs, but I can handle those bad feelings and tough them out.

5. (Not getting down on yourself) Even though I have an unrealistic aversion to bugs, I don't want to punish myself for that.

6. (Not blaming someone else) I don't want to waste time blaming anyone else, or the bug, for the fact that this bug is here.

Which of the following is an example of "not getting down on yourself?"

A. It's not so bad – I can handle it.
or

B. I made a mistake, and I'm imperfect, but it won't help to punish myself for that.

251. Now we continue our example of the twelve thought exercise, with the second six thoughts, about the same situation as before.

7. (Goal-setting) My goal is to get over my unrealistic fear of bugs. I want to be able to relax and stay cool, especially when the bug isn't the stinging type.

8. (Listing options and choosing) I could look away. Or I could deliberately watch the bug, to do prolonged exposure. I can relax my muscles. I can remind myself of the lack of danger. I can check my SUD level every so often. I think I'll do all of these except looking away.

9. (Learning from the experience) I learned that in situations like this, there's a chance of seeing a bug, so it's good to get used to seeing them.

10. (Celebrating luck) I'm glad that I happened to have this opportunity to do some prolonged exposure.

11. (Celebrating someone else's choice) I'm glad that people have done research finding that prolonged exposure can help you get over fears,

because that helps me now with my fear of bugs.

12. (Celebrating your own choice) I'm glad that I was able to stay cool about this situation and make a good choice of what to do. I'm really glad I didn't try to escape.

The Twelve-thought Exercise makes clear that:

A. There is only one correct way of thinking about a situation.
or
B. There are several different ways to think about any situation, and you can use the thoughts that will help you handle the situation best.

252. It's often fun to do the Twelve-Thought exercise with someone else, and to make a social activity out of it. To do this, you pick a situation, and then the two people go through the twelve thoughts in order, taking turns making up the next thought about that situation. So, the first person gives an example of awfulizing, the second person an example of getting down on yourself, the first blaming someone else, and so forth.

The author is recommending

A. one person goes through all 12 thoughts with one situation, and the other person goes through the 12 thoughts with a different situation,
or
B. the two people take turns so that each of them makes up 6 thoughts about one situation?

253. I recommend doing the Twelve-thought Exercise many, many times with the situations listed in the rating scale for fears at the end of this book. The more you can increase your flexibility of thinking, the more you can make good choices about how you want to think about a certain situation.

In this section the author recommends using the rating scale for fears that is an appendix to this book

A. as a source of situations to practice the Twelve Thought Exercise with,
or
B. as a way of monitoring progress in getting over fears?

The four-thought exercise

254. Going through all twelve thoughts is a very important exercise. But we need a shorter exercise in addition, one we can do more quickly. When a real-life situation arises, you usually won't have time to think in all twelve ways. But with practice, you can learn to go through four of these

thoughts very quickly. You can do such practice via the Four-thought Exercise. In this exercise, you use

1. not awfulizing,
2. goal-setting,
3. listing options and choosing, and
4. celebrating your own choice.

When a courage choice point comes up in real life, you usually can flash all four of these types of thoughts across your mind, especially if you cultivate the habit of thinking about them quickly.

What are the four thoughts that we use in the Four-thought Exercise?

A. not awfulizing, goal-setting, listing options and choosing, and celebrating your own choice,
or
B. not blaming someone else, learning from the experience, getting down on yourself, and celebrating luck?

255. Let's go over why these thoughts are so useful in response to courage choice points. Let's think about not awfulizing. Fear and aversion are responses to threats and danger. The more we think that something horrible has happened or is about to happen, the more intensely we feel fear. On the other hand, if we recognize that the situation is a lot better than it could be,

or that we can handle it, or that we are not in great danger, we are less likely to be intensely fearful.

Why is not awfulizing so useful in fear and aversion reduction?

A. We naturally don't feel so scared about situations that we realize aren't very bad threats to us.
or
B. It's impossible to be fearful after uttering the sentence, "It's not awful."

256. Let's think about goal-setting and listing options and choosing. These are the types of thoughts that help you decide how best to handle the situation, how to cope best. One of the greatest antidotes to fear and aversion is having and carrying out a good plan for what to do. This is especially true if you feel competent in handling the situation; this means that you feel confident that your goal is a good one and that your choices have a good chance of allowing you to reach your goal.

When you are very well practiced in goal-setting and listing options, and you have a high expectation that you will make a good choice, the emotion that is likely to replace fear or aversion is

A. confusion,

or
B. confidence?

257. When practicing listing options and choosing, I recommend usually listing only ethical, nonviolent options. Although thinking of an outlandish or funny option may sometimes free up your creativity to think of a good option you wouldn't have landed on otherwise, thinking of violent and hostile options usually just wastes your energy.

Which of the following types of option lists does the author prefer?

A. Let's see: I could knock everybody down and run out of here, or I could just relax my muscles;
or
B. I could ask this person who criticized me to make his criticism more specific, or I could excuse myself and spend some time speaking with someone else?

258. The fourth thought in the four-thought exercise is celebrating your own choice. When you think, "Hooray for me; I did something brave!" you are rewarding yourself; if you are lucky and have practiced enough, this celebration of your own choice will make you feel good. And feelings of pleasure are a very strong antidote to fear and aversion. So for example,

when someone thinks, "I celebrate my own courage in deciding to face this scary situation," any pleasure that comes from this thought reduces fear.

The reason the author gives in this section for celebrating your own choice is that

A. the pleasure you feel from congratulating yourself tends to reduce fear,
or
B. rewarding yourself for good things tends to make you do those good things more frequently in the future?

259. When people do the Four-Thought Exercise together, I recommend that they take turns, not with thoughts, but with situations. Each person goes through all four thoughts with one situation, and the other person goes through all four thoughts with the next situation. In this way they can practice going quickly through all four thoughts.

The author recommends that when two people make a social activity out of the four-thought exercise,

A. they take turns so that each person comes up with two thoughts for each situation,
or

B. one does all four thoughts with one situation, and the other does all four thoughts with the next?

260. Let's look at some examples of the Four-thought Exercise. Imagine that someone who has an aversion to touching dirty clothes has laundry that must be done.

Not awfulizing: Yes, these clothes are dirty, but they are very unlikely to give me an illness. I think my aversion to touching them is unrealistic, and I'm not in danger.

Goal-setting: My goals are to get this laundry washed and also to get over my aversion to dirty clothes.

Listing options and choosing: I can just bravely pick them up and put them in the washer. I can do some more prolonged exposure than that, by holding some of the dirty clothes for a longer time. I can wash my hands after loading the clothes in, or I can not. Since I'm short on time now, I'm going to choose to load them in quickly, and later do some prolonged exposure. I'll wait a good while before washing my hands to prolong the exposure to the feeling of dirty hands.

Celebrating your own choice: Hooray, I think I made good choices.

In the goal-setting part of this, the person set

A. one goal,
or
B. two goals?

261. Here's another example. The situation is that someone is lying in bed alone, in darkness, waiting to fall asleep.

Not awfulizing: I'm very safe here, so any uneasiness that I might feel represents unrealistic fear. Nothing bad is likely to happen at all.

Goal-setting: My goal is to get enough rest so that I'll be refreshed tomorrow, and another goal is to get very comfortable with this situation.

Listing options and choosing: I could actually try to stay awake for longer than usual, just to get used to this situation. I could relax my muscles. I could do the "pleasant dreams" exercise, where I make up fantasies of beauty, kindness, and peacefulness. I think I'll choose to do all of these.

Celebrating your own choice: I'm glad I made these choices!

Why do you think the person in this example decided to try to stay awake a little longer than usual?

A. to make the exposure more prolonged,

or

B. to watch out in case something dangerous happened?

262. Here's an example of the four-thought exercise with the situation of riding on an airplane.

Not awfulizing: The chance of danger is so small that it's not worth worrying about.

Goal-setting: I'd like to get some work accomplished on this flight. I'd like to reduce my fear of flying.

Listing options and choosing: I can work on some of my school work during the flight. I can just take in everything going on around me, to try to get the most out of this exposure. I can relax my muscles. I can read, during the flight, about ways of reducing anxiety. I think I'll read the anxiety book, relax my muscles, and take in everything around me, including looking out the window. Later on I might do some school work.

Celebrating your own choice: Hooray, I think I made some good choices.

The person in this example "not awfulized" by giving himself or herself a reminder that

A. the probability of an accident was very small,

or

B. the "disutility" of a plane crash was very large?

263. The situation for the next example is one in which the person gets the urge to procrastinate on writing an article for a school assignment.

Not awfulizing: There are more pleasant things to do than write this article, but I can handle it. It isn't that bad.

Goal-setting: My goal is to get the article written on time. Also I want to do a good job on it. I also want to increase my enjoyment of writing and reduce any unrealistic aversions I have to it.

Listing options and choosing: I can try not to be too perfectionistic, especially at the beginning. I can reward myself in my mind, often, for the work I've done. I can do the writing in stages, where at the beginning I'm just trying to get the ideas down without worrying about how they sound and the grammar and spelling and so forth.

I can give myself an external reward, like the chance to read my new magazine or take a walk, when I've gotten the ideas down in outline form. I'll do all these.

Celebrating your own choice: I'm glad I thought of these strategies!

This person's listing options and choosing illustrates the fact that

A. you can choose to do several options,
or
B. you must pick one option from the ones you list?

264. In the next situation, the person is in a conversation with someone, but the person can't think of anything to say.

Not awfulizing: This isn't so terrible. The other person isn't saying anything either. Nobody made a rule that you have to be talking every instant.

Goal-setting: I want not to let this bother me, but to continue to enjoy the conversation.

Listing options and choosing: I can look at and listen to what's going on around me, and make a remark about that. I can think of something the person was talking about before, and

ask them to tell me more about that. I can just look at the person and smile. I can mention an article I read in the newspaper today that interested me. I think I'll first just smile at the person, and then mention the article I read.

Celebrating my own choice: Hooray, I think I made a good choice!

Which option did the person NOT think of, in this example?

A. Saying goodbye, and walking away from the person.
or
B. Asking the person to tell more about something the person was talking about before.

265. If you do the four-thought exercise enough times that you create a "reflex" of doing these four thoughts in stressful situations, you will have developed a very valuable habit. I recommend doing the four-thought exercise at least dozens, and probably hundreds, of times, to develop this reflex.

The author feels that

A. when you've done one four-thought exercise, you've done them all,
or

B. the four-thought exercise is
probably worth repeating hundreds of
times?

Chapter 7: Choosing Emotions for the Situations You've Listed

266. We've talked about listing situations, arranging them in order of how unpleasant they are, and giving a SUD rating to each. For the person with test anxiety, one of those situations may be taking an important standardized test. For the person with social anxiety, one of those situations may be going to a party and looking for people to chat with. For the person with a work aversion, where the negative emotion is not fear but boredom, one of the situations may be sitting and doing homework for an hour.

Taking a test, going to a party, and working at homework are three different

A. emotions,
or
B. situations?

267. This chapter asks you to ponder the question, "How would I *like* to feel in this situation?" Perhaps for a big test or a party, you would prefer a feeling of confident excitement. This would certainly be much preferable to terror, and it would even be preferable to sleepy calmness. Perhaps while working on homework, one would prefer feelings of determination, alertness, and pride in the work already done. Again, these feelings may be preferable to dreamy relaxation.

This section illustrates someone answering which of the following questions?

A. What's my best use of time at this moment?
or
B. How would I prefer to feel in this situation?

268. Paul has a fear of bugs, such as beetles and potato bugs. Paul thinks, "How would I like to feel around these bugs?" Paul decides that he would like to feel curious about the bugs. He also decides that he would like to feel some compassion for the creatures.

Both curiosity and compassion are fairly *incompatible* with extreme fear – in other words, you're not likely to feel lots of curiosity and compassion while feeling very scared at the same time. (Worry, shame, guilt, and anger are much more compatible with fear.)

The person in this section decided upon alternative feelings to fear, and they were

A. fierceness and valor,
or
B. curiosity and sympathy?

269. Molly has a fear of talking with people by telephone. She thinks, "How would I rather feel?" She decides that feeling friendly and sociable is greatly preferable.

Tom fears dentists' work on his teeth. He decides that while in the dentist's chair, he would like to feel very calm, relaxed and dreamy, and in the mood for pleasant fantasies.

Karen has a fear of getting fat. She has an aversion to the idea of herself being even in the normal weight range. She looks at pictures of people who are of normal weight, and decides that she would like to associate the image of herself looking like that with a healthy feeling, an "in control" feeling, and a self-satisfied feeling.

Three emotions that the characters in this section chose were to feel

A. friendly, calm, and proud of themselves,
or
B. determined, cool and calculating, and curious?

270. Ron feels very nervous and self-conscious in social situations such as eating lunch with others or hanging out in groups. He discovers, however, that he has a quick wit, and he decides that he would much rather feel lots of hilarity and humor. He prepares to do fantasy rehearsals of joking and laughing and seeking out people who also like to be funny.

Tara also feels nervous in social situations. Unlike Ron, her strength is not her ability to be humorous; she is, however, an excellent listener and very kind. She decides that she would do best to aim for feeling caring and friendly in social situations, because she is likely to succeed at this.

A point made by this section is that

A. the fear of social situations can subtract a lot from people's happiness,
or
B. when looking for feelings that are to be replacements for fear or aversion, it's a good idea to take into account your own strengths.

271. When you are choosing what emotions you'd like to feel, keep in mind that you have lots more choices than just highly excited terror and a very low arousal relaxed state. Deep relaxation is only one of the emotional

states that are incompatible with unpleasant anxiety. There are lots of positive emotions that involve high excitement. The emotion we call *fun* more often goes along with excitement than with calm and serene feelings.

What's the main point of this section?

A. It's good to be able to turn up or down your level of excitement.
Or
B. You have lots of choices for emotions, other than deep calm: sometimes high-excitement emotions, like having fun, are the best alternative to fear.

272. If you have the chance to do some biofeedback using your skin conductance level as a measure of your excitement, you will quickly find that if you get yourself scared, the conductance goes up; it also goes up when you laugh; it also goes up when you feel like pumping your fist in triumph over having succeeded in something. These observations tell us that emotions incompatible with fear, such as humor and triumphant pride, can involve high excitement.

This section makes the same point as the previous section, only backing up the point with

A. examples from a study in which people were given adrenaline,
Or
B. examples from experience with skin conductance biofeedback?

273. What makes high excitement sometimes experienced as pleasant and sometimes unpleasant? A major difference is in our expectations of how things will turn out. For example: Consider two people who take a ride on a roller coaster.

The first screams at the scary parts, and then laughs. The roller coaster is great fun. Somewhere in the back of the person's mind is the expectation of getting together with friends afterwards and laughing together about how scary it was and how loud someone screamed and so forth. The underlying idea is, "It's going to turn out OK."

The second person rides on the roller coaster, but this person is thinking, "Am I sure a little screw couldn't come loose on this car? Is it possible that I could go hurtling down to my death? Yes, it's very possible." The fear that this person feels doesn't get translated into hilarity and fun, because the person has the underlying idea, "It could very possibly NOT turn out OK; in fact it could end in disaster."

What's the point of this example?

A. Our thoughts and expectations make the difference in whether we experience high excitement as fun or terrifying.
Or
B. A high-arousal expectation of bad outcomes is called fear; a low-arousal expectation of bad outcomes is called depression?

274. At one time many mental health counselors thought that it was futile to try to control or change your emotions. It was argued that the main challenge was to accept whatever emotions you had.

But the truth is that some emotions – most often fears and aversions – often get in the way of happy and effective living. And the second truth is that you *can* deliberately change how you feel in certain situations. You do this partly by deciding how you would like to feel instead, and then practicing feeling the new way rather than the old way, in many, many rehearsals.

The point of this section is that

A. all feelings are good, and you can't change your feelings,
Or
B. some feelings hinder you more than help you, and you can change your

feelings by practicing different ways of feeling?

275. Here is a brief menu of some feelings you may want to choose as alternatives to fear or aversion, in various situations. These, as well as others not on this list, are possible answers to the question, how would you *like* to feel in this situation?

Determination
Confidence
Courage
Cool and Calculating
Curious
Compassionate
Having Fun
Humor and Hilarity
Happy-go-lucky
Peaceful
Calm, Serene
Proud
Grateful
Relieved
Loving or liking
Indifferent

The central belief underlying a menu of feelings is that

A. you can choose how you want to feel in a certain type of situation, and cultivate the habit of feeling that way, or

B. since there's not time for
everything, you need to arrange your
uses of time into order of priority?

Chapter 8: Relaxation and Meditation

276. Let's briefly review the idea of the Yerkes-Dodson curve that we spoke about earlier. For any given task, there is some level of excitement that will help you perform the task best. If the task is running away from bad people, you probably want the highest level of excitement you can get; if the task is discussing a conflict with your husband or wife, you probably will do best remaining calm.

The idea of this section is that

A. a lower level of excitement is better for all tasks,
or
B. for any given task, there's a level of excitement that is not too much or too little, but just right?

277. As we've discussed before, many experiences of anxiety and aversion are accompanied by high excitement, high activity of the sympathetic nervous system. Adrenaline is flowing throughout our bodies, and we are excited. What if we could simply turn that excitement up or down, just as we turn up or down the volume level on a music player? The truth is that we *can* learn to turn excitement up or down. This skill is not easy. But through lots

of practice, we can cultivate that skill to a high degree.

The author's attitude is that

A. learning to control your level of excitement is something you can learn quickly and easily, if you read this book,
or
B. learning to control your level of excitement usually takes lots of practice and work?

278. As we discussed in the last chapter, choosing our emotions is not just about turning up or down the level of arousal. You can have pleasant and unpleasant emotions at all levels of arousal. If you can learn to make relaxation and meditation pleasant for yourself, you can get lots of practice at the sorts of pleasant emotions that are the opposites of fears and aversions.

The benefit of relaxation and meditation practice that the author is referring to in this section is

A. learning to turn down the level of arousal or excitement whenever you want to,
or

B. practicing pleasant emotions that are the opposite of fears and aversions?

279. Hundreds of studies have found that people benefit from learning relaxation and meditation techniques. In some of these, studies, the researchers intended that relaxation would be an ineffective treatment, compared to something else the researchers thought would be more effective! If you search the Internet, you can find those studies indexed using the words "relaxation," "meditation," and sometimes "mindfulness."

Relaxation and meditation practice has proved useful for headaches, stomach aches, problems with the jaw joint, cold hands and feet, anxiety, depression, addictions, and a wide variety of other medical conditions. One could write a large book just reviewing the studies that have been carried out.

What's the author's attitude toward the research on relaxation and meditation training?

A. It's inconclusive, because not enough research has been done yet.
or
B. There's enough research for us to know that relaxation techniques are very useful for anxiety and several other related problems?

280. The techniques in this chapter can be described as ways of "meditating" as well as ways of relaxing. The word *meditation* can refer to many things; usually it refers to activities of the mind that people do by themselves, without getting lots of external stimulation. (Often people sit with their eyes closed while meditating.) Usually meditation is for the purpose of calming oneself, coming to deeper awareness of important things, creating inner peace and serenity, and so forth. Thus listening to a rock concert or riding a roller coaster are usually not called meditation; sitting and mentally reviewing the multiplication facts before taking a test is not called meditation; sitting and generating images of kindness, peace, and beauty is called meditation.

The purpose of this section is for the author to

A. make the point that we are too dependent on stimulation, and we need to turn our attention more to our own thoughts,
Or
B. to tell what he means by the word *meditation*?

281. For all anti-anxiety techniques, it's important to practice them when you DON'T need them. If you try them only in moments of high anxiety, two things are likely to happen. First, they will be unlikely to work, because you haven't had enough practice. Second, you may even learn to associate these techniques with more anxiety, rather than with relaxation, because you have used them only under circumstances of anxiety.

Therefore, it's wise to practice relaxation on some sort of regular schedule, even when you are already feeling relaxed and calm and peaceful. In fact, those times may be the best times to build up the skill of getting even more calm and peaceful.

What's the author's advice in this section?

A. If you don't feel anxious, don't relax – why fix something that isn't broken?
or
B. Practice relaxing even, or especially, when you're already calm.

282. One logical time to practice relaxation is after you've gone to bed, before falling asleep. But this should not be the only time you practice relaxation. You want to have a major goal of learning to be relaxed while alert. This is why many traditional instructions for practicing relaxation advise sitting rather than lying down, and sometimes while sitting up fairly straight. The erect posture is to keep you from getting sleepy or falling asleep. If the only time you practice relaxation is when waiting to fall asleep, you're missing out on the full benefit of this skill.

The author recommends in this section that at least some of the time, you

A. practice relaxation without becoming sleepy or falling asleep,
or
B. practice relaxation while running?

An important preliminary: exercise

283. It's very difficult to practice a method of relaxation that involves, say, sitting still with your eyes closed, when you're feeling restless from having sat still in school classes or at work all day long. (A technique that may get around this problem is the "meditation with movement" technique I describe below.)

It is often very useful to exercise before relaxing, for example by going for a walk or a run. The first priority is to give the body what it needs: the chance to move and relieve the restlessness that comes from having to stay seated a long time.

The author feels that if you're restless after sitting in class for a long time,

A. relaxation techniques are an excellent way to get rid of restlessness,
or
B. before practicing relaxation, it's good to exercise so you won't feel so restless?

An even more important preliminary: attitude

284. Many of the people who benefit the most from learning relaxation or meditation techniques cultivate a certain attitude, consisting of certain thoughts and positive expecations. Here are some of them:

There are people in the world who have used these techniques to become calm, focused, effective, and happy individuals, and I want to do the same.

These techniques can be very powerful in making life better for me.

Using these techniques is a skill that I want to gradually cultivate.

When I get skilled enough, doing these techniques will be not only useful, but quite pleasant.

What's the point of this section?

A. People who benefit from meditation and relaxation tend to have certain positive attitudes toward the activities.
or
B. Using self-discipline tires people, and they need ways of renewing their stores of self-discipline.

285. Here are some more of the thoughts that go along with success at using meditation and relaxation techniques:

I am cultivating the ability to control my own state of mind. I will be able to take on not just relaxed sleepiness, but also calm, peaceful, serene, alertness, that can be useful in waking activities.

This activity can refresh me, "recharge my batteries," and leave me with a fresh supply of self-discipline.

Each time I use these techniques, I deserve to feel good, and not to feel that I have "failed."

I am both imagining and wishing that this technique will strengthen me in a way that I need or want to be strengthened.

And sometimes: I want to view whatever pops into my mind with serenity, interest, curiosity, and good will.

What's a summary of the thoughts that are listed?

A. Meditation and relaxation have certain effects on the brain that are able to be detected with modern technology.
or
B. Meditation and relaxation can be both useful and pleasant.

Muscle relaxation

286. The first technique for increasing or decreasing your excitement level is based on the finding that when you are more excited, your muscles get tenser, and when you are calmer, your muscles get more relaxed. Conversely, you can make yourself more or less excited by raising or lowering your muscle tension.

   Fortunately, tensing and relaxing muscles is something we can do voluntarily, because we do it every time we move. However, lots of times we're not aware of how much our muscles are straining against each

other while not moving. Sometimes it takes some practice to recognize muscle tension. One way of learning to recognize muscle tension is to tense muscles on purpose, notice the feeling, and then to relax the muscle and notice the contrast.

In the second paragraph of this section, the author advises tensing your muscles

A. to get yourself more excited,
or
B. to learn to recognize better what the feeling of muscle tension feels like?

287. Many people tense their jaw muscles when they are anxious, without even realizing that they are doing this. Sometimes they get so much in the habit of doing this that they damage their teeth or their jaw joints by pressing or grinding their teeth together so hard. Sometimes the habit is so strong that they keep clenching their teeth even while they are asleep. Becoming aware of how tense your muscles are by purposely tensing and relaxing them can help prevent such problems.

The point of this section was that

A. muscle relaxation tends to produce a calm feeling,
or

B. being aware of tension can prevent problems such as damage to teeth and jaw joints from too much teeth-clenching?

288. There are many sets of recorded instructions on relaxation, including tips on how to relax your various muscles. I made one of these; the script is included as an appendix to this book. This explains some of the motions that different muscles make. Another way to learn how to relax your different muscles is to experiment. The arms and legs are pretty easy. The head, neck, face, shoulders, and back can be trickier. With your hands, feel the jaw muscles on the side of your face, and figure out how to make them tense or loose. Do the same with other regions until you feel confident that you know how to relax any given region of your body.

The goal of the instructions and experimentation described in this section is to

A. maintain focused concentration, or
B. know how to relax all the muscles in your body?

289. I have had several operations (four wisdom teeth removed, a sebaceous cyst removed, some moles cut off) without anesthesia, as experiments to see how much effect fear-reduction techniques could have. Muscle relaxation was one of the most effective techniques I used during these operations. I concentrated on not flinching or tightening up, partly because I did not want to disturb the surgeon's motions. The intense concentration on keeping the muscles as loose and limp as possible tended to put me in a state of relaxation that was not disrupted by pain.

This section contains

A. an example from the author's life of how muscle relaxation was an effective technique to control fear and pain,
or
B. an explanation of how muscle relaxation has its effect on the brain regions that affect anxiety?

290. One option is to sit and focus on muscle relaxation for anywhere from one to twenty minutes without doing anything else. Pick a length of time so that the relaxation time is pleasant and not boring. As you relax your muscles, cultivate a feeling of pleasure from the restful feeling that muscular relaxation brings.

Another option is that throughout the day, you take several "five second vacations" in which you relax your muscles, rest, and then go on about your business. Even very brief relaxations can provide a healthy break from sustained stress and striving.

If you use very short relaxation breaks, I recommend also trying longer practice periods. I recommend including both in your "courage skills workout regimen."

This section

A. tells about using mental images of meditation gurus as role models,
Or
B. tells about using very brief (five second) periods of muscle relaxation several times during the day?

Breathe and relax

291. The word *mantra* refers to something that you focus your attention upon when you are relaxing or meditating. One technique I find pleasant is to focus attention on the breath going in and out. In the "breathe and relax" technique, you don't concern yourself with how deeply you're breathing, or try to time the lengths of inhaling or exhaling. You simply observe your breathing, and every time your breath goes out, you try to relax your muscles somewhere in your body, just a little bit more.

One benefit of this technique is that as you focus on your breathing, you realize how slowly you can breathe when you are really relaxed. As we'll discuss in another chapter, slowing down your breathing is very useful in avoiding "attacks" of anxiety or panic that are really consequences of breathing too fast.

As with all mantra techniques, if your mind strays from focusing on your breathing and relaxing your muscles, don't worry. Just gently swing your attention back to your breathing and your muscle-relaxing.

To use the technique of this section, you

A. inhale on the count of 5 and exhale on the count of 3,
or
B. simply be aware of your breathing, and relax your muscles each time you breathe out?

Observing what comes to mind

292. We can classify meditation techniques into two groups: in one, you are trying to focus on something (such as your breathing, or relaxing your muscles.) In the second group, you are not trying to concentrate on

anything in particular, but you're letting your mind drift as it will.

In the "Observing What Comes to Mind" technique, (which overlaps greatly with how some people use the word *mindfulness*) you let your mind drift. But you save a little of your mind to observe what the rest of it is doing! What's more, as you observe, you do it with an attitude of calmness and serenity and good will.

Thus, you sit back and become aware of what thoughts and images come into your mind. If they are pleasant, you enjoy them. If they are worrisome or distressing, you observe them with interest and curiosity and with a calm attitude, wishing the best for yourself and for all others involved.

To use the meditation technique described in this section,

A. you relax your muscles as you focus on some object,
or
B. you let your mind drift, while watching with calm curiosity to see what does come into your mind?

293. Here is only one reason why this technique is so useful for many people: Many of the our most troublesome and disabling fears are of our own thoughts and memories. Are we trying to avoid memories of unpleasant or traumatic events of the past? Are we trying to avoid thinking about some unpleasant truth about our lives? Are we trying to deny that we have certain urges or impulses that come into our minds? Facing such aspects of our own minds with calmness, curiosity, good will, and a feeling of peace is a habit very much worth cultivating. At the same time, being able to find pleasant daydreams, pleasant memories, joyous anticipation of future events, and enjoy these products of our own minds is also a tremendously useful skill.

This section expresses the idea that

A. observing what comes to mind hopefully allows you to become more serene about distressing thoughts and memories, and to take more enjoyment in pleasant ones,
or
B. observing what comes to mind helps you to label more accurately what you are feeling at any given moment?

294. Here's another reason why this technique is useful. Many people are troubled by boredom, and by the need to seek stimulation in order to get rid of their boredom. If they can learn to turn their attention to their own thoughts, and find ways of being

stimulated by their minds' own productions, they won't be so dependent on something or someone else to relieve their boredom.

The author seems to hope that

A. relaxation and meditation techniques such as this one will help people get over stress more readily, Or
B. relaxation and meditation techniques such as this one will help people not to be bored so much?

The word one as a mantra

295. To use this technique, you sit down and relax, close your eyes, and repeat to yourself silently, the word *one*, every few seconds. You keep going for some preset length of time (say, 1 to 20 minutes). As with other mantras, you don't "try hard" to keep focusing on the mantra; if you notice that your attention has strayed, you gently bring it back to repeating the mantra.

The purpose of this section was to

A. tell what effects meditation has on the brain and the rest of the body, or

B. describe the technique of meditating using as a mantra the word *one*?

296. Whoever got the idea of doing this? Apparently meditation by repeating a word has been done for many centuries in Eastern cultures such as in India. In the 20th century, researchers looked at its effects and found that meditation by repeating a word to oneself was helpful in many ways. Herbert Benson, a Harvard researcher, had his research participants use the word *one*; it appears to be good enough. Probably many other words would work as well!

There are several ideas about why it should be useful to repeat a mantra to yourself. Here's one: there appears to be something about a low-level, rhythmically repeated stimulus that is relaxing, for nonhuman animals as well as for people. The practice of repeating a word takes advantage of this fact.

This section mentions the fact that

A. a low-level repetitive stimulus tends to be relaxing, or
B. the word *one* gives people a feeling of "oneness" with the universe?

Meditation with movement

297. We've just spoken about meditation using a "repetitive stimulus" – something we experience over and over. What about making that something a movement rather than a word? Doing this can achieve the positive effects of exercise and meditation at the same time.

What's the main point of this section?

A. If you meditate while moving, you can accomplish the benefits of exercise and meditation simultaneously.
or
B. One of the benefits of meditation using a repetitive stimulus is that you increase your resistance to boredom.

298. There are different ways of meditating while moving. One is to use the movement as a mantra: you pay attention to the movement you are making, and if your mind strays onto other things, you gently return your focus to the movement pattern you're making.

The second way is not to focus on the movement, but to use one of the other techniques listed here while you're moving. For example, you can let your mind drift while performing the movement, and to take an interested and curious and accepting attitude to how it does drift. This is really the same as doing the "Observing What Comes To Mind" meditation, only moving rather than sitting while doing so.

What's a summary of this section?

A. There are different ways of meditating while moving: first, focusing on the movement (using it as a mantra), and second, not focusing on the movement, but using a different mental technique while moving.
or
B. If you carry out the movement while thinking, "This is stupid," then that's not meditation at all.

299. Here's one movement I've used. I press my hands together, or clasp them and pull them apart, so as to be using the muscles of the upper body. I bend the knees, and at the same time move the clasped hands down as though picking up something. Then I straighten out the knees, while bending the arms at the elbow and raising them, and then straightening them out to be stretched out overhead, as though handing something to someone over me. It's roughly the same movement someone would make from picking up something and putting it on a high cart, bending at the knees rather than bending the back.

The purpose of this section is

A. to convince the reader that this movement is the best one to use,
or
B. to describe one possible movement that can be used while meditating?

300. If you start to get uncomfortably tired while doing this, slow down, bend the knees less, and/or don't pull or push the hands so intensely. If you want to work yourself harder, do the opposite. If you want to work your abdominal muscles while doing this, breathe out using your "abs" rather than your chest. You can alternate your weight between one leg and another. You can alternate between pushing with your hands and pulling. You can relax your facial muscles while you are exerting your other muscles. You can close your eyes and observe what comes to mind while doing this. This one movement permits lots of variation, if you want it.

What's the point of this section?

A. There are ways to vary the movement that was described, to make it harder or easier or to involve different muscles, or to include some muscle relaxation or other mental techniques.
or

B. Meditation has been found helpful in at least six studies with people trying to break addictions to alcohol and drugs?

301. There are many other movements that you can use as a mantra.

For those who like to practice balancing, here's another movement I've used: you stand on one foot, and slowly move the other leg and your arms to be outstretched straight out in front of you. Then you smoothly move the same leg and your arms to be outstretched behind you, as you counterbalance yourself by moving your upper body forward and slightly bending the leg you're standing on. Then you repeat the motion using the other leg. The latter part of this movement gives good exercise to your lower back. If you do this with your eyes closed, I think it's a good idea to have at least one hand on something stationary like a wall or a bannister or sturdy chair.

The purpose of this section was to

A. make the case that practicing balancing tends to prevent falls in older people,
or
B. describe another movement involving balancing on one foot, that the author has used for meditation while moving?

302. In addition to these, you can use almost any dance step.

If done with the right attitude, walking, running, cycling, and so forth can be ways of moving while meditating. (You will need, however, to pay attention to your surroundings enough that you don't run into something!)

The important thing is to have the same attitude as with any other meditation: you are striving to cultivate a feeling of peace, relaxation, and calm alertness that can exist despite any stresses going on in life. You want to imagine and wish that the technique you are using is strengthening you in the ways that you need to be strengthened.

A summary of this section is that

A. many movements can be beneficial, as long as you have the "meditative attitude" toward them,
or
B. meditation has proved very useful for people who need to improve their emotional regulation skills?

Visualizing relaxing scenes

303. Are there places, real or imaginary, that are associated in your mind with a feeling of peace and relaxation? If so, a useful technique is to go, in your imagination, to one of those places and take it in, letting the conditioned association do its work.

Here's a short catalogue of scenes – are any of them relaxing for you?

Being warm while snow gently falls

Being near a clear flowing mountain stream

Standing on a mountaintop

Lying on a beach, listening to ocean waves

Seeing a starry sky at night

Seeing the colors in autumn leaves

Lying in bed on a morning when you have no responsibilities

Someone patting you on the shoulder

The technique described in this section is to

A. take scenes that at first are not relaxing to you, and make them relaxing,
or
B. find scenes that are already associated with relaxation for you, and call them to mind when you relax?

Biofeedback

304. Biofeedback is a way of measuring your level of excitement. Excitement and relaxation are not things you do with your brain only – many parts of the body get into the act. When we get more excited, at least three things happen. First, our muscle tension goes up. This, as we've discussed before, is meant to get us more ready to fight or flee.

Second, our fingertip temperature goes down. Why? When we get excited, the small blood vessels in the hands constrict. This keeps the heat from the rest of the body from being conducted as much to the hands and feet.

This section implies that with greater relaxation,

A. heart rate goes down and respiratory rate goes down,
or
B. muscle tension goes down and fingertip temperature goes up?

305. As we get more excited, our hands sweat more. Because sweat conducts electricity better than dry skin, we can measure sweatiness by seeing how well the skin conducts a tiny current of electricity (much too small to feel). Thus sweatiness of the fingertips is called "skin conductance."

Muscle tension, fingertip temperature, and skin conductance are very practical to measure.

One of the details in this section lets us conclude that when people get more relaxed,

A. their skin conductance levels go down,
or
B. the variability in their heart rates goes up?

306. Here's the way biofeedback works. You hook yourself up to a device that measures a variable like muscle tension, skin conductance, or fingertip temperature. Then you play with various techniques of relaxing or exciting yourself, to try to make whatever you are measuring go up or down. You fiddle around with changing your own level of arousal, and watch what happens on the biofeedback display. Gradually you learn to make the level go up or down at will. When you do this, you have brought under voluntary control a part of your physiology that was at one time thought to be "involuntary" or uncontrollable.

The main point of this section is that

A. biofeedback is not a technique you use just when you are anxious – you practice it when you are not anxious, or
B. by playing around with various techniques and watching what happens on the display, you gradually learn to control something going on in your body?

307. I use the word "playing" on purpose when I talk about biofeedback. Some people are very oriented to success or failure; they approach biofeedback with an idea like, "I must get that temperature to go up fast, and if possible, faster than anyone else has done it!" Such an attitude often produces arousal that has the opposite effect from that which they desire. When they notice the temperature falling rather than rising, they get frustrated and upset and conclude, "This technique is not for me!"

This section gives an example of someone who

A. used a visualization technique to help out with biofeedback, or
B. was so driven to success versus failure that the person found biofeedback frustrating?

308. A more useful way to think about biofeedback is as a series of experiments. If you find that intently willing your temperature to go up causes it to go down, that's a useful finding. You log away in your memory that a certain type of mental activity resulted in a lowering of temperature. Then you try doing something else with your mind, and see what happens with the second type of mental activity. With this attitude, there's no way to "fail." Even if you find that whatever you are measuring sits on one value without budging, no matter what you do, that's an interesting finding in itself. You've learned what sorts of changes in mental activity don't make any difference in what you are measuring!

This section advises that when you do biofeedback,

A. muscle tension is easier to change than fingertip temperature, or
B. you not worry about success or failure, but just experiment and notice the connection between what goes on in your mind and what happens on the display?

309. Despite my caution against approaching biofeedback with an attitude of driven intensity, we can name certain levels for the three

easiest parameters to measure, so that "if you are at this level, you are very likely to be relaxed." I can with some, but not very much, confidence, advise people to keep playing around with and practicing biofeedback at least until they can obtain these levels at will, fairly consistently.

Fingertip temperature is only meaningful as a measure of relaxation versus arousal if you are in a room that is around 70 to 74 degrees Fahrenheit (or possibly a little cooler, if you are wearing a sweater). In such a room, a fingertip temperature in the neighborhood of 90 to 95 degrees Fahrenheit is usually "relaxed."

One of the points this section makes is that

A. a fingertip temperature above 95 degrees Farenheit, when the room is 70 to 74 degrees, often is associated with feeling relaxed;
or
B. heart rate depends on how good physical condition someone is in, in addition to how relaxed the person is?

310. For muscle tension, one common site for measurement is at the forehead. Potential differences under 2 microvolts indicate relaxation, and those under 1 microvolt indicate even greater relaxation.

Skin conductance depends upon how much sweat is on the fingertips. This in turn depends upon both the temperature and humidity of the environment, and possibly also on how calloused the hands are and other variables. But a conductance level under 2 or 3 micromhos represents the dry fingertips associated with relaxation. For skin conductance, being able to move up or down from wherever you are at present seems more useful than striving for a particular level.

The purpose of this section is to

A. tell the levels of a couple of physiological parameters that are often associated with relaxed feelings,
or
B. tell the advantages of heart rate variation as a measure of relaxation?

311. In the previous section I mentioned "some, but not very much, confidence" about recommending the above levels as standards. This is because when you are using biofeedback, you think not only about the absolute level of what you are measuring, but also its change from whatever you started with. Different people have baselines that run higher or lower than other people. If your fingertip temperature starts at 75 degrees Fahrenheit and moves up to

90 degrees, you may have relaxed more than the person who starts at 93 and stays there. For this reason, things are a little too complicated for us to view the number displayed as a straightforward measure of how relaxed or excited you are.

What's the point of this section?

A. Biofeedback would be much more widely used if more people were willing to take the time to practice with it.
or
B. Since some people have higher or lower "baselines" than others, you have to think about the change in a biofeedback number. You can't view one reading as a foolproof measure of how relaxed you are.

312. When biofeedback was first introduced in the 1960's and 1970's, the measuring devices were quite expensive. Now they are inexpensive enough that individuals can own them. An Internet search of the phrase "biofeedback thermometer" will yield models costing about $20. There are devices to measure skin conductance for around $80, and computer programs (e.g. "Journey to Wild Devine") measuring skin conductance in addition to heart rate variation, (and displaying the results in great graphics rather than simply numbers) costing

about $300. The best measures of muscle tension cost several hundred dollars at the time of this writing. The company Biomedical Instruments Incorporated is a source of biofeedback materials.

The purpose of this section was to tell the reader

A. that it is possible and affordable to purchase some biofeedback devices, and where to find them,
or
B. that many more than the three parameters of muscle tension, skin temperature, and skin conductance have been used in biofeedback?

313. Biofeedback is usually best used in conjunction with one or more of the other techniques described in this chapter. You can experiment with any of these techniques, and see what happens to some physiological measure.

What do you conclude if a certain technique makes you feel much more pleasantly peaceful and calm and secure, but it doesn't cause what you're measuring to go up or down much? Then my advice would be to believe how you feel rather than the numbers on the display. The physiological measures are not necessarily the gold standard of whether you are relaxed. How the techniques affect your thinking and feeling is just as important, if not more so. Usually, but not always, the measures will be correlated with your feelings.

The main point of this section is that

A. if a certain relaxation technique affects your thoughts and feelings in valuable ways, you should use it, no matter what it does to some physiological measure,
or
B. the main reason why people are not helped by biofeedback is that they do not spend enough time at it?

Imagining acts of kindness

314. As I explain in another chapter of this book, I believe that an extremely important antidote to anxiety is to be a member of very positive social relationships, where people are kind and loyal and supportive to one another. Just the imagining of acts of kindness has, in my experience, a soothing and calming effect for most people.

To use this technique, then, you get in mind (or on a piece of paper) a list of different types of acts of kindness, such as the one in the next section. Then you go through this list one by one, and for each type of

act, you imagine someone doing a specific act of kindness of that sort for someone else. Thus you are making up very specific images that are examples of the general categories. The examples can be memories of your kind acts toward others, others' kind acts toward you, acts you have witnessed, acts you have read about, or acts you simply make up during the meditation session.

To use the technique described in the last section,

A. you remember or make up specific examples of several different types of kind acts,
or
B. you simply think about the general concept of kindness, without landing on specific images?

315. Below is an incomplete list of types of kind acts. Feel free to add to it.

Types of Kind Acts

1. Helping
2. Complimenting, congratulating
3. Expressing thanks
4. Being a good listener
5. Teaching, and learning from
6. Forgiving
7. Consoling

8. Spending time with, keeping company, inviting
9. Being cheerful, approving, funny, or fun-loving with someone
10. Being affectionate
11. Giving
12. Doing fun things with someone
13. Working together
14. Working to benefit someone else
15. Being assertive, not spoiling

How does the author recommend that you use this list in a meditation technique?

A. Look at the list, and visualize someone doing an example of each of these things with someone else,
or
B. read the phrases to yourself slowly, over and over?

316. The last item on the list of kind acts deserves some explanation. How is "being assertive, not spoiling," a way of being kind? Sometimes the kindest thing to do for people is to say no, to withhold giving, to deny giving people their way.

For example, suppose a child in a rude voice demands, "Mommy! You buy me that candy, right now!" The most loving and kind thing for the mother to say would be something like, "Sorry, I don't reward that kind of talk."

What's another example of the kind assertiveness that this section talks about?

A. Someone sees a person who is hurt, and stops to help that person,
or
B. A person wants to borrow money to support his gambling addiction, and the person he is asking says, "No, it wouldn't be kind for me to 'enable' this unfortunate habit of yours."

317. What is the point of the "visualizing acts of kindness" meditation? Much of the fear and aversion that we feel is rooted in acts of cruelty and hostility between people, either real or imagined. Thinking about people being kind, caring, and considerate to each other is in many ways the direct opposite of the sense of danger or oppression that is at the root of fear and aversion.

The purpose of this section is

A. to point out that the more vividly and concretely you imagine, the more effective this technique is,
or
B. to explain that acts of kindness between people may be the most powerful anti-anxiety events?

The good will meditation

318. This technique also uses the fact that kindness and good will between people bring about a feeling of calm and security.

For this technique, you begin with yourself, and wish three good things for yourself:

1. May I become the best that I can become.
2. May I give and receive kindness.
3. May I live with compassion and peace.

After this, you visualize another person – perhaps a family member or friend. You wish the same three things for that person. You let your mind go from one person to another, wishing these things for each one of them. I find that it feels good to wish these things even for people I don't particularly like, perhaps because wish number 1 provides a gratifying image of this person's changing and developing in positive ways. (It is probably much more calming to wish for positive change than to plot revenge!)

A summary of the technique described here is that you

A. visualize beautiful and relaxing scenery,
or
B. wish for one person after another to do good things and have good things done to him or her?

The pleasant dreams technique

319. Can you imagine having a very pleasant dream – not one like an exciting action movie, but one filled with soothing images of peacefulness, kindness, beauty, safety, and security? It would be a dream that would not tend to wake you up, and you would not want to wake up from it. The pleasant dream technique of relaxation is to make up for yourself such a fantasy, while you are awake, and let it continue to unfold for as long as you want.

The pleasant dreams technique is done by

A. sitting and letting any fantasies come to your mind that happen in,
or
B. purposely constructing fantasies of peacefulness, kindness, and beauty?

320. Here's an example of what a fantasy might sound like if put into words while using the pleasant dreams technique.

"I'm on a huge lawn, and the cool grass feels good on my bare feet.

It's evening; I can just begin to see a star start to come out, but it's still light enough to see well. I have with me a dog who is very loyal to me, very energetic, and totally joyous. I throw a ball and it goes a huge distance over this lawn, and the dog leaps after it with huge strides. Now he has the ball and he's running back to me, and I hug him. Now we're both running together over the huge lawn. I find that I can run like the wind, and I leap from grassy knoll to knoll. It's a great feeling to have such energy. When I'm through running I have a very pleasant relaxed and slightly tired feeling, the way I often feel after exercising.

The person who is constructing this pleasant dream-like fantasy is keeping in mind that

A. stories that people enjoy tend to have some conflict in them,
or
B. in the pleasant dreams activity, you want to have a feeling of safety and security from start to finish?

321. The pleasant dreams narrative begun in the previous section continues.

    "Now I come upon an area with trees and stone benches and small hedge mazes and little caves, and I somehow know that I am in a game of hide and seek, where several people

are hidden, and I am looking for them. But these people are not just random people – these are the people who have loved me the most and have been most kind to me throughout my whole life, present, past, and future. I look around and find them, one by one, and then I'm able to walk and talk with each one, while time is suspended. As I talk with each one, I thank them for the kindness they have shown me. To each I say farewell for now, knowing I will meet that person again soon, and search for the next one. It gives me a great thrill to find them, and a great feeling to talk to each of them."

In this example of the pleasant dreams technique, there is

A. a great deal of suspense and danger,
or
B. not much suspense and no danger, but lots of positive feelings?

322. When you are using the pleasant dreams technique, you don't have to worry that things are consistent. The time, the setting, or the characters, or even who you are in the dream can shift for no apparent reason, just as in real dreams.

    At first it may be difficult to make up stories like those you want to use in the pleasant dreams exercise. But composing for yourself these fantasies of beauty, peace, kindness, and security is an art that can improve with practice. And, I believe, the better you get at this skill, the greater an underlying feeling of calm and peace you can achieve.

I think that the pleasant dreams exercise is an especially good one to do while lying in bed waiting to go to sleep. This is especially true once you have practiced enough that it's very easy to come up with the pleasant fantasies. But I recommend also practicing this technique in the daytime, when you are fully awake and alert.

The author feels that making up fantasies for the pleasant dreams technique is

A. effortless, from the beginning, or
B. a skill that takes practice to cultivate?

The psychological skills meditation

323. To use this technique, you get in mind (or on a sheet of paper) the following psychological skills:

Productivity
Joyousness
Kindness

Honesty
Fortitude
Good individual decisions
Good joint decisions or conflict-resolution
Nonviolence
Respectful talk

Friendship-building
Self-discipline
Loyalty
Conservation
Self-care
Compliance
Positive fantasy rehearsal
Courage

These are the psychological skill groups that form the outline for most of my writings. (This book is primarily about courage and fortitude.)

This section

A. tells how to do the psychological skills meditation, or
B. tells the psychological skills that you will use for the meditation, but does not tell how to do the meditation?

324. To do the meditation, you sit quietly and relax. Then you let the word "productivity" come to mind, and then you let come into your mind an image of yourself or someone else

doing something productive. You imagine celebrating the productive act. The act can be a real one, or one that is purely the product of your imagination. Then you let the word "joyousness" come to mind, and a concrete, specific image of joyous behavior, with celebration of that. And so on, through the complete list of skills.

A summary of this technique is that

A. you sit quietly with eyes closed, and observe whatever thoughts come into your mind,
or
B. you go through a list of psychological skills, visualizing a positive example of each and imagining celebrating it?

Reading, and contemplating, inspiring quotations

325. From the beginning of recorded history, people have written down words that impart meanings to life – ways of thinking about life's situations that enable an optimistic, courageous, or calm spirit. The essential truth of this technique is that "You needn't reinvent the wheel." You can collect writings that have inspired others, and run their ideas through your mind in ways that make you feel more confident and courageous. To use this technique, you simply sit and read these selections, and contemplate them.

The main point of this section is that

A. a technique of relaxation or meditation is to sit and read selections of writings you find inspiring,
or
B. you don't need to have your eyes closed in order to be "meditating?"

326. Here's an example of a short poem that is in my personal collection of inspiring writings. The narrator has a beautiful dream, and then awakens to remember all the work that it's necessary to do. The narrator is tempted to feel that the beauty of the dream is a sham and that the only reality is never-ending toil. But then the narrator decides to adopt a courageous attitude, and to let the beautiful images of the dream give inspiration and meaning both to the work and to the pauses in it. What sort of courage is the narrator demonstrating? It's the courage not to give in to feeling hopeless about the responsibilities and demands of life. Here's the poem, by Ellen S. Hooper:

I slept and dreamed that life was Beauty:

I woke and found that life was Duty:
Was then my dream a shadowy lie?
Toil on, my heart, courageously,
And thou shalt find thy dream to be
A noonday light and truth to thee.

In the poem reprinted in this section,
the narrator

A. courageously faces both physical
and social danger,
or
B. courageously faces the temptation
to get demoralized by all the work that
must be done?

327. As I have mentioned before, I
believe that an orientation to kindness,
both from others and to others, is a
powerful antidote to anxiety. The
following statement is attributed to
William Penn, who by the accounts I
have read was a good person:

 If there be any kindness I can show,
or any good thing I can do to any
fellow being, let me do it now, and not
defer or neglect it, as I shall not pass
this way again.

The author suggests that there's an
anti-anxiety message in a quotation
that says

A. don't pass up a chance to be kind,
because the same opportunity won't
come again,

or
B. my soul is tough enough to endure
whatever hardship life can offer me?

328. We've spoken of the fear of
failure, the fear of making mistakes,
and how these fears can keep people
from taking the risk to try things, and
so make failure more inevitable. The
following brief proverb is from
Alexander Pope:

To err is human; to forgive, divine.

Forgiveness of oneself for one's own
mistakes is part of the divine ability of
which Pope speaks.

A paraphrase of the quotation given in
this section is

A. courage often consists in resisting
what a crowd of other people would
expect you to do,
or
B. everyone makes mistakes, and it's
great to be able to pardon yourself and
others?

329. The "serenity prayer" has
inspired many toward courage. It was
originally advanced by Reinhold
Niebuhr, who worded it as follows:

...Give us grace to accept with serenity
the things that cannot be changed,
courage to change the things which

should be changed, and the wisdom to distinguish the one from the other.

A paraphrase of the quotation in this section is

A. be brave enough to improve those things you can and should improve, but don't waste your energy on things you can't control;
or
B. you will feel braver if you keep your energy focused on a certain specific goal?

330. Eleanor Roosevelt was a great humanitarian, who had to overcome fear in order to make the accomplishments she did. Here are some quotations from her about the process of reducing fear:

 You gain strength, courage and confidence by every experience in which you really stop to look fear in the face. You are able to say to yourself, "I lived through this horror. I can take the next thing that comes along." You must do the thing you think you cannot do....
 I believe that anyone can conquer fear by doing the things he fears to do, provided he keeps doing them until he gets a record of successful experiences behind him.

The above quotations from Eleanor Roosevelt reveal that, despite the fact that most scientific research on anxiety occurred after her death, she understood the value of

A. relaxation techniques,
or
B. prolonged exposure to, and practice of successful strategies with, the feared situation?

331. A very major fear for many people is the fear of loss of love. What if a loved one dies, or what if a loved one rejects me? Alfred, Lord Tennyson, wrote the following words, that give inspiration to endure such losses:

I hold it true, whate'er befall;
I feel it, when I sorrow most;
'Tis better to have loved and lost
Than never to have loved at all.

The words of Tennyson seem to suggest that

A. losing love should not hurt you,
or
B. the pain of loss of love is something we often must courageously endure in exchange for the privilege of loving in the first place?

332. The essential truth of cognitive therapy is that our thoughts and judgments on situations, and not just the situations themselves, greatly influence our emotional responses. We can decide whether we want to focus our attention on the positive part of a situation, or the negative part. These ideas were grasped by stoic philosophers centuries ago. One was Epictetus, who wrote:

What disturbs our minds is not events but our judgments on events.

Another was Marcus Aurelius, who wrote:

Your disposition will be suitable to that which you most frequently think on; for the soul is, as it were, tinged with color and complexion of its own thoughts.... Your life is what your thoughts make it.

A paraphrase of the idea that you can choose the way you want to think about things, as Epictetus and Marcus Aurelius pointed out, was also offered by

A. A Japanese proverb that says, "You can either complain that rose bushes have thorns - or rejoice that thorn bushes have roses,"
or

B. Benjamin Franklin, who wrote, "Dost thou love life? Then do not squander time; for that's the stuff life is made of."

Simple rest

333. The last "technique" is simply taking a few minutes and resting, in whatever way you want. You don't try to do anything in particular, other than to take it easy and do nothing! One study I saw found that this worked as well as meditative techniques that were taught.

This may be harder than it appears. For many people in today's technological society, an opportunity to rest gets translated into checking text messages and emails, turning on the television, plugging into a music player, starting up an electronic game, or looking at a movie trailer. This is not what was referred to as "simple rest" in the study I read! Resting means stopping activity for a while rather than directing activity to the closest electronic device.

This section implies that

A. When people try to rest, many of them end up getting distracted by electronic technology,
or

B. resting is most useful when you
have first done something productive?

334. This chapter has explained
several techniques of relaxation or
meditation. I recommend that you try
out each of them. Often as little as one
minute is long enough to get the flavor
of the technique. You can gradually
work your way up to longer periods of
practice of the technique.

      There is one major reason why
these techniques don't work: that the
amount of time the person "logs in" to
practicing them averages about zero
per day. If you want these to work,
you will have to spend time practicing
them and focusing on them.

The author believes that the major
reason that techniques of relaxation
and meditation don't work is that

A. some people just don't have the
physiology that will be helped by
learning to meditate or relax;
Or
B. people don't invest the time it takes
to benefit from these techniques?

Chapter 9: Breathing, and Avoiding Hyperventilation

335. The flight-or-fight response is meant to help us avoid danger. As we discussed before, the activity of the sympathetic nervous system can be life-saving when we need extra energy to fight a predator or run from danger. Adrenaline and noradrenaline turn up our muscle tone, our heart rates, our sweating, and our rate of breathing, in preparation for extreme physical exertion. The effect of fear on breathing rates has very much to do with the subject of this chapter.

The reason for jumpy, trembly, and tight muscles, a pounding heart, sweating, and faster breathing when we are nervous is that

A. these are symptoms of a disease,
or
B. these are ways that our body prepares us to run or fight well when we perceive ourselves to be in danger?

336. When our bodies produce the flight or fight response and we don't run or fight, sometimes we get into vicious cycles that can be very unpleasant. A "panic attack" is one possible result of these vicious cycles, where activated muscles, a pounding heart, and fast breathing, as well as a feeling that something horrible is

about to happen, seem to turn themselves up and up to the point of great discomfort.

This section made the point that

A. in a panic attack, vicious cycles turn up the flight-or-fight response to very unpleasant levels,
or
B. it is important to practice relaxation even when one is not feeling particularly anxious?

The vicious cycle of hyperventilation

337. There is one vicious cycle that operates in most people who have panic attacks. It often plays a role in anxiety that doesn't reach the panic attack level. Understanding it can help enormously in preventing future panic attacks. This is the vicious cycle of hyperventilation.

Hyperventilation simply means breathing too fast. The vicious cycle of hyperventilation means that for some people, breathing too fast signals our bodies to breathe even faster. The result is a very unpleasant feeling, that largely contributes to the unpleasantness of a "panic attack."

Fortunately, we can control our rate of breathing. If you can thoroughly understand how breathing influences panic and anxiety symptoms, this knowledge can help you avoid bad panic attacks for the rest of your life!

This section starts discussing the vicious cycle where

A. thoughts that something horrible is happening lead to emotions that create more evidence that something horrible is going on,
or
B. breathing too fast signals the body to breathe even faster?

338. If you have panic attacks or anxiety, and you're not sure whether you breathe very fast when episodes occur, you can watch yourself very closely the next time an episode happens. But since so many people hyperventilate without realizing it, my advice is to read this chapter carefully and to practice the exercises that it recommends, whether or not you are sure you hyperventilate. If you don't hyperventilate, none of this will do you any harm; if you do, this will help you tremendously.

The author's advice is to

A. not do any exercises until you are sure you hyperventilate,
or
B. to learn what's in this chapter and do the exercises, whether or not you're sure you hyperventilate?

CO_2 excess and CO_2 deficit

339. Let's think about the effects of breathing. We learn in science classes that as our bodies generate energy, we use oxygen to "burn" fuels that come from the food we eat. Those fuels have carbon in them, and the by-product of making energy from them is carbon dioxide. Our bodies continuously need to get the carbon dioxide out, and to get oxygen in. This is the purpose of breathing. With every breath, we take in oxygen and "blow off" carbon dioxide.

This section presents

A. the reason for panic attacks,
or
B. a summary of what happens when we breathe?

340. If we breathe too slowly or not at all, we build up *too much* carbon dioxide: we have what we will call a CO_2 excess. If we breathe too fast, we blow off too much carbon dioxide, so we are left with *too little* of it in our

bodies. Hyperventilation produces a CO_2 deficit. Our bodies are built so that neither of these states feels good. We get unpleasant feelings from carbon dioxide excesses or deficits. The purpose of those unpleasant feelings is to motivate us to get the carbon dioxide into the right range, where there is "not too much, not too little, but just right."

What's the main point of this section?

A. Both deficits and excesses of CO_2 produce unpleasant feelings, which motivate us to keep carbon dioxide in the right range?
or
B. CO_2 excesses make the blood more acidic, whereas CO_2 deficits make the blood too alkaline?

341. The unpleasant feelings of deficits and excesses of CO_2 are different from each other. Have you ever swum underwater, and experienced that increasing feeling of air hunger that makes you want to come to the surface and gasp for breath? Or have you held your breath for any other reason? The increasing unpleasant feeling you get from breath-holding is the feeling of CO_2 excess. This feeling is meant to tell our brains, "Breathe! and breathe fast!"

This section tries to communicate

A. why CO_2 excess makes the blood more acidic,
or
B. what the feeling of "CO_2 excess" is like?

342. The feeling of CO_2 deficit is different. This occurs when we breathe fast, but do not flee, fight, or produce a lot of carbon dioxide from some other form of exercise. Even ten very fast very deep breaths can produce a little of this feeling.

Some people describe the feeling as being light-headed, or dizzy. It's not a spinning type of dizziness, but a feeling that you're on your way to feeling faint. If you keep hyperventilating, there can get to be tingly or numb feelings around the mouth or in the hands and feet, and these too are unpleasant. These unpleasant feelings are trying to tell us, "You have too little carbon dioxide!" "Don't breathe so fast!"

The point of this section is that

A. breathing fast without exercising leads to the unpleasant feeling of CO_2 deficit,
or
B. the flight-or-fight response probably still helps people survive, but less frequently than long ago?

343. Probably almost all of us respond to fear by starting to breathe faster. Why would our bodies do this? Because if we are going to flee or fight a predator, we're going to be exercising strenuously, and producing lots of carbon dioxide. Starting to blow off that carbon dioxide gives us an advantage in the fight or the flight.

However, if we don't need to exercise strenuously, normally something tells us, "You don't need to breathe so fast." Probably most people sense the feeling of CO_2 deficit and slow down their breathing some, without even thinking about what they're doing.

This section

A. describes why people get panic attacks,
or
B. describes what normally happens when we start to breathe faster when afraid, but then automatically slow down the breathing, in response to feelings of CO_2 defect?

The mistake that makes the vicious cycle of hyperventilation

344. But for those people who have a gene or something else that disposes them to panic attacks, something different happens! The bad feeling of CO_2 deficit can get misunderstood. The brain feels those unpleasant signals from too little carbon dioxide, and misinterprets them as "I'm not getting *enough* air." Thus the person breathes even faster! Some people are not even aware of doing this; others are very much aware of thinking, "I can't get enough air!"

Now a vicious cycle has begun. The faster the person breathes, the more the person feels the need to breathe fast, and the worse and worse the person feels!

The crucial thing that makes a vicious cycle happen is that

A. the person starts feeling tingling around the mouth or in the hands or feet,
or
B. the brain interprets the bad feelings of CO_2 deficit as not getting enough air?

345. Why should the body make the mistake of feeling that too much breathing is really too little? Let's think about how you would design a brain if you were focused on survival. You might think, "If the person really isn't getting enough air, but feels that he should slow down his breathing, that could kill him. On the other hand,

if he really is getting enough air, and feels that he should speed up his breathing, that won't kill him. It will feel very unpleasant, but I'm interested in survival, not in preventing unpleasant feelings. Thus I'll design the brain so that if there is any doubt about whether to breathe faster or slower, the person will breathe faster."

Centuries of evolution have designed the brain with survival in mind. For this reason, there are lots of people where breathing faster leads to breathing faster. I don't hear of those for whom breathing slower leads to breathing slower – probably because the genes for that problem have been selected out. If you have hyperventilation problems, you can attribute your problem to the fact that your body has been designed to "err on the side of caution" when it comes to deciding whether to breathe faster or to breathe more slowly.

The point of this section is to

A. give specific ways of learning to breathe more slowly,
or
B. explain how evolution probably has favored hyperventilation over breathing too slowly?

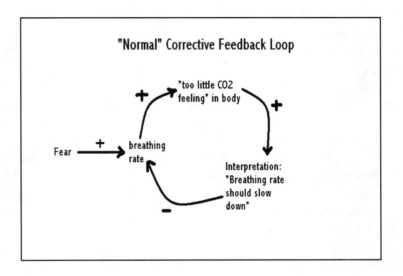

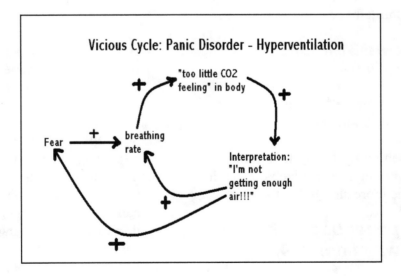

346. The diagrams on the previous page illustrate the process we've been describing. For people without hyperventilation problems, fear tends to increase the breathing rate; this causes a feeling of CO_2 deficit; the breathing slows down to correct this. But in people with hyperventilation problems, the feeling of CO_2 deficit is mistakenly interpreted as "I'm not getting enough air!" This leads to faster breathing, an even greater CO_2 deficit, more of a feel of suffocation, and still faster breathing! If you understand, either from the diagrams or from the words, that the crucial remedy for hyperventilation is realizing that you need to breathe more slowly, then you hold the key to eliminating hyperventilation episodes.

The diagrams referred to by this section illustrate that

A. when you get CO_2 excess, your blood gets more acidic,
or
B. when you get CO_2 deficit, the crucial thing is to realize you should breathe more slowly?

The paper bag technique, and why I don't like it

347. In the past, many emergency room physicians used the "paper bag treatment" to help people who come for help with panic episodes. (I don't recommend it, for reasons we'll discuss later. But it helps to understand what goes on with hyperventilation.) Physicians asked the person to hold a paper bag around their mouth and breathe into it. Why did this work? Because the carbon dioxide that the person breathed out stayed in the paper bag, and the person then breathed it back in again. Thus the carbon dioxide level rose in the blood, and this helped end the hyperventilation episode.

The purpose of this section was to

A. recommend that you breathe into a paper bag as a treatment for hyperventilation,
or
B. describe the paper bag treatment, to illustrate that in hyperventilation episodes, what the body needs is more carbon dioxide?

348. Why do I not recommend the paper bag treatment? If you use a bag that is too air-tight, and hold it with too good a seal around the mouth, you can use up the oxygen in the bag. You don't want to exchange too little carbon dioxide for too little oxygen! But if the bag is not air-tight enough, the carbon dioxide will escape and the bag treatment won't work. So the paper bag treatment isn't good

enough, because it creates a mixture of gases that is not controlled well enough.

In addition, when you're with people, it looks a little strange to take out a paper bag and breathe into it. Fortunately, there is a much better way to stop a hyperventilation episode: simply breathe more slowly.

This section argues that if you start to hyperventilate, you should

A. breathe into a paper bag,
or
B. breathe more slowly?

The best cure for hyperventilation: breathe more slowly!

349. Why does it work to breathe more slowly, when you're in the vicious cycle of hyperventilation, or starting to go into it? When you breathe very slowly, the CO_2 has a chance to build up, because you aren't blowing out the CO_2 so quickly. Your slow breathing cures your CO_2 deficit. Your body returns to its normal state.

The author stresses that when people, as part of a panic attack, start hyperventilating, they need

A. to let more oxygen get in,

or
B. to let more CO_2 build up?

350. Would it also work to start exercising, in order to generate more carbon dioxide? This also should work: it furnishes the exercise that the body expects to accompany the flight or fight response, and builds up carbon dioxide by generating it more rapidly. So far, we've accumulated lots less experience with how this works for ending hyperventilation episodes. (If you try it, please email me and let me know how it worked out! My address is on page 2.)

One reason we have less experience with exercise as a way of breaking the hyperventilation cycle is that often it looks strange socially to start running in place or doing jumping jacks unless we're in a gym. (Maybe some day the world will improve to the point where this is no longer true.) But breathing more slowly is a treatment or preventive for hyperventilation that you can use anywhere, in any circumstance.

Both points below are true, but what's the *main* point of this section?

A. Exercising should help relieve CO_2 deficits and thus help end hyperventilation cycles, but we know more about the helpful effects of

simply slowing breathing, partly because you can do it anywhere.
or
B. The author would love to hear the results if you experiment with exercising for breaking hyperventilation cycles.

351. When people start to get anxious, other people often tell them to "Take some deep breaths." Taking *slow* deep breaths can be helpful, but what helps is that the breaths are slow, not that they are deep. In fact, taking fast deep breaths is usually worse than taking fast shallow breaths, because fast deep breaths blow off carbon dioxide even faster. What people should say to people who are getting anxious is, "Take some *slow* breaths."

The point of this section is that

A. you should usually take deep breaths when you get anxious,
or
B. you should usually take *slow* breaths when you get anxious?

352. What do we mean by slow breaths? Some time when you are relaxed, count your breaths, or at least pay attention to the rate and rhythm. When at rest, most adults take somewhere in the neighborhood of 10 breaths a minute; children breathe a little faster. And these breaths are usually not very deep. You can notice how fast you breathe when you are not scared or exercising. When you are scared, you may need to breathe a little faster or deeper, because you are using up a little more energy with your muscles' being tight and jumpy. On the other hand, if you have already been hyperventilating, you can sometimes go for a minute or so with very little breathing until you build up more carbon dioxide. But your resting breathing rate gives you a guideline of what is meant by "breathing slowly."

The point of this section is to

A. try to communicate more concretely what is meant by "breathing slowly,"
or
B. convince you to breathe with your abdominal muscles and diaphragm rather than your chest?

353. "An ounce of prevention is worth a pound of cure." If you can learn to nip hyperventilation in the bud before it turns into a panic attack, things go much easier. Thus the goal is to notice CO_2 deficit as soon as it starts, and to breathe more slowly as soon as you feel that CO_2 deficit. You want to learn to distinguish very clearly between CO_2 excess (the feeling you get when you hold your breath) and CO_2 deficit (the feeling you get when

you breathe faster than you need to). These are learnable skills, and you can get better at them with practice! And this is wonderful news for anyone with hyperventilation or panic symptoms! The exercises that follow are meant to help you learn these skills.

The goals of the exercises that will follow are to

A. slow your heart rate and make yourself sweat less,
or
B. help you tell the difference between CO_2 excess and CO_2 deficit, and slow down your breathing when you start to get a CO_2 deficit?

Exercises for avoiding hyperventilation

354. The first exercise is "hold your breath and correct." This is short for "hold your breath to create a CO_2 excess, then correct that by breathing." In this exercise, you simply stop breathing for a few seconds. You don't take a deep breath first (because if you do, you have to waste more time sitting and waiting until you get the feeling of CO_2 excess.) You gradually feel what some call "air hunger": the urge to take a breath. This is the same feeling people get

when they swim under water, and need to come up and breathe. It's also the same feeling you get when you run really fast and get "out of breath." Notice what this feels like, and particularly, as you do this over time, notice how it feels *different* from the feeling of CO_2 deficit. But as soon as you feel the tiniest amount of discomfort from CO_2 excess, go ahead and breathe; you'll naturally breathe fast enough to correct the CO_2 excess. Then breathe at a normal rate again, and you're done with this exercise!

The first exercise, in a nutshell, is to

A. hold your breath a few seconds, notice the CO_2 excess feeling, and then breathe to correct that state,
or
B. hyperventilate a little, then exercise hard to make the CO_2 deficit feeling go away?

355. The point of this exercise is not to hold your breath a long time. It does no good to subject yourself to unpleasant extremes of CO_2 excess. You accomplish all you need when you feel a slight feeling of air hunger and then correct it by taking a couple of quick deep breaths.

This section told you that

A. in doing the "hold your breath and then correct the CO_2 excess" exercise, you don't need to hold your breath very long,

or

B. most of the time your breath should not command your attention, but simply go on automatically?

356. The second exercise is called "hyperventilate and correct." This is short for "hyperventilate to create a CO_2 deficit, then correct that by breathing very slowly." In this exercise you purposely blow off carbon dioxide, feel the CO_2 deficit feeling, and then make that feeling go away by breathing slowly.

This section

A. gives a very brief summary of what the "hyperventilate and correct" exercise is,

or

B. explains how hyperventilation affects how tightly your blood cells hold on to oxygen?

357. Here's how you do "hyperventilate and correct," in detail. You breathe as fast and deeply as you can, for somewhere between 5 and 15 fast deep breaths. You want to hyperventilate on purpose, just enough that you get a tiny bit of the "weird feeling in the head" that comes from

hyperventilation, but not enough of it to be very unpleasant or uncomfortable. For some people, 5 deep breaths will be plenty.

Then you sit and notice what CO_2 deficit feels like. Notice how it feels *different* from CO_2 excess! Meanwhile, you breathe very slowly. If you go for several seconds without even feeling the urge to take a breath, don't worry – this is natural. Breathe very slowly until the tiny bit of lightheadedness goes away, and then breath naturally. You have now corrected the CO_2 deficit by breathing slowly, and you have done one repetition of the exercise!

A summary of the "hyperventilate and correct" exercise is to

A. hyperventilate just enough to feel a little different, and then breathe slowly to make that feeling pass,

or

B. breathe at whatever rate is natural, and relax some group of muscles each time you exhale?

358. You can combine both of these exercises if you want. Here's the way you do that: you take a few deep breaths, and feel the CO_2 deficit. Then you stop breathing, notice the CO_2 deficit feeling go away, and notice a little feeling of CO_2 excess start. As soon as it starts, breathe enough to

make this feeling go away, and you're done.

In this combining of the two exercises, you

A. first feel CO_2 deficit, and then a little CO_2 excess, and then correct?
or
B. first feel CO_2 excess, and then make that feeling go away without ever feeling a CO_2 deficit?

359. None of these exercises should be unpleasant. You want to produce just the tiniest bit of CO_2 deficit or excess, and then correct these conditions by breathing slower or faster. These exercises are meant to prepare you for what you need to do in real life: to notice when you start to get CO_2 deficit or excess, to tell the difference between these, and to correct either condition as soon as it occurs.

Why do I advise you to produce just a tiny amount of carbon dioxide deficit or excess? It's not that you will harm your body or do something dangerous if you go beyond the tiniest amount. It's just that if you make these exercises unpleasant by hyperventilating too much or holding your breath too long, you won't want to do them. If you stop hyperventilating or holding your breath very early in the process, the exercises will be tolerable enough that

you will do them. Also, you want to practice nipping carbon dioxide deficit or excess in the bud, not waiting until later.

The purpose of this section is to

A. explain why you stop hyperventilating or holding your breath sooner rather than later,
or
B. to explain why "no pain, no gain" is the motto for these exercises?

360. Sometimes people who aren't aware of the principles described in this chapter have panic attacks that are so bad that they hyperventilate to the point of losing consciousness. Then the automatic reactions take over, and the person breathes more slowly, and as far as I know there is not permanent damage to organs. At other times people simply keep hyperventilating for a while, feel very uncomfortable, and eventually stop hyperventilating. Unless the person already has a seizure disorder or a serious heart condition, there is much more discomfort than there is physical danger.

The purpose of this section is to communicate that

A. hyperventilation, though very unpleasant, is not very dangerous,

or

B. biofeedback devices that measure exhaled CO_2 have been used to help people with hyperventilation?

361. Keep in mind that the flight or fight response, even with hyperventilation, can be unpleasant, but is not dangerous. If you remind yourself of this, you can interrupt another vicious cycle that often occurs in panic attacks. People often think, "I wouldn't be feeling so bad if something horrible were not happening to my body! Something terrible and unknown is going on, that I have no control over!" These, of course, are very scary thoughts, that only increase panic. When people understand the principles of this chapter, they can say to themselves very different sentences. They can say, "I am feeling some discomfort from the flight or fight response. I may be getting a carbon dioxide deficit. This is something I can control. By breathing more slowly and relaxing, I may be able to make it go away sooner. Even if I'm not skilled enough to control it this time, I'm facing something that is unpleasant but not very dangerous, something that will go away eventually." These thoughts are MUCH less fear-inducing, and the good thing is, they are true.

The point of this section is that

A. you are now able to prevent every panic attack for the rest of your life, or

B. with an understanding of the principles, you can have thoughts about flight-or-fight responses you feel that are much less scary?

362. There are some therapists or gurus who feel that most people do not breathe "correctly" and that people should work a lot on "proper breathing techniques." I am somewhat skeptical about these claims, so far. As long as we are getting air in and out of our lungs fast enough but not too fast, we are doing a perfectly fine job of breathing. Breathing mostly occurs automatically, without our paying attention to it, and that's the way it should be! We have lots of other things to attend to in life without worrying about the correctness of every breath we take!

The major time we need to pay attention to breathing is when we start hyperventilating; at that time, it's very important to think, "I recognize that feeling! Time to breathe more slowly!" Otherwise, my recommendation is to enjoy the fact that we don't have to think very much about breathing.

In this section the author expresses an attitude toward many teachings about right and wrong ways of breathing that is

A. enthusiastic,
or
B. doubtful and skeptical?

363. Some people have been able to permanently get rid of bad panic attacks just by using the principles described in this chapter. When you combine these principles of breathing with lots of practice in turning down your own level of arousal through relaxation exercises, lots of practice in taking control of your own thoughts and imagery, lots of fantasy rehearsal of handling unrealistically feared situations bravely and calmly, lots of prolonged exposure to the unrealistically feared situations, lots of skill-building in whatever it takes to be successful in the scary choice points, and a few other techniques, the chances of success become quite high. Knowledge and work provide power, if you know why and how to do the work you need to do.

The main point of this section is that

A. evidence that genes contribute to anxiety comes from studies of twins and adopted people,
or
B. the principles of this chapter, especially when combined with others,

really can be effective against panic and anxiety?

Chapter 10: Doing Exposure and Fantasy Rehearsal

When rehearsals don't work, it's usually because they're not done.

364. If you've really decided to start doing lots of exposure, fantasy rehearsal, and real-life rehearsal in order to reduce an unrealistic fear or aversion, you've come to a momentous decision. This decision could greatly improve the course of your life.

Some people can't bring themselves to believe that they can learn new and better responses to situations by practicing, both in real life and in imagination. Some say, "That's stupid, it won't work."

There are many, many research studies documenting that people can make these techniques work. What's the number one reason that rehearsals don't work? It's that they're not done. I have seen people hang on to fears or aversions for years, not doing rehearsals, while other people get over their fears or aversions in weeks, or sometimes even days, through doing lots of rehearsals.

The author's point of view in this section is that

A. Exposure and rehearsal are very effective IF people actually put out the time and effort to do them.
or
B. Everyone who hears about this wonderful new technique has fantastic results almost immediately.

365. One excellent way to do fantasy rehearsals is to speak them aloud. That way you can make sure you're staying on task. Plus, if you're working with someone else, that person can hear your fantasy rehearsals.

Another very useful way to do fantasy rehearsals is to write them out, and then read them, often. It will probably help to read them aloud.

It's useful, when you're getting good at the art of making up fantasy rehearsals, to read examples that someone else has made up. For that reason, there are several such examples in this chapter.

The technique the author did NOT mention in this section was

A. writing out fantasy rehearsals and reading them aloud,

or
B. sitting silently and visualizing yourself handling the situation well?

The "STEBC" of fantasy rehearsals

366. There are several steps to doing a "complete" fantasy rehearsal. We can remember by these thinking about the STEBC: Situation, Thoughts, Emotions, Behavior, and Celebration. You describe the situation you are in, as if you are experiencing it now. You say the thoughts you'd like to think in this situation. You imagine feeling the emotions you'd like to feel, and report on them. You imagine yourself doing the behaviors you'd like to carry out. And then, having responded to the situation in a really good way, you celebrate your good choices.

The main point of this section was to

A. describe the "STEBC" of a complete fantasy rehearsal,
or
B. remind you to celebrate your good choices?

367. What if you don't get around to rehearsing thoughts, emotions, behaviors, and celebration, but only do one or two of these? These "incomplete" fantasy rehearsals can also be very useful. The more you can rehearse *any* positive response to the situations, the better off you'll be.

Doing the four-thought exercise is really a type of fantasy rehearsal. You imagine the situation and rehearse useful thoughts. In so doing, you also think about what behavior you want to do, (when you list options and choose) and you celebrate your choice. So the four-thought exercise has a lot in common with doing fantasy rehearsals with all the STEBC.

The author's attitude is that the four-thought exercise

A. is completely different from a fantasy rehearsal,
or
B. is a type of fantasy rehearsal?

Mastery and coping rehearsals

368. We speak of two types of fantasy rehearsals: *mastery* rehearsals and *coping* rehearsals. Mastery begins with the letter M, as does the word *miracle*; this is a way of remembering that in a mastery rehearsal, you imagine that a "miracle" has occurred so that you are immediately able to handle the situation with no fear or aversion. You breeze through the

situation with comfort and confidence, and with no pain or suffering. This is the way you usually want to handle the situation, eventually.

In the mastery fantasy rehearsal, you imagine yourself as

A. being very nervous, but doing what you need to do anyway,
Or
B. feeling confident, and handling the situation just like someone who has no fear or aversion to it?

369. It may take a while before you can handle the situation with complete comfort. For this reason, it's good to fantasy rehearse feeling nervous, but still making yourself confront the situation and handling it well. You practice feeling the fear or aversion, but doing what you choose anyway. Because you are coping not only with the situation, but also your unpleasant feelings about it, this is called a *coping rehearsal*. But in it, like a mastery rehearsal, you see yourself behaving just as you would like to behave.

What is the difference between a mastery and a coping rehearsal?

A. In a coping rehearsal, you imagine yourself coping with feelings of unrealistic fear or aversion, whereas in a mastery rehearsal you see yourself as confident and comfortable.
or
B. Both mastery and coping rehearsals ask you to imagine behaving very appropriately in the situation.

370. Which are worth doing, mastery or coping rehearsals? The answer is both. The advantage of mastery rehearsals is that you get to practice the comfort and confidence that you eventually want to have in the situation. And mastery rehearsals are a great way to start out, because they tend to be a fairly painless way of doing exposures and practice. The advantage of coping rehearsals is that when you get around to practicing the situation in real life, you won't be thrown off guard if you still feel nervous or otherwise uncomfortable, because you've prepared yourself to deal with your own feelings of discomfort.

The author's attitude is that it's best to

A. do only mastery rehearsals – why even imagine discomfort if you don't have to?
or
B. do both mastery and coping rehearsals, so that you can deal not only with the situation, but also with any discomfort that you may feel with it.

371. As a general rule, you want to follow up your fantasy rehearsals with real-life rehearsals, whenever possible. Sometimes finding real-life practice opportunity is easy – for example, when someone rehearses going to school, doing math, or lying in bed in the dark. But sometimes you can go a whole lifetime without real-life practice, as for example when someone uses rehearsal to handle the fear of nuclear war, rejection from all one's friends and family members, or being in an airplane about to crash.

Which is closer to the attitude expressed in this section?

A. You should always follow up fantasy rehearsal with real-life exposure and practice.
or
B. Use real-life practice when it is desirable and possible, but for some fears, fortunately, it will not be.

Examples of fantasy rehearsals

372. Frank is very much afraid of dental procedures. He does a rehearsal of an item close to the bottom of his hierarchy of situations. He imagines himself looking at a character in a drawing, and imagines that the character is waiting to see the dentist! The rehearsal goes like this:

> I'm sitting at the back of a big, empty auditorium, looking at a drawing at the front of the auditorium, where there's a stick figure sitting in a chair. The person is waiting to get some dental work done. He can smell the "dental office" smell.
>
> He's thinking, "This is no problem, I'm just going to get my teeth cleaned. I want to enjoy my time. I think I'll make up a pleasant dream-like story while I'm getting my teeth worked on. I like that choice." He's feeling happy about how clean and fresh his mouth is going to be, and he's also feeling happy about having some time to imagine fun things. He sits and relaxes in his chair and waits to be called. He thinks, "I like the way I'm handling this!"

Was this fantasy rehearsal "complete," in that it contained a description of the situation, thoughts, emotions, behaviors, and celebration?

A. Yes,
or
B. No?

373. Now suppose Frank has worked his way up to close to the top of the hierarchy. Here goes another fantasy rehearsal.

I'm sitting in the dentist's chair, and the dentist is preparing to give me a shot of local anesthetic.

I think to myself, "This will hurt some, but I can handle it. A major goal is holding still. I also want to keep cool, because that will be a big accomplishment. One option is that I can concentrate on relaxing my muscles, and another is that I can remind myself that the pain doesn't mean I'm being harmed – I don't need to protect myself. I'll do both of those! I'm glad I chose to do that."

I'm feeling alert, and determined, just the way I've practiced feeling.

Relaxing the muscles helps me feel calm. I open my mouth and relax my jaw muscles as the needle goes in. I'm holding still and staying relaxed even as I feel some pain and then some numbness. Without the fear, the pain isn't bad at all! And now that's over.

Hooray for me, I feel really proud of how I handled that!"

Because Frank didn't imagine feeling nervous or scared at all, this was a

A. mastery fantasy rehearsal,
or
B. coping fantasy rehearsal?

374. Janelle is very much afraid of public speaking, but she has a speech to give. Here's a fantasy rehearsal for a situation low on her hierarchy:

I'm going into the classroom where I'll give this speech, but there's nobody here. I have this time to practice, all by myself.

I think, "It's really nice being able to get into the room to practice. My goal is just to relax and read my speech. I don't even need to practice looking up at the audience yet. That can come later."

Even in this practice situation, I feel excited. I can feel my heart beating a little faster than usual. But that's good, because I can get used to that feeling.

I pull out my written speech and just start from the beginning, and read it off. "Thanks for coming tonight. I'm glad to be able to talk with you about this very important subject!..."

Hooray for me, I'm getting some great practice done!

Do the Situation, Thoughts, Emotions, Behaviors, and Celebration each get one paragraph in the above section, and in that order?

A. No,
or
B. Yes?

375. Now Janelle has worked her way up to the top of the hierarchy.

I'm sitting up front, facing the audience, and now someone is introducing me. I see all the people looking toward the front.

I think, this is a real opportunity to make a triumph. And all I have to do is to read my speech, just as I have in practice lots of times! Remember to use enthusiastic tones, remember eye contact with the audience.

I'm feeling excited but confident. I'm feeling super energized, but that's just going to help me be a better speaker!

Now the introduction is over, and I walk to the podium. I look to the audience and smile. I begin speaking without even looking at my speech, because I remember it so well. But I look at the speech all I need to – I don't have to remember it all.

Yay, I'm having a triumph!

If Janelle had wanted to make this more of a coping rehearsal, she would have

A. imagined feeling very relaxed, or
B. imagined feeling not only excited, but very scared, but giving a good speech anyway?

376. Janelle decides to practice with a fanciful answer to "What's the worst that could happen when you give your speech?" The fantasy rehearsal goes like this:

I'm giving my speech, and some people are hissing and booing. Some have fallen asleep. Some are talking with each other, and some start playing video games. Someone loudly says, "This speech is really boring!"

I'm thinking, this is going to make an interesting story to tell. This is their problem, not mine. What are my options? I can keep going as if nothing happened. I could finish the speech immediately and walk out quickly. I think I like this option best: finish up, but challenge the audience to defend why they're acting as they are.

I'm feeling angry at them for their rude behavior, but also very curious. I'm not feeling bad about myself in the slightest.

I say to them, "OK, the speech ends here. But before I leave, I'm curious to hear from you – why are you acting as you are? Do you disagree with what I'm saying, and are you trying to protest? Or did you never want to hear about this in the first place, or what?" I'm packing up my stuff, waiting for someone to reply. No one does, and I walk out.

I feel really good about the way I handled this!

For most speakers, this fantasy rehearsal would represent which of the following two?

A. Preparing for a situation unlikely to occur, in order to make the speaker feel more confident about being prepared for every possible outcome, or
B. preparing for the most likely outcome?

377. Ralph is afraid of flying on airplanes. He's working on a situation fairly low on the hierarchy. He imagines the following:

I'm allowed to walk onto and explore this plane, which is parked in the airport and not turned on. I'm allowed to sit and read a book until I want to get off.
It's really great that I have this opportunity to practice. I'm in no danger at all, and I have a chance to do some prolonged exposure. My goal is to get used to this situation as thoroughly as I can, and also to get used to any discomfort that I feel.
Even though I'm in no danger at all, I can feel myself getting really activated. My heart is going faster. I'm shaking a bit. I feel nervous.

I'm walking around the plane for a long time, looking at the seats, and the baggage containers, and the bathrooms, and looking out the window at the wings. Now, I sit in one of the seats, and start reading my book. Every once in a while I imagine that the plane is in the air, just to make the exposure more useful.
Gradually, I calm down. Hooray for me! I've done a really useful practice!

The fact that Ralph imagines himself feeling nervous, with some trembling and heart-pounding, means that this is a

A. Mastery rehearsal, or
B. Coping rehearsal?

378. Ralph decides to practice with the very top item of his airplanes hierarchy.

I'm riding along on the plane, and all of a sudden I notice that both wings have fallen off. The plane is now hurtling toward the ground. It's totally certain that the plane will crash.
I'm glad I have a few seconds left. This will give me time to be thankful for the chance to be alive. What a miracle life is, in the first place. I really appreciate having had the chance to take part in it.

I'm feeling strangely serene and calm. I could get myself really upset, but since I only have a short time left, I want to feel this serene feeling. I feel grateful for everyone who has loved me and whom I've loved.

I relax and close my eyes.

Hooray for me, I'm handling this situation well, and it's a fairly difficult one!

This is a

A. mastery rehearsal,
or
B. coping rehearsal?

379. Francine is afraid of situations where she has to say "no" to people. She does the following rehearsal:

I answer the phone, and it's a telemarketer for a charity that I actually have supported in the past. But I don't want to be interrupted at home.

This situation gives me a good opportunity to practice saying no. My goal is to practice being assertive in a very polite way.

I feel relaxed, because nothing bad is going to happen, and confident.

When the person asks if I would like to make a donation now, I sweetly say, "No, I wouldn't." The marketer asks if I can make a donation later, and I say, "No, not at any time." The marketer starts explaining why the cause is so important, and I say "Those are good points, but I don't want to donate." The marketer says, "Do you mind if I ask why?" I say, "I don't want to make a donation to any organization that interrupts me by phone, and I'd like to be put on the do not call list, please." The marketer says OK and finally says good bye. I say, "Have a nice day."

Hooray, I was very polite, yet assertive!

This was a

A. Mastery rehearsal,
or
B. Coping rehearsal?

380. Ronnie has a fear of sleeping over at other people's houses. He imagines a scene that is not very high on the hierarchy.

To practice sleeping over at someone else's house, I'm practicing sleeping in a different room of my own house. I have a mattress on the floor in the living room, and it's time to go to sleep.

This isn't a bad situation. The mattress is comfortable. If I don't get to sleep right away, that won't be awful. My goal is to make use of the chance to practice this situation, as long as I'm awake. What are my options? I can relax my muscles. I can drift into pleasant fantasies, and do the "pleasant dreams exercise." I think I'll do both of those.

I'm feeling calm and drifty.

I'm relaxing my muscles. Each time I breathe out, I try to get another muscle group more relaxed. I imagine myself singing with my friends. Now I imagine my friends and me floating slowly through the air, above our town, looking all around, amazed by what a beautiful night it is. We drift down and knock on the door of another friend, and this friend joins us, and now we all start again, floating around through the air.

Hooray, I'm handling this situation in a very pleasant way!

When Ronnie says, "I'm feeling calm and drifty," he is rehearsing

A. a celebration,
or
B. an emotion?

381. Ronnie has decided that one of the things he likes least about the idea of sleeping over is that he may not be able to sleep, even though it's dark and everyone else is asleep. He decides on a strategy to deal with this, and rehearses it.

I'm spending the night with my friend Zeke, and now everyone is asleep except me.

I'm glad to have the chance to practice with this situation. I may have a lot of time to get used to it.

I feel proud that I prepared for this situation.

I take out my little flashlight and my science book from my backpack, and I start reading. I'm learning the stuff I'm eventually going to be tested on in school.

Even if I'm up for hours, I'm going to learn a tremendous amount that is going to help me. I feel good about the way I've handled this!

The major feeling that Ronnie imagines having during this rehearsal is

A. being proud of himself,
or
B. feeling nervous and tense?

382. Rick has a very unpleasant aversion to the sound of silverware scraping against plates or bowls.

I sit down to watch a television show, and I've resolved that I'm going to scrape a fork against a plate the whole time I'm watching the show. I'm starting out rubbing the plate very lightly against the plate.

This is an opportunity to be really tough and strong. I don't want to be a wimp. I want to be like those army guys in the movies who were tortured by the enemy but still didn't tell the secrets.

I'm feeling very determined. I feel excited about doing this; if it works, it will be a major triumph. Starting out, I feel the SUD level very high, but I'm going to push through it.

I keep scraping and scraping, a little harder and harder as time goes by, so that the noise is as loud as it needs to be to give me all the exposure I need. I find that I can enjoy the TV show and still keep this up. Every once in a while I forget to keep scraping, but I start right back up again. Over time, my SUD rating is going down! I keep on.

Now it's the end of the TV show, and my SUD rating for the scraping noise is WAY down from what it started at, maybe 9 down to 2. In one session! What a triumph this was! Hooray!

This was a

A. Mastery fantasy rehearsal,
or
B. Coping fantasy rehearsal?

383. Rochelle has a hand-washing compulsion. She does a fantasy rehearsal as follows:

I will wash my hands before supper, but that won't be for another hour and a half. I'm not going to let myself wash my hands until then. I'm going around and touching doorknobs, and table tops, computer keyboards, and even the toilet bowl seat. Now I'm touching the things at my desk, which according to my former way of thinking, would contaminate them, too.

But I'm finding that a miracle has occurred! I don't have any more worry about contamination than someone without OCD has. I think, this is no big deal, this is just the way you act, and you don't get any dread disease.

It feels wonderful not to have to worry about contamination.

I sit at my desk and do my work, and I get lots done. I don't even have the urge to get up and wash my hands.

I'm so glad I don't have to waste so much time hand-washing! This feels great!

This was a

A. mastery fantasy rehearsal,
or
B. coping fantasy rehearsal?

384. Tim has a compulsion about having things be symmetrical. One of

these is having his socks pulled up to exactly the same height. He does a fantasy rehearsal, as follows:

I deliberately pull one of my socks up as high as it will go, and push the other down a little bit. One is a lot higher than the other now.

This is not terrible. Nobody is going to die. Nobody is even going to be harmed. It will not make any difference. My goal is to get used to it. If I can do that, I will save a lot of energy, and I will have had a real triumph.

At first, I have a very uncomfortable feeling. It's not exactly fear – maybe closer to disgust? I feel a very strong urge to pull up the other sock. The SUD level is about 8. But I hang in there. I feel determined.

I do some work, and every once in a while I turn my attention back to my socks. I'm not touching them.

Now it's several hours later, and my SUD level has gone down to 1! I feel so proud of myself for doing this long exposure, and for having a triumph!

The emotions Rick felt at various points in this story were

A. fear, worry, and relief,
or
B. disgust, determination, and pride?

385. Jeremy has an aversion to eating foods that have touched each other on his plate. He does the following rehearsal:

I have some nice beans and some corn, very separate on my plate. They look good. Now I'm taking my fork and deliberately mixing them all together. Now they're all mixed up!

Before, it would have been very difficult for me to eat them. But now, a miracle has happened! The mixture looks very appetizing.

I'm feeling hungry, and I can't wait to eat that mixture of corn and beans. I feel delighted that my aversion has totally gone away.

I'm eating the corn and beans, and they taste great! They taste even better than either of them by itself would taste.

Hooray, I'm so glad I decided to take advantage of this miracle!

This was a

A. mastery rehearsal,
or
B. coping rehearsal?

386. Lucinda has a "body dysmorphic disorder" problem. She decides that one aversive situation is seeing in the mirror her own image. She decides on the way she would like to respond if a

"miracle" occurred, and she does a fantasy rehearsal.

I'm dressed up, ready to go out, looking at myself in the mirror.

I think, "Hey, I look just fine. There's nothing wrong with the way I look! I'm attractive enough!"

I feel excited and confident about going out and seeing people.

I'm going out and greeting other people, and I'm enjoying being with them!

Hooray, I'm glad I'm able to feel just fine about how I look!

This was a

A. mastery rehearsal,
or
B. coping rehearsal?

387. Lucinda decides on another specific situation: looking at her own arms. She does a fantasy rehearsal in which she starts to do her usual response, but catches herself.

I notice my arm, and I see that it is fatter and a little flabbier than that of the models I see. I reflexively start to think, "That's disgusting."

But then I think, "No, it isn't. It's perfectly OK. I'm so lucky that it works well, it's able to move in every way that an arm should. I'm so lucky that it isn't in pain. I'm lucky that it hasn't had to be amputated."

I feel a very small amount of regret that my arm doesn't look like the model's, but a very large amount of happiness that my arm is perfectly healthy and there's nothing wrong with it.

I'm going about my business of trying to do something good for someone else or myself, without worrying about how I look!

Hooray, I'm glad about the way I handled this situation!

Lucinda got the urge to do a lot of getting down on herself. Which thought pattern did she substitute for this, in her rehearsal?

A. Listing options and choosing,
or
B. Celebrating luck?

Real-life exposure and rehearsals, and the celebrations exercise

388. The "gold standard" for overcoming fears and aversions is successful real-life rehearsal. It's amazing how much fantasy rehearsal can make it easier to handle the feared situation in real life. Sometimes you have imagined so vividly that the fantasy rehearsal has prepared you thoroughly for real-life exposure.

But sometimes, despite lots and lots of fantasy rehearsal, once you get into the real life situation, something is different. There's a plane that really could crash. There's another human being that really could get mad at you. There's food you are now really going to put into your mouth. You find more fear or aversion than you did in your fantasy rehearsals.

What's the main point of this?

A. Sometimes real-life exposure is difficult, despite lots of fantasy rehearsals.
or
B. People with very vivid imaginations may benefit more from fantasy rehearsal.

389. Most people have a tendency to think that they have done "lots of fantasy rehearsals" when they have done ten or fifteen of them. I would recommend defining "lots of fantasy rehearsals" as hundreds or even thousands of them. If you have truly done "lots" of them by this bigger definition, you will probably find yourself much better prepared for real-life exposures.

What's the point of this section?

A. You'll find that fantasy rehearsals are more likely to have prepared you for real-life exposure when you have done hundreds or thousands of them.
or
B. Along with just doing exposure, you want to practice successful handling of the situations.

390. If despite "lots" of fantasy rehearsals you find that real life exposure is still scary or aversive, you simply work your way up a hierarchy of real-life exposures, practicing the same positive responses you practiced in fantasy rehearsals. You celebrate that because you have done coping rehearsals, you are prepared for the fear or aversion you have to put up with along the way.

What's the main point of this?

A. Sometimes an important way to move down the hierarchy of difficulty in real-life exposure is to have someone you trust along with you.
or
B. If real-life exposure is still scary or aversive after "lots" of fantasy rehearsals, you just work your way along a real-life exposure hierarchy.

391. As you do real-life exposures, one of the most important ingredients for success is self-reinforcement. You want to feel as good as you can about every success experience, every step toward mastery. The "celebrations

exercise" is recalling the positive steps you've taken, writing them down or telling someone about them, and revisiting them in memory with as much positive feeling as you can muster. The person you tell about them should be someone who will really feel good with you. As you do your exposure and practice, be sure to celebrate your successes. This will have two effects: 1) you will tend to have still more successes, and 2) you will feel good more often.

The celebrations exercise that the author speaks of here is

A. holding a party, with several people in attendance,
or
B. recalling and feeling good about and writing down or telling someone else about your success experiences?

Chapter 11: The Roles of Social Support and a Positive Emotional Climate

People's needs for social support

392. When I was listing the major ways of overcoming anxiety and aversions, we spoke about "allies." Allies are people who are on your side, friends or family members whom you can count on to help you, people who like you and will stick up for you. Having lots of strong allies has been called having "social support" or a good "social support system."

Social support simply means

A. having structured organizations that you are an official member of,
or
B. having enough friends and/or family members that you can count on to help you?

393. Social support, alliances, and friendships travel on two-way streets. If you want to count on people to help you, you usually need to let the others count on you to help them. So the better you are at providing social support to others, the more you can feel comfortable receiving it for yourself.

The point of this section is that

A. if you want to receive social support, get skilled at providing it to others,
or
B. social support probably reduces anxiety for reasons that are built into the human brain?

394. Why is social support so strong an antidote to anxiety? Part of the reason probably depends upon the evolutionary past of the human race. Throughout millions of years, human beings and their ancestors have lived among predators – either other animals, or predatory humans. Part of the business of life has been defense against predators. Imagine four or five people who have agreed to help defend one another, carrying sticks or spears. If they encounter a wildcat or a bear or a threatening human being, their unity brings them protection and perhaps the difference between life and death. Facing the same situations alone would be far more dangerous. For this reason, the human brain probably evolved a part that gives the

signal, "I need to belong to a pack," and "When I'm on my own, I'm in greater danger." The signal of danger from being without a supportive pack is anxiety.

What's the main point of this section?

A. Because throughout centuries, danger has been greater for loners than for those in groups, anxiety is a signal of danger when people lack or lose social support.
or
B. human beings have probably been more dangerous to other humans than animal predators have been?

395. Even in the present, people are in greater danger, primarily from human predators, when they travel alone. If you imagine yourself walking through a fairly rough section of a city, late at night, would you prefer to go by yourself, with one other person, or in a pack of ten or fifteen allies? Even in the present day, social support helps in defending against predators. If you have no allies, the danger is greater.

The point of this section is that

A. the need for allies has been selected for in our brains throughout many centuries,
or

B. even today, people often need to rely on allies to help defend against predators?

396. People need a social support network for reasons other than protection against predators. Whom do we depend on when we get very sick, or hurt? How about when there is a problem we can't seem to make progress on by ourselves? How about even when we need to move an object that's too heavy or bulky for one person? What about when something breaks or runs out and we need to borrow something from someone? What about when the rent is too high for one person to pay by himself or herself? How about when some storm or flood comes, and the work is too much to be done by one person alone? And importantly, what about when all the work is done and the problems are at least on hold, how do we go about having fun? (Watching television by ourselves just doesn't seem to supply that essential something.) All these things go better when we have supportive friends and/or family.

The main point of this section was that

A. in these times, housing costs are so high that people need to share them rather than live alone,
or

179

B. people need social support for all sorts of reasons other than protection against predators?

397. What if you are super-competent at doing things for yourself, by yourself? What if you have figured out very effective ways of getting enjoyment from life, all by yourself – from reading, or writing, for example? Then you will be less dependent upon other people for your needs. You have less need to be anxious if your social support system is running low. However, the most secure position is to be very competent at taking care of yourself, AND to have a very good social support system. When the going gets tough, you have two engines to use to survive and prevail, not just one. This is why skill-building and allies are both important techniques for overcoming anxiety.

The point of this section is that

A. even the person who is most skilled and independent can sometimes get so sick that he or she needs help, or
B. skill-building and allies work together to reduce anxiety – the better off you are with each of them, the more secure your position is.

Positive emotional climates

398. What makes a group of people supportive? They don't provide each other much of a feeling of security and safety if they are constantly resenting each other, criticizing one another, and making each other unhappy. If, on the other hand, they speak kindly to each other, take pleasure in one another, and help each other, they do their jobs of social support and anxiety-reduction much better.

The main point of this section is that

A. to be a good support system, people need not just to be together, but to be kind and helpful to one another, or
B. the more skilled and competent you are at useful work, the more people will want you to be in their support networks?

399. When people are in the habit of acting kind and cheerful and respectful to one another, we can compare the good effect on life to that of good weather, living in a place without hurricanes and floods and droughts. We can say they live in a positive "emotional climate," or a favorable "interpersonal climate."
    But the emotional climate is much more important for people's happiness than the climate that results

from weather. When people are part of a kind, loving, mutually supportive group, they can remain happy despite lots of bad weather.

The main purpose of this section was to

A. cite two studies showing that people are less anxious when their family members are nicer to them,
or
B. define an idea called the "emotional climate" or "interpersonal climate" which names how kind and supportive people in a certain group usually are toward each other?

400. What goes on in very negative emotional climates? People feel mad at each other, but they can't resolve their conflicts. They may yell at each other, or hit each other, or otherwise be violent. Or they may silently resent and avoid each other. Someone may boss others around, and often at least one person is very critical and insulting to the others. When one has a success, the others are jealous or angry. When someone fails at something, the others may make fun of that person. The talk that goes on often has a tone of arguing or whining or complaining. People often frown at one another, seldom smile, and when they do smile, they are often making fun of the other's shortcomings. When

there is work to do, they feel that the others should do it.

One of the things this section mentioned that goes on in negative emotional climates is that

A. they are physically violent,
or
B. they come into each other's presence without saying "Hi," or anything else?

401. Here's more of what goes on in negative emotional climates.
        When there are good things to be shared, each thinks, "I am not getting my fair share!" They compete with each other, and the usual feeling is, "If the other person gets more, that will mean less for me." When there are decisions to be made together, the usual pattern is that someone will be in favor of an option, the other will be against it, and no other options are listed. They fight over that one option for a while, and then they get off the subject onto why things are the other person's fault. If they are asked the question, "What do you do together that both of you really enjoy?" they can't come up with much. If they are asked, "When you have fun conversations with each other, what do you talk about," the question often "doesn't compute." When people

don't get what they want, they often "go ballistic" as a way of trying to pressure others to give them what they think they need. There are many more disapproving tones of voice than approving ones.

The main purpose of this section was to

A. describe what goes on in bad emotional climates,
or
B. let you know how to make a bad emotional climate better?

402. On the other hand, what goes on in very good emotional climates? People let each other know they are glad to see each other by their cheerful greetings. They have fun and interesting conversations, and when one has something to say, the other is a good listener. They often help each other on tasks, without being pressured or forced to do so. They enjoy working together. They compliment each other and thank each other for their positive actions. When one has a success, the other feels genuinely glad, partly because the group has been honored, and partly because he takes pleasure in the other's happiness.

One of the things this section mentioned is that in positive emotional climates,

A. people feel fine about lending things to others, knowing the other will be careful to give whatever is borrowed back unharmed,
or
B. people celebrate and feel good about each other's successes?

403. What else goes on in positive emotional climates?
When there is a problem to solve, people can think about several different options and discuss them calmly. People can stick up for their own rights without yelling at or insulting the others. They think more about the advantages and disadvantages of different courses of action than about whose fault something is. They often smile and laugh together. They have many things that they enjoy doing together, including very simple and inexpensive things like walking and talking. Someone would hear many more approving tones of voice than disapproving ones in this group.

The purpose of this section was to

A. make the point that people in positive emotional climates are less lazy,

or

B. list a bunch of things that people in positive emotional climates tend to do?

404. A central difference between positive and negative climates has to do with reward and punishment. In negative emotional climates, people very often influence one another by punishing each other – most often by saying disapproving words or using a disapproving tone. In positive emotional climates, people very often influence each other by rewarding each other – most often speaking with kind words and an approving tone. I have for a long time advised people to aim for a 4 to 1 ratio of approval to disapproval. If there are four times as many approving statements as disapproving ones, you can be pretty sure you are in a positive emotional climate.

This section focused on one major difference between positive and negative emotional climates, which was

A. that in positive emotional climates, people have a much more favorable attitude toward doing work,

or

B. that in positive emotional climates, people give each other much more approval relative to disapproval?

405. Strong feelings of social support do not develop overnight. People need to know each other for a good while before they have accumulated enough of a "behavior sample" to feel that they can count on the other person. Loyalty grows over time, not right away. The most supportive emotional climates are cultivated over years, not days or weeks.

The main point of this section is that

A. it's important for people to feel loyal to each other,

or

B. the security people feel from positive relations takes time to cultivate?

406. Because relationships take time to cultivate, and support systems take time to grow, people often find themselves more anxious when they have uprooted themselves from their social support systems. For example, when someone moves to a town where she knows no one, you would expect her to feel less safe and secure. When someone leaves a supportive family and friends to go off to college with a bunch of total strangers, you would expect him to feel less supported.

The main point of this section is that

A. college can be stressful, partly because of temptations to drunkenness,
or
B. when people uproot themselves from a support system, they are more likely to be anxious?

Improving emotional climates

407. How do you make the emotional climate better, for the groups and the relationships to which you belong? There are two ways: first, picking wisely the people to be in your social network, and second, contributing to the emotional climates of the networks you are in, by your own positive influence.

The two ways that the author mentions for getting yourself into a positive emotional climate could be referred to as

A. selecting well, and influencing well,
or
B. giving well, and taking well?

408. In the appendices to this book, there are three rating scales having to do with the emotional climate. There are two alternate forms of a scale giving a list of the characteristics that distinguish positive and negative environments. The third scale gives a list of things that people say to improve the emotional climate. These scales are more of the same ideas we have already talked about in this chapter.

I believe that it's a good idea to examine these scales closely, and to get the items into your mind. Then, when you are selecting people to hang out with, try to choose people who tend to create positive emotional climates.

The advice in this section is to

A. choose your friends at least partly on the basis of how much they tend to create positive emotional climates,
or
B. pay lots of attention to how much you contribute to a positive emotional climate?

409. You can select friends, but it's harder to select relatives! However, even within your family, you may be able to select whom you want to spend more time with and less time with. Many families contain aunts, uncles, grandparents, cousins, and so forth whom you can choose to stay in touch with, or not. With phone and other

electronic communications becoming cheaper and easier, you have the chance to be in touch often with more distant family members who want to be part of your social support network.

The main point of this section is that

A. you can't select your parents,
or
B. you can probably select which family members you want to spend time talking with?

410. What if you feel you can't be very choosy about the members of your social support system, because not many people seem to want to be your friend? Then 3 actions may be in order:

1. Get very good at social skills, particularly social conversation.
2. Develop very useful skills that people value highly – academic, work, athletic, artistic, etc.
3. Don't be afraid to issue invitations to people, and don't be too upset when people turn you down.

The three actions listed in this section are meant to

A. help you strengthen your social network of friends and family members,
or

B. be all you need to succeed in life, quickly and easily?

411. An important way to become part of a positive emotional climate is to make very positive contributions in relationships you already have. Can you increase the fraction of the time you use tones of approval? Can you say "Thanks" and "Congratulations" more often? Can you become a better listener? Can you offer to help people in ways that they appreciate? Can you become an expert in social conversation? Can you get to be a very rational resolver of conflicts? Can you have an infectiously cheerful mood? Almost all people can stand to improve in these behaviors.

This section lists

A. some benefits you get from improving the emotional climate of your own relationships,
or
B. some ways to make a more positive contribution to the emotional climate of the relationships you're in?

412. I have a guess; maybe you can help me test to see how often it's correct. The Emotional Climate Act Frequency Scale, near the end of this book, lists lots of things people say that may improve the emotional climate. My guess is that any one

person can unilaterally improve the emotional climate of many relationships or groups, simply by enthusiastically saying these things more often. This is not always true. For example, some people tend to punish or make fun of others for being cheerful and approving. And some people seem not to have the capacity for approval in their repertoires. But for many groups, an upbeat, enthusiastic, kind attitude is contagious. When you notice it spreading from yourself to others, you can feel really good about this contagion!

The author's guess is that for many, but not all groups,

A. cheerfulness, helpfulness, kindness, good listening, and so forth spread from one person to another in a group, or
B. the harder you work at whatever the group is doing, the more respect you get?

413. A great deal of research has shown us that positive emotional climates protect people from all sorts of mental health problems, not just anxiety. They tend to protect against depression and anger problems as well. Almost all psychological problems are less troublesome when people are in supportive social networks!

The author's point is that

A. being in positive emotional climates seems to help prevent drug and alcohol problems, or
B. being in positive emotional climates seems to help for almost all types of psychological difficulties?

414. Improving your social support system may take a great deal of time and effort. Compared to taking an anti-anxiety pill, it is slow to have its effects. Many, perhaps most, anxious people do not even recognize that anxiety is connected with their social support systems. But in the long run, the process of shoring up your social support system and improving the emotional climates in which you live may be the most rewarding way to decrease anxiety and aversions, as well as to increase happiness.

This section implies that getting into a very positive emotional climate

A. is quick and easy if you have read this book, or
B. can take lots of time and effort, but can be very rewarding?

Chapter 12: Overcoming Social Anxiety

415. Social anxiety is fear connected to things that people do and say with one another. The fear of social situations is more complicated than fear of elevators or of flying in an airplane. There are different types of social situations; sometimes people feel very comfortable with one type of situation, and very uncomfortable with another.

 Below I list a few of the sorts of social situations that can make people uncomfortable. There are learnable skills that help with each of these sorts of situations.

social conversation
rejection and exclusion
getting criticized
being teased or harassed
physical harm
conflicts and provocations
performances and fear of failure
secrets revealed
needing to get help
needing to be assertive
getting close to someone
being independent or on your own
being in charge of what others do
having someone in authority over you

One of the main points of this section is that

A. there are several different sorts of social situations, and skills for dealing with each of them,
or
B. there is evidence that the world is moving gradually toward more kindness and less violence in social relations, despite the bad news that we hear constantly?

Social conversation

416. What do people do when they're together? While they're doing almost anything else, they talk with each other. When there's no business that needs to be carried out by talking, they talk for the fun of it. People who are fun to talk with tend to make friends more easily and have better relationships. They tend to run into fewer unpleasant social situations, and they tend to be able to solve them more easily because people like them.

 Getting really good at social conversation is one of the major ways of overcoming social anxiety. The sections to come will quickly summarize some tips on social conversation.

This section is sort of a sales pitch on

A. getting good at social conversation, or

B. doing a daily workout of exercises for courage skills?

417. In conversations, many people greatly fear not being able to think of something to say. But most people in the world, it seems, would rather be around a good listener than a good talker. It's really pleasant to be around someone who really encourages you to say what's on your mind, and reinforces you for talking, and brings out a part of your experience that is really interesting.

The main idea is

A. If you want to have good conversations, learn to be a very good listener.
Or
B. If you want to have good conversations, think of funny things to say that don't hurt people's feelings.

418. Let's talk about four things that good listeners tend to do. One is to make reflections, or paraphrases of what the other person said. Reflections are to make sure that you understood correctly, and to let the other person know you understood. Here's an example:

Isabel says, "I've decided that trying to get into the best college in the world just isn't worth it. I don't want to make myself miserable."

Alicia says, "So you're saying that you don't want to sacrifice having fun all through high school, to get into a higher-rated college?"

One of the ideas in this section is that

A. The tone of voice with which you make reflections is very important, or
B. If you make an accurate reflection, the other person can rightly think, "She is listening, and she understands."

419. If you summarize something someone else said with a sentence that starts in any of the following ways, you are probably making a reflection:

So you're saying

_____?
What I hear you saying is

_____.
In other words, _____?
So if I understand you right,

_____?
It sounds like _____.
Are you saying that _____?
You're saying that _____.

Which of the following would be a reflection?

A. If I understand you right, you've been learning a new way of thinking about people, so that when they do annoying things, you pretend that they're giving you a puzzle to solve?
or
B. What I hear you saying reminds me of a time that something really funny happened to me.

420. In order to do reflections well, you have to really concentrate on what the other person is saying. It feels good for most people to know that they are understood. Reflections are also nice because they don't direct the person – they leave it up to the person what to say next.

Reflections are particularly useful when someone is saying something complex, where the person might wonder if what she said really did get across. It often sounds strange to reflect a very simple statement. For example, suppose person A says, "I like popcorn," and person B says, "If I understand you right, you enjoy the taste of popcorn?" Person A is likely to think, "That's a weird response!"

Which of the following statements is complex enough that the person would probably appreciate an accurate reflection?

A. That bus is too loud!
or

B. I want to be an achiever and get a good job and all, but I feel like I'm spending my whole life doing school work. And it would be different if it were more fun.

421. A second listening response is called a facilitation. It is something like "I see." or "Humh!" or "OK," "Uh huh," "Yes," "Right!" "Oh?" "Ah!" or the like. Most facilitations mean, "I'm still listening; please go on." And if the facilitation is spoken in an enthusiastic tone, the message is, "I'm not just still listening; I'm also enjoying doing so!"

An example of a facilitation would be

A. Huh!
or
B. If I understand you right, you have so much homework that you don't have enough time to enjoy life?

422. A third listening response is a follow-up question. This is a question asking for more information about what the person just said.

Maria says to Juanita, "Something really exciting is going to happen to me this week end!"

The most natural thing for Juanita to say is "Oh, what is it?" That's a follow up question.

An example of a facilitation, followed by a follow-up question, is

A. That's a good point!
Or
B. Uh huh! And then what happened next?

423. A fourth good listening response is positive feedback. Examples of this are as follows: "Good point!" "I'm glad you told me that!" "That's very interesting!" "Thanks for telling me about that." These sorts of sentences reinforce or reward the other person for telling you something.

The four listening responses we have talked about are

A. reflections, facilitations, follow-up questions, and positive feedback, or
B. not awfulizing, goal-setting, listing options and choosing, and celebrating your own choice?

424. In your conversations, pay attention to your tones of voice. Suppose someone says something, and you reply, "Huh, that's interesting." Think of three different possible tones in which you can say this. There's a monotone "Huh – that's – interesting" that doesn't sound as if you're very interested at all. We can name this "neutral." Then there's a pleasant,

somewhat enthusiastic, "Huh, that's interesting!" that we've named "small to moderate approval." Then there's a really enthusiastic, "Huh! THAT'S INTERESTING!!" that conveys much more emotion – we call this "large approval." Then, of course, there are tones of small to moderate disapproval and large disapproval as well.

Good conversationalists tend to use a lot of small to moderate approval, and some large approval every once in a while. They don't tend to use neutral tones for a long time, and they don't tend to use lots of disapproval toward their listeners.

The main idea is

A. People get an idea of approval from facial expressions as well as tones of voice, or
B. People whom other people like to talk to tend to use a lot of small to moderate approval, and some large approval at times?

425. Tones of voice are a very important way for people to show approval or disapproval toward one another. A great chance to use tones of approval is *greeting rituals* and *parting rituals*. If you read the following aloud, be conscious of your tones of approval. Hi Jim! Good morning, Chris! What's up, Nora!

Hey, how are you! See you later, Paul! It was good talking with you, Jane! Bye Sara, have a safe trip home! Thanks for coming over!

Greeting and parting rituals are a very important way to let people know you care about them, that you are not ignoring them, and that you value them at least enough to speak to them.

The point of this section is that

A. If you want good relations with people, use greeting rituals when you see them, and parting rituals when you leave them, with some approval in your voice.
or
B. If people reject you, keep in mind that there are "more fish in the sea." This means that there are other people to have relationships with.

426. In social conversations, of course you don't just listen – you also tell about your own experience. You also bring up new topics and invite the other person to talk about them. What do you talk about? I like to divide the subjects into 5 categories, which you can remember by the word PAPER:

Places: Where do you live, where you have lived, where you've visited.

Activities: What you like to do, what you have done, what you don't like to do, what you're planning to do.
People: What friends you know, who is in your family, what you think about certain other people, what your relationships are like.
Events: What has happened to you, what events are coming up in your life, good things and bad things you've experienced. Also, current events, happenings in the news, or events of history, or anything you've read. Interesting stories.
Reactions and Ideas: How you react to, or what your ideas are, about any of the things above, or anything else. Or anyone else's ideas that you find interesting.

What you just read is a way of classifying

A. four ways of listening to another person,
or
B. five subjects that people talk about when telling about their own experience?

427. When choosing what to talk about or what to ask the other person about, you want to be sensitive to the cues that tell you whether the person is finding the topic interesting, or wanting to switch to a different topic. When you're telling about your own

experience, you have to stop frequently and let the other person react. If the other person doesn't seem very interested, maybe it's time to go to a different topic or let the other person tell about his own experience.

What's the main point of this section?

A. As you tell about your own experience, check frequently to see whether the other person is interested.
or
B. Feeling that you are expert, or at least competent, at social conversation eliminates lots of the anxieties that people feel in social situations?

428. What are the cues that let you know the other person is interested in what you are saying? Here are some.

First, they are giving you eye contact, looking at you a fair fraction of the time, rather than looking around at something else.

Second, they are doing some facilitations or follow-up questions, or maybe even some reflections or positive feedback occasionally, with an interested tone of voice. For example, if your listener says, "I see, keep going!" or "And what happened next?" or "Oh, that's interesting, tell me more!" you are getting a very clear signal to just pick up where you left off, and continue.

Third, your listener might tell you some of their own experience with or ideas on the same topic.

On the other hand, if when you stop talking, your listener changes the subject, be glad that you stopped and gave them the chance to do so. You don't want to spend your time talking about something that doesn't interest your listener!

The purpose of this section was to

A. list some ways to tell whether your listener is interested,
or
B. list some ways of responding to criticism?

429. When you talk, don't make "overlong statements." It's important to stop fairly often and give your listener a turn. What do we mean by "fairly often?" I would recommend not talking for longer than one minute without giving a turn to the other person.

As you listen to other people chatting with each other, and as you participate in chats yourself, pay some attention to how long people talk before they give the other person a turn. If you pay attention to this every so often, you can get a gut feeling (if you don't already have one) for when it's time to stop talking and give the other person a turn.

In this section the author

A. makes the point that the length of time you can talk without stopping varies greatly according to what type of conversation it is,
or
B. recommends stopping to give the other person a turn at least once per minute?

430. We've mentioned things to do in social conversation. Three things that people do often make social conversation unpleasant. These are commands, criticism, and contradictions. For examples:

"Stop moving around so much. Take your coat off. Quit looking at those other people so much. Stand up straight. Tell the other person about this. Don't slur your words so much. Shut up." These are commands.

"Your voice sounds weird. Your hair looks funny. You don't know much about that, do you? You're really mixed up, I can tell. You aren't even listening to what I'm talking about. You never pay attention to people. You're stupid." These are criticisms.

"No, that isn't right. That isn't the way it happened, at all. What you just said is wrong. That's a crazy idea – just the opposite is what's true." These are contradictions.

The main point of this section is that

A. It is often important to criticize and contradict people who are saying wrong and bad things, whether they enjoy it or not.
or
B. People tend not to enjoy social conversations where they are commanded, criticized, and contradicted very much.

431. We can summarize a fair amount of what makes social conversations pleasant by the mnemonic REFFF versus CCC.

This means: **reflections**, telling about your own **experience**, **facilitations**, **follow-up questions**, and positive **feedback**, versus **commands**, **criticisms**, and **contradictions**.

The purpose of this section was to

A. go into detail about ways of responding to criticism,
or
B. give a way of remembering some of the important tips for social conversation?

432. Another thing that good conversationalists seem to do fairly often is to say something funny or laugh at something the other person

said that was funny. The art of humor is very complex. It's important not to be hurtful to other people in an attempt to be funny. It's also important not to joke around when it's not appropriate, such as when a job needs to get done urgently. But if someone can do non-hurtful humor fairly well, it's a great source of fun and pleasure.

What's the main advice of this section?

A. In addition to the other tips, add some humor to your conversations when appropriate.
or
B. An attitude of kindness and empathy toward the other person is behind most of the tips on social conversation.

433. Here's a useful thought about social conversation: Silence is not a sin or a tragedy. In other words, if you are talking with someone and neither of you has anything to say at a certain moment, this is not awful. You can just smile at the other person. Or you can just gaze out into the distance, and then back at the other person. You can make a remark about the weather. The point is that the world will not cave in if there is a lull in the conversation. Sometimes if people can convince

themselves of this, they remove a lot of social anxiety.

The main advice of this section is that

A. If there's a lull in the conversation, do some "not awfulizing."
or
B. Think of a few things to remark on in case there is a lull in the conversation.

434. Another tip on social conversation is to watch and listen to people who do social conversation well, and study how they do it. Do they follow the advice given in the sections above? How do they go about exploring a topic together? How much pleasure do they each seem to get from the conversation?

It is sometimes hard to find people who model doing social conversation really well. There are some made-up dialogues in an appendix to this book, which model social conversations.

This section recommends that the reader

A. observe models of good social conversation,
or
B. use self-reinforcement for good examples of social conversation?

435. Finally, if you are interested in improving the art of social conversation, you can do an exercise called the social conversation role-play. There are several ways to do it. In the first, you decide upon two characters, and make up and write down a social conversation, like the ones in an appendix to this book. Second, you compose a social conversation, acting out both parts, speaking aloud rather than writing. And third, you let someone else play one part, and you play the second part, making up a social conversation between any two characters you want to portray. The point of this exercise is to practice coming up with good social conversations.

The main point of this section is

A. You can practice social conversation by writing out dialogues, speaking both parts as you make them up, or improvising them with another person.
or
B. It's important in social situations to realize that people are not solely consumed with judging you.

Dealing with rejection, exclusion, and disapproval

436. People are wired to try to form alliances and relationships with others. They like it when other people accept them and like them and form good relationships with them. They don't like it when people reject them and exclude them from groups and think or say critical things about them. It takes fortitude to handle rejection, exclusion, and disapproval.

Here are some examples of exclusion:

- Jane sits down at lunch with a group of people who are talking with each other. They don't talk to her or even say hi, and they just keep talking with each other as if Jane doesn't exist.

- Keisha has been in a group of four friends. But the other three seem to decide to kick her out of the group. They start getting together without inviting Keisha.

A main idea of this section is that

A. people don't like it when their bids for good relationships with others are rejected,
or
B. sometimes the quest for relationships can crowd out the

activities that are supposed to be the purpose of work or school?

437. Here are some more examples of the rejections, exclusions, and disapproval that require the skill of social fortitude to handle:

- Larry makes a mistake at work and says something really inappropriate to someone. Now that person and all that person's friends won't have anything to do with Larry.

- There's an important group project that Carl is doing with three other co-workers. When Carl has an idea, the other three criticize it or ignore it. But when one of the others has an idea that's not even as good, the other two enthusiastically support it.

Situations like these all have in common the fact that

A. The person who experienced the tough situation did absolutely nothing to bring it on or "deserve" it.
or
B. The tough situations have to do with being disliked, rejected, disapproved of, teased, or not wanted as a friend?

438. Here are some more "social fortitude" situations.

- Ling notices small groups of other people looking at her and pointing and laughing. When she looks at them, they stop. When she looks away, they burst into giggles again.

- Alonzo is in a group of five others. He tells the rest about something he read about that was really interesting. The others roll their eyes and say, "Yeah, right, Alonzo, that's really interesting, isn't it?" in a very sarcastic way.

- Martha starts to sit by another girl on a bus, but the other girl says, "You can't sit by me! I don't want you here!"

The three situations you just read about had to do with

A. being physically pushed around, being dared to do dangerous things, and having rumors spread about you,
or
B. being laughed at, having your ideas put down, and being told to go away?

196

439. Many of the situations requiring social fortitude involve a betrayal of trust. For example:

- Jean likes a certain guy in her class at school, and she confides in her friend. Her friend lets the word out to everyone in class. The guy himself finds out, and when he sees Jean, he puts his hand in his shirt and moves it to look like his heart is pounding. He makes faces like he is swooning; this act gets big laughs and his classmates want him to do it over and over. Jean feels embarrassed and humiliated, but also very much betrayed by her friend whom she trusted.

- Stephanie is very angry at another girl, Britany. Stephanie "blows off steam" and says some pretty mean things about Britany to a friend. Her friend tells other people what Stephanie said, and it gets back to Britany. Now Britany and all her friends treat Stephanie as a mean bully, and even parents and teachers take Britany's side.

In the difficult situations we just described, people found out the hard way that

A. A common characteristic of human beings is not being able to keep secrets.
or
B. Sometimes people exclude you or make fun of you for reasons that are totally mysterious to you.

440. Is it possible, or even desirable, to prevent all criticism, rejection, and exclusion? In other words, do we aim to get so good at dealing with people that no one ever disapproves of us or opposes us? The answer is no. People are human, and sometimes they will give us some criticism or rejection for no good reasons whatsoever. Even if someone were "perfect," there would probably be lots of people who would hate that person out of sheer envy. The person who desperately tries never to get any disapproval or rejection is locked into going along with the crowd, being a conformist, even when they know what's right and should stick up for what's right.

- Joanna is with two friends who are making really mean and vicious remarks about a classmate. Joanna says, "This talk is getting too mean! It's time to stop!" She risks disapproval and rejection by her friends, but she feels good about what she's done.

- Barbara has a group of friends who all get into smoking marijuana, and pressuring Barbara to do so. Barbara says, "No, I'm not interested, and I think you're making a mistake." She knows she would have gotten more approval from them by saying, "OK, cool!" But avoiding disapproval and rejection is not her main purpose in living!

The main point of this section is that

A. To avoid all disapproval and rejection is not possible or even desirable.
or
B. Marijuana smoke is just as bad for the lungs as cigarette smoke is, and it often does bad things to the brain?

Define success by how you act, not by others' actions to you

441. Here's the an important tip on social fortitude: it has to do with how you define a "successful day," or how you define your goal. You define these things in terms of what you CAN control, and not in terms of what you CAN'T control. You can't control how nicely people act toward you. You can control how friendly, kind, decent, and wise are your actions toward other people. Sometimes people will continue to be unkind to you about things you did in the past, which you can't change. Sometimes people will be unkind for no good reason at all. But if you cultivate the habits of acting as a friendly, empathic, respectful, trustworthy person, in the long run you will probably have good relationships. And in the short run, you will have reason to celebrate every good day you have, and every positive move you make.

According to this section, which is the better daily goal?

A. "Today, I want to have people give me approving messages and signal that they like me, and for no one to reject me."
or
B. "Today, I want to act the part of a person who is good for people to be friends with: nice, fun-loving, caring, empathic, and wise."

Fantasy rehearse handling rejection

442. Fantasy rehearsal is a great way of practicing the positive patterns you want to do more often. Here's a useful exercise for fantasy rehearsal. Imagine someone who for some reason is totally rejected by everyone in the person's class, or neighborhood, or workplace. Despite this, the person manages to act cheerful, speaking in an upbeat and enthusiastic tone of voice. The person makes eye contact with people and smiles at them, despite the fact that they often roll their eyes and look away. If they don't roll their eyes and look away, the person does appropriate "greeting rituals," for example by saying "Good morning, how are you!" If anyone does actually talk to him, he is a very good listener. He often thinks to himself, "I am getting to practice something really useful! If I can continue being cheerful, even when people are rejecting to me, I am building up a strength that will be useful the rest of my life!" He feels good about each day that he is able to do this.

This section

A. Made the case that you should act nicer to the people who act nicer to you.
Or
B. Gave an example of a fantasy rehearsal of an image of someone's

acting friendly and cheerful despite being totally rejected.

An option: turn your focus to your work

443. Sometimes a good way to deal with rejection, exclusion, or disapproval is to focus much less on the social world where you are experiencing the problem, and to concentrate on academic or work success. Sometimes people can get caught up in worrying full time about what other people think of them, when no matter how nicely they act, there simply is no way that they can make most people start accepting them and treating them kindly any time soon. But if they work really hard, they can do well on the science or social studies test coming up later this week, or the records they have to keep for work, or the article they are writing. Becoming a good student or worker probably has more impact on their future than their popularity rating in any given group.

The point of this section is that

A. Having friends is a very important long-term goal.
or
B. Sometimes it's best not to worry so much about what classmates or co-workers think of you, but to focus on

having success in the work you are doing.

444. Trying to figure out and fully understand exactly what went wrong in social relations is sometimes such a complex task that it can fully occupy your mind, and not leave any time and energy for work. Why is this person not seeming to like me? Is it that I said this to that other person, and the other person distorted that message in repeating it to this person, or is it that the person saw me looking at this person and thought that I was thinking this, and felt threatened for this reason ... or is it another possibility? You can "spin your wheels" on this sort of thing for hundreds of hours if you let yourself. (Often the simple solution of asking the person what's wrong and getting a clear answer is difficult for at least one of the people to carry out.)

An alternative to this is to focus energy on being polite to everyone, and to focus most of your energy on learning as much as you can in your school subjects, or accomplishing as much as you can in your work.

The advice of this section is that

A. If someone explains to you why she is mad at you, it's best to just listen and repeat back in your own words what you hear, rather than arguing against the other person or trying to defend yourself,
or
B. Sometimes the best strategy is to avoid trying to figure out the complexity of what happened, and to focus on being nice to everyone and working really hard on your schoolwork.

Criticism or disapproval provides an opportunity to practice at least one of two useful responses

445. When someone gives you criticism or disapproval, it's often useful to think about a responsibility pie chart. How much of the responsibility for the criticism is yours; how much is the critic's; and how much is someone else's?

For example: someone I don't even know and haven't even seen before says, "You're stupid." 100% of the problem lies with the critic, and none with me.

On the other hand, I get lazy and copy someone else's work, and someone says, "You did something dishonest." 100% of the problem is with me.

In the two situations we've seen so far, who held the responsibility for the criticism?

A. It's impossible to say, because the situations are too complicated.
or
B. The critic in the first situation, and the person being criticized in the second situation.

446. Here's an example of what more often happens: I make a little teasing comment, that I didn't mean to be hurtful, but the other person happens to be much more sensitive in that area than I thought, and the person gets very hurt and angry about what I said, and criticizes me. The problem is partly, perhaps 50% mine for teasing, and partly, perhaps 50% the other person's, for reacting the way she did.

Here's something even more complicated. I say something about Nancy, to Jean. Jean repeats to Nancy what I said, but makes it sound much worse than it was. Nancy is mad at me and criticizes me. Some of the responsibility for the problem is mine; some is Nancy's; and some is Jean's.

In the situations mentioned in this section, who held the responsibility for the criticism?

A. Both the critic and the person being criticized, and in the second situation, a third person as well.
Or

B. The critic in the first situation, and the person being criticized in the second.

447. What's the purpose of figuring out how much is my responsibility and how much is someone else's? It is not that the person who is found guilty should be punished. We are not in a courtroom situation. Rather: if the problem was my responsibility, I have an opportunity to improve myself by learning from this experience and working on not making the same mistake in the future. I also might want to apologize to someone, or make restitution for the harm I've caused. On the other hand, if the problem is totally the other person's responsibility, I have the opportunity to practice handling unfair criticism and disapproval. I have the opportunity to practice saying to myself, "This is just someone else saying false mean stuff, for their own reasons. This isn't my problem."

The main idea is that

A. Restitution means trying to undo any harm that you have done.
Or
B. Figuring out responsibility helps me to decide whether to make amends or to practice ignoring unfair disapproval.

Have it in your repertoire to apologize

448. All of us make mistakes at times and say and do things we wish we hadn't. Sometimes people's rejection and disapproval are because of smoldering resentment over something we said or did to them. Apologizing often is the key to getting the relationship back on a good footing. Sometimes it takes nothing more than a sentence like these:

- I'm sorry I acted the way I did.

- I apologize for what I said. I don't mean those things.

or just,

- I'm sorry.

- I apologize.

Sometimes a little note with these words on them makes things lots better.

The point of this section is that

A. it's good to be able to apologize for your mistakes,
or
B. you don't want to get into the habit of apologizing over and over and groveling for forgiveness?

449. Why is apologizing important? It communicates some very important information to the other person. For all the other person knows, you could feel fully and totally justified in what you said or did, and intend to act that way proudly, from now on. If this is not the case, and you regret the way you acted and intend to act better, this makes a big difference.

The main point is that

A. You shouldn't apologize to people who are just being mean, when you have no responsibility for the problem. or
B. When you've acted in a way you regret, apologizing gives the other person the important information that you don't intend to repeat the behavior.

Avoid raising your voice in anger

450. One of your goals is to minimize the amount of disapproval and rejection you get that is your responsibility. You want to give other people little reason to be legitimately mad at you. One of the major ways to do this is to cultivate the ability to stay cool and rational, not to "lose it," not to "freak out." If you can follow this

202

one rule, you will go a long way toward avoiding losing friends: Don't raise your voice in anger. Don't yell at people when you're mad. Don't insult people. When you're really angry and feel like yelling at someone, try to get apart from that person and cool off, and then calmly decide what to do about the problem.

The main point of this section is

A. Don't speak loudly or scream when you feel hostile.
or
B. The notion that by "getting your feelings out" you make yourself less angry has been disproved by lots of careful research, of several different designs.

You don't need to defend yourself against every accusation

451. People like to have power. If, any time someone accuses you of being dumb, mean, ugly, clumsy, dishonest, or anything else undesirable, you feel that you have to prove to that person or anyone else that you are really OK, then the accuser has lots of power over you. The accuser has the power to mobilize much of your energy in figuring out how to prove that you're really a good person, when you might have needed that energy to put into your algebra homework! You can avoid giving accusers such power, by the use of one sentence – "You can think what you want to." This sentence is often best delivered with a shrug. You often don't even need to say it to the other person, if you say it to yourself. This sentence implies, "Someone who insults or criticizes me does not create an automatic obligation for me to prove them wrong!"

The main idea of this section is that

A. There are times when you will want to debate against a critic or accuser, particularly if you are accused in front of an audience,
or
B. You don't want to give everyone the power to make you feel you have to defend yourself.

452. "You can think what you want to," is an all-purpose response to critical statements from other people. Another all-purpose response to mean statements from other people is, "I'm sorry you feel that way about me." Almost always, when someone is mean or rejecting to you, you will wish they didn't feel the way they do, so you can say this statement with total honesty and sincerity. The statement is often best said with a tone

and a facial expression of concern, but not devastation – a matter-of-fact statement that you wish things were not like that. Then you go on about your life. The advantage of this response is that it doesn't fuel the flames of the other person's hostility or criticism, and it is sympathetic and not hostile, but at the same time, you don't get pulled into the trap of having to defend yourself.

The author recommends saying, "I'm sorry you feel that way about me," with a tone of

A. irony and sarcasm, to let the other person know you really don't care what they think,
Or
B. sincerity and concern, to let them know you really would prefer friendly comments, but at the same time communicate that you are not devastated?

453. When responding to mean or critical statements, you want to avoid reinforcing critics by showing how much power they have. If their statement moves you to make a very loud counterattack, they have often been rewarded by finding out how much power they have to touch off a very emotional response in you. If saying something very mean elicits a mean statement back from you, they

have found that they can start up a game of "Who can insult the other most effectively," whenever they want to, and this is sometimes the object of their game in the first place. For some people, strangely enough, it's reinforcing that someone else is threatened by them enough to yell hostile things at them. It shows that they make a difference, that they're not a nobody. For this reason, when responding to mean and critical statements, it's good to think first, and then speak softly and slowly. This is usually not very reinforcing for someone who is trying to stir up something stimulating.

The author recommends making quiet responses to critical statements

A. to avoid reinforcing people who find high emotion rewarding,
Or
B. to avoid getting in trouble with teachers in school?

454. Linda is trying to be nice, standing around chatting with people, and hoping to make friends. All of a sudden two other girls come up to her, looking mean, and one of them says, "You look like a slut!" Which of the following responses is more in line with what is recommended for not reinforcing people who are looking to get the stimulation of a big argument?

A. "Well, I'm sorry you don't like the way I look." (Then she walks away and gets into a conversation with someone else.)
Or
B. "YOU are telling that to ME? Get real. Go look in a mirror somewhere and criticize yourself first."

Whom do you want to appoint as your judges?

455. Sometimes it's useful to choose someone to help you decide whether you are doing the right or the wrong thing, whether you are acting appropriately, whether you are being a good or bad friend, whether something you've written communicates clearly, or whether you look good in a certain outfit or with your hair a certain way. Feedback from other people is often useful. You judge your own actions, but sometimes it's useful to get some help from others in the important task of deciding whether you're on the right track or not.

The author feels that

A. It makes no difference what others think – you are the only one who has any useful information about what your choices are.
Or

B. Sometimes it's very useful to get other people's reactions and opinions, when you are making choices.

456. The important thing to remember, though, is that you are the one who decides whose feedback you want to use. You want to choose people who are wise, who know about the situation or the choice, and who you think will be helpful. You don't hand out the power to judge you to random unqualified people!

Sarah is planning to go to a party where she knows hardly anyone. She thinks, "As soon as I walk into the room, they're going to be judging me! What if they all think I'm stupid or awkward or unattractive or mean or all of the above?" This thought creates a lot of anxiety.

But then she thinks again: "Wait a minute. I haven't appointed all these people who don't even know me to be my judges. Most of them will have better things to do than to judge me. If any of them have really negative reactions to someone walking in and just acting nice, that's their problem, not mine." When she thinks in this way, she isn't so anxious.

The main point of this section is that

A. At parties, it's good to follow the rule of "If you can't say something nice, don't say anything at all,"

Or

B. It's good not to give to just anyone the power to be your judge, for example strangers at a party.

Avoiding trouble with secrets

457. Suppose that you have some strong feelings, positive or negative, about someone you know. You want to talk about this, but you would be totally mortified if what you said got broadcasted to other people you know, or to the person you were talking about. Whom should you talk to about it? The worst choice is a peer who is also a friend of the person you're talking about. The temptation is just too strong for that person to blab to their friend. People are human, and you shouldn't expect most people to use great self-discipline in keeping secrets.

Better choices would be a parent, another relative who does not know your friends, a friend who lives out of state, a counselor, or anyone else who is not a member of your social group.

This section's main idea is that

A. It's usually unreasonable to ask someone to keep a secret from a person that person knows well.

or

B. Talking over difficult situations with someone you trust can often really help you sort things out; one of the major benefits is just being able to put things into words.

458. It's good to be able to feel sticky secrecy situations coming and to head them off quickly. Suppose someone says to you, "If I tell you something, do you promise not to tell anybody?" For most people, the first impulse is to say "Sure, I promise! What's the secret?" But most people really shouldn't make such a blanket promise. What if the secret is something that really would help a certain friend of yours to know, and you are much more loyal to that friend than to the one telling you the secret? What if the secret-teller is doing something wrong, and by keeping the secret you are being made an "accomplice to the crime?" What if the secret-teller is putting herself in danger?

One option is to say, "Before you tell me, make sure the secret won't force me to be disloyal to another of my friends, or keep quiet about some dangerous situation, or have some other sticky dilemma. Otherwise maybe it would be best for me not to know." Now you are putting some reasonable conditions on your guarantee of secrecy.

This section's main idea was

A. Don't reveal secrets that other people tell you, without a very good reason,
or
B. Don't make unqualified promises to keep secrets, to anyone who wants you to keep a secret.

The fear of physical harm, and invoking the rule of law

459. If people aren't seeming to like you, if they aren't smiling at you, if they aren't inviting you to their parties, there's not a good strategy to force them to do so. However, if they are physically hurting or endangering you, calling you bad names, insulting you, playing mean pranks on you, and doing other mean things actively, they can and should be forced to leave you alone. No one should have to endure active bullying. If these things are going on, the best course of action is usually not to take the law into your hands and try to retaliate or sabotage. Usually the best course of action is to have a conversation with those who are in authority. For students, these will be parents and teachers and principal and if necessary other school administrators involved in enforcing the rules against bullying. For

workers, it's a supervisor, or if the supervisor is the bully, the supervisor's supervisor. Or sometimes you will need to get a lawyer to help you. Not being bullied is your right. Schools and workplaces have an interest in enforcing these rules, to keep bullying from escalating into violence.

The main idea here is that

A. If you are being verbally or physically abused, try to figure out what will avoid reinforcing the bullies for doing this,
or
B. If you are being verbally or physically abused, get the authorities involved in enforcing the rules against bullying?

460. Tovanda walks through the halls at school. As she passes a certain place, a couple of girls do something to her every day. One day, one of them makes gross noises and the other acts as if Tovanda did it. Another day, they make oinking noises at her. Another day, one of them bumps into her and makes her drop what she is carrying.

Tovanda thinks about her options. She considers trying to carry out "vigilante justice" by getting a cup of scalding hot water and purposely spilling it on them. But instead, she talks to the associate principal about what is going on. The associate principal waits from a hidden place around a corner and sees and hears what the girls do to Tovanda. She catches them in the act, scolds them thoroughly, takes them to the office, and calls the girls' parents in for a conference. The parents and the girls are informed that this incident has already affected the recommendation letters that the girls will get from the high school when they apply to college or work, and if further incidents like this occur, the students may be expelled. The bullying stops.

Which advantages of using the "rule of law" rather than "vigilante justice" do you think this author finds more compelling?

A. That Tovanda herself did not risk getting blamed, and that the rule of law is strengthened for the benefit of other students.
Or
B. That the revenge is sweeter the way it turned out?

Doing the four-thought exercise

461. When developing "social fortitude," it's good to do the four-thought exercise that we discussed in an earlier chapter. You take a certain social situation and practice four useful ways of thinking about it. Let's give an example.

Here's the situation. In the hall, I pass Carmen, whom I thought was a really good friend. With fairly large approval and enthusiasm, I say, "Hey Carmen! How's it going!!" With neutral tones, she says, "Hi," gives almost no eye contact, and keeps moving.

Not awfulizing: "Well, that wasn't a very friendly greeting, but I can handle it. Maybe there's something temporarily on her mind. Maybe she just had a bad experience. Or perhaps she even permanently doesn't want to be friends any more, but either way, I can handle it."

Goal-setting: "My main goal is not to get too bothered by this, and to keep on having a successful day of school."

Listing options and choosing: "I can just not give this another thought, and go ahead to class and concentrate on doing well. Or I can put on my mental to do list to chat with Carmen some and see how she's doing. Maybe she needs some support. Or I can work on making other friends. I think for the time being, I want to turn my attention to my next class, and maybe try to check out how she's doing later if I get around to it."

Celebrating your own choice: "I think I made an OK choice!"

Do you think that in this example

A. the person thought of all the goals and options that could have been considered,
or
B. there were various other goals and options that the person could have thought of?

462. No matter how well you do the four-thought exercise, there are probably goals and options that would be even better than the ones you think of. But the good thing about life is that you don't necessarily have to come up with the best possible response to every situation you face. If you come up with a reasonably OK one, you're in much better shape than most people.

Here's another example of doing the four-thought exercise. Catarina hears from a friend that someone has started a rumor that she is in love with a certain guy in her class that she doesn't dislike, but considers kind of immature and definitely is not in love with.

Not awfulizing: "Well, I wish I weren't getting attention in this way. But I can handle it. At least this isn't a rumor that I've done something bad."

Goal-setting: "I want to let this little drama run its course without stirring up more drama. I want not to hurt anybody's feelings. I want not to distract myself too much from my work."

Listing options and choosing: "I can just keep cool and say to people things like, 'No, not true,' if they are curious. I can not get very excited about this one way or the other. I can focus really hard on studying for the math quiz coming up today. If people ask me how I do feel about this guy, I can not say anything bad or good. I don't want to protest too much, because that will just get people more interested. I can just shrug and say, 'There's not really much very interesting about my feelings on that one way or the other.' I think all these options are good, and I can do them all."

Celebrating your own choice: "I think I made an OK choice."

The person in this example

A. wanted to get the spotlight off her as soon as possible,
or
B. enjoyed being in the spotlight, and wanted to entertain herself by stirring things up as much as she could?

463. When you do the four-thought exercise, keep in mind certain principles as you set your goals and list and choose your options. I believe that it's a good idea to hold yourself to

high standards of honesty and kindness, but not to expect others to have the same standards. That way you cultivate good habits in yourself, but you are not terribly upset when others don't act in the way you feel that people should act. If someone becomes your enemy, take into account that if you get vicious in seeking revenge, your own personality is being pulled into bad habits. Watch out that you don't fall into the trap that someone described by saying, "Pick your enemies carefully, because you will come to resemble them."

At the same time, it's wise to be nicer to the people who have been kind to you than to the ones who have been mean to you. If you have some favor that you can do or some reward you can hand out, give it to the ones who have stuck by you rather than wasting it on the ones whose approval you've wanted but have never been able to get. You want a certain minimal level of civil and polite behavior even to those who obviously don't like you, but save your best prizes for those who do like you.

The purpose of this section was to

A. describe another exercise,
or
B. tell some principles to be guided by when doing the four-thought exercise?

464. There's another thought that is really useful in dealing with social hard knock situations: Learning from the Experience. For example:

Su Li has a friend that seems not to be as friendly to her as before. Su Li gets very worried, and repeatedly asks the friend what's wrong. The friend gets irritated with so much asking, to the point that now she really doesn't want to hang out with Su Li as much. The friend points this out to Su Li. Su Li thinks to herself, "I learned something from this. I learned that sometimes it's best just to let people be distant for a while and not bug them about it. This learning will help me from now on." That type of thought is Learning from the Experience.

If you have the attitude that learning about human relations is a lifelong task, and every mistake you make has a lesson embedded in it that can help you for the rest of your life, the knocks you take in the social world have a consolation prize attached to them.

The consolation prize that the author is referring to is

A. the sympathy you get from people when things don't work out,
or
B. the learning that you can get when you make a mistake?

210

465. Blanca is with a friend at a play. Blanca's friend sees several of her friends, who don't know Blanca. These friends all form into a circle, that leaves Blanca out, and they talk animatedly about things they have in common. Blanca looks for the opportunity to introduce herself, but no one even so much as glances in her direction.

Blanca decides that as long as she is as if invisible, she will take the opportunity to do some learning. So she listens very carefully to the conversation she is being excluded from. She analyzes who in the group seems to have the most power, and who seems to be most liked. She notices what sort of listening responses people make. She notices how people compete with each other for the chance to talk. She observes what topics people talk about, and which topics people seem to enjoy the most. She notices the tones of voice that people use. She has fun learning from her experiences.

Which type of thought is being promoted in this section?

A. Not getting down on yourself, as in "It's not because of any defect in me that they aren't paying any attention to me, so I don't need to feel ashamed or embarrassed."

Or

B. Learning from the experience, as in "Interesting, the people who use the most animated and enthusiastic tones seem to be the ones that the others seem to pay most attention to. That's a piece of learning that could help me at some point."

A suggested project

466. This chapter has mentioned various difficult social situations, social choice points. There are more listed in an appendix to this book. How many more can you list? If you can make a growing list of choice point situations, you can think about these situations and deliberate what is the best response. You can return to them over and over – with time, your ideas about what the best response is will probably change as you learn from your experiences. Doing the four-thought exercise with these situations is usually very useful. And listing these situations and thinking about them lets you get a little distance on them. Thinking about them at times other than when you are involved in them gives you a chance to apply a clearer head to them. If you can start seeing them as puzzles to solve, some of the painful emotion is removed.

The project that is being suggested in
this section is

A. To make a growing list of social
choice point situations, and to practice
the four-thought exercise with them
repeatedly.
or
B. To practice relaxing until you can
get yourself calmed down at will, so
that you can apply a clearer head to
whatever situation you are dealing
with.

Chapter 13: Reducing Worry

The thoughts and beliefs that cause worry, and the ones that undo It

467. If you have worried, you may remember the types of thoughts that go along with worrying. What if this bad thing happens? I might really mess up on this. I might have already messed up really badly. What if I make the wrong decision and the consequences are terrible? What should I do about this -- it's very important that I make the right decision, but I don't know what I should do.

The purpose of this section is to

A. give an example of some typical worrisome thoughts,
or
B. convince the reader that worrying is unpleasant?

468. It's hard to be very worried without having at least one of the following thoughts or beliefs. Often, worry is accompanied by all of these beliefs:

1. Something bad might happen.

2. The stakes are high – we're thinking about something very bad that may happen.
3. I need to do something to keep something very bad from happening.
4. I don't know, or can't decide, what to do to keep this very bad thing from happening. AND/OR
5. I do know what to do to keep this very bad thing from happening, but I'm incompetent to do it.
6. Despite the fact that I'm not making progress in deciding about this, I'd better think about this right *now*. OR
7. I'd rather not think about this right now, but I can't keep from doing so.

This section presents

A. how to stop worrying,
or
B. seven thoughts or beliefs, at least one of which is almost always present when anyone worries?

469. Sometimes it's possible to reduce or eliminate worrying by changing your thoughts, or self-talk, so as to dispute one of these ideas. For example, someone finds himself worrying that something he said might have slightly offended a stranger he spoke to at a party. He tells himself, "It's possible, but the person can

handle it, and in any case it's of very little consequence – the stakes are very low." Realizing this turns down the worry.

This section gives an example of someone's

A. turning down worry by realizing he is very competent to carry out what he's decided,
or
B. turning down worry by affirming to oneself that the stakes are very low?

470. Here's another example of reducing worry by changing self-talk. Rashad will be taking a test tomorrow. He finds himself worrying in a very unpleasant way. But the idea above that he disputes through his self-talk is the idea, "I'm incompetent to keep something very bad from happening." He thinks, "I've done numerous practice tests already, and I've shown myself over and over that I'm competent. All I have to do is to recreate the performance of any of my recent practice tests, and I'll do well enough. I have what it takes!" These thoughts help him to relax and enjoy himself.

The idea that Rashad affirmed to himself was

A. that the test didn't make much difference,
or
B. that he was competent to handle the challenge of the test well?

Worry can be seen as energy to be harnessed and used productively

471. What do we do when we worry? We use our brains intensely. We work very hard. We can't relax and let our minds drift peacefully. Something in us cries out to our brains, "Don't just sit there, do something!"

The worrying state is not one of laziness. We feel energized, and we want to use our energy. The only trouble is, the expenditure of energy doesn't seem to move us much of anywhere except around in circles.

The author seems to feel that when worrying, we

A. have given up, and have no energy to spend,
or
B. have the urge to use our energy?

472. When we find ourselves worrying, therefore, we might first celebrate that we have energy to spend and have the urge to spend it. When there are problems, it is a great advantage to feel energized rather than

to feel depleted and unable to get oneself to move. After celebrating this motivation, we might then ask the question, "How do I use the motivation I have in a way that really gets me somewhere?" If we can take the motivation that propels worrying and harness it in ways that help us make good decisions on what to do about the situations that are bothering us, we have solved the problem.

The sections that follow will describe one strategy in attempting to use our "worrying energy" productively.

The two thoughts that this section advises are a celebration and a question. They are:

A. hooray that things are not worse than they are, and how did things get to be this way,
or
B. hooray that I have motivation, and what's the most productive way for me to harness my motivation?

Turning worry into productive decision-making, through writing

473. In the process of worrying, we flash upon bad things that might happen in the future and feel bad about them. We might think of a possible way to keep one of those bad things from happening, but then we think of a disadvantage of that solution and a reason to why it might not work. Then we might flash on some other bad thing that might happen. Then our mind might go around from one problem to another. We land on each problem just long enough to get concerned about how things might not turn our well, or perhaps to get a sense of foreboding and dread. But, we don't follow through with figuring out the solution to the problem thoroughly enough that we have a sense of closure and completeness that lets us quit stewing about the problem.

In the process of worrying the author has described,

A. a decision was made,
or
B. no decisions were made because the problem was too complicated?

474. The important thing for us to realize is that worrying is usually *incomplete problem solving.* We grapple with problems enough to where we get the bad feeling of realizing the possible bad consequences, but not enough to get to the satisfied feeling of coming up with the best solution we can arrive at.

Why do we all seem to do this, some of us more than others? Why don't we take on one problem at a time, think about it very systematically, come to a systematic decision, and then move onto the next problem? Why, instead, do we flit around from one situation to another in a rather disorganized but unpleasant way?

The question the author is raising in this section is

A. what causes people to need to make decisions,
or
B. when we worry, why don't we systematically finish making a decision?

475. I believe that the answer to this is that many of the problems that we face are so complicated that a systematic decision process overwhelms our memory resources. A complete, systematic, organized approach to the problems we are facing would require holding too many things in memory at once. Since we can't hold all those things in memory, our minds flit around from one thing to another.

The answer the author proposes to the question of why worrying usually doesn't result in completed decisions is that

A. we are afraid to commit ourselves to any solution,
or
B. the problem is complicated enough that we don't have enough memory to solve it?

476. Let's give an analogy to this situation. Suppose that we lived in the days where there were no computers or calculators. Suppose that a situation came up where it was very important that we found an exact answer to the problem, 4,296 x 6,167. We'll imagine that we knew how to carry out this multiplication but had no pencil and paper or electronic device or anything else to write with. What would be likely to happen? We would get part of the way into the problem, trying to solve it in our heads. But part way through, we would forget some of what we had done earlier. Then we would have to go back and do that part over again. But when we did that part over again, we would realize that we have now forgotten the next step that we had done after that. So we have to do that over again. This process could go on indefinitely, in a very unpleasant way.

The author uses the example of the multiplication problem

A. to show that you should work at getting proficient in mental math,

or
B. to illustrate that some problems are very difficult to figure out because they require too much memory?

477. The obvious solution for the person with the complicated multiplication problem is to get pencil and paper, or write with a finger in the dirt, or to otherwise record the steps of the problem solving process so that they don't overwhelm memory resources. By the simple use of pencil and paper, an extremely troubling and difficult problem would be made easy.

We should be using the same solution much more of the time for our worries: We should write down our thought processes. This enables us to stay organized. It enables us to proceed from beginning to end with the decision making process rather than going around in circles.

The author is advising

A. that when you worry, you try to remember what you need to, as if you were writing things down,
or
B. that when you worry, you really get out a pencil and paper or a computer and start writing?

478. Thus I recommend that you actually write your thoughts, to turn disorganized worrying into organized decision-making.

When you write out your thoughts you use an organized procedure that is able to be generalized from one problem to another. You can use the same outline each time. Here's the outline:

1. Situation (what it is, how high are the stakes)
2. Objectives (what are your goals?)
3. Information (What can I find out more about the situation?)
4. Listing Options
5. Advantages and Disadvantages of the options – weigh them, to make your choice
6. Doing the option you pick (what did you decide to do; what did you actually do?)
7. Learning from the experience

(mnemonic: SOIL ADL)

In this section, the author recommends that

A. you write in an unstructured way, because each situation is different,
or
B. you get into the habit of writing about decisions using a similar outline each time?

479. First you describe the situation. You might start out the situation by

posing a question to yourself: What am I going to do about this problem? Then you write about the situation in as much detail as you want to. You may find it very useful to analyze what caused the situation to come up. You may want to think about how different things cause one another in this situation. Analyzing the situation may bring up other problems to mind, and if so, you write down these questions in a separate space. You come back to your first question, and you describe the situation in great enough detail that someone else would have the ability to think productively about what to do in it.

The author advises that when you write about the situation you are in,

A. that you be very brief,
or
B. that you go into as much detail as is helpful, sometimes very great detail?

480. As you write about the situation, tell how high the stakes are. How important is it that a good decision is made for this problem? If the stakes are very high, you want to invest a lot of energy, if necessary, into the solution to this problem. If the stakes are fairly low, you don't want to waste a lot of time on it. Deciding that the stakes are low is similar to the "not awfulizing" part of the four-thought exercise. Deciding that the stakes are high, but that you can handle it, even if it doesn't come out the way you want, is also a part of "not awfulizing."

The author is recommending in this section that as you write about the situation, you include some thoughts about

A. when you should have made the decision in the best circumstances,
or
B. how high the stakes are for this decision?

481. Next in the process of writing about the decision is stating what your objectives, or goals are. What are your priorities? This is often a very important decision in and of itself. Is your goal to prove your point and win an argument, or to strengthen a relationship? Is your goal to get publicity, or to avoid embarrassment? Do you want to strengthen your support network, or to stick to your principles even if everyone in a certain group is alienated from you? What options you list and eventually choose depends to a very large extent on what you are wanting to accomplish.

The author in this section is advising you to

A. think about your objectives, without writing them down, or
B. to write down your objectives for the situation you are working on?

482. For the next step, you often get onto the Internet, or go to a reference book, or to the library, or to an expert consultant, and get information about the situation. Or, you plan an experiment that will let you gather information directly. The more you know about it, the better you will be able to decide. For some complicated decisions you will need to read and study quite a bit if you want to make the best decision. You may wish to return to this step several times in the course of the decision – it's not necessarily all finished when you log off.

The author implies that

A. once information is gathered, you should not keep getting more, or
B. for important decisions, you may need to get more information at various times, over and over?

483. Now you list options. You write about the possible courses of action you could take. This is the part where you brainstorm, trying to get as many different ideas as you can. You concentrate on listing, trying not to overlook any good options.

The next step is writing advantages and disadvantages of the options. If you've written your options in a computer file, you can come back up and make a list of advantages and disadvantages underneath each option. I recommend writing advantages and disadvantages only for the best options, especially if you have generated lots of them. If you are convinced that a certain option isn't workable, you don't need to waste time explaining to yourself. But for the top candidate options, it's worthwhile to write the pros and cons.

The two steps in the decision process that were described in this section were

A. landing on a good choice, and acting upon what you choose, or
B. listing options, and writing advantages and disadvantages for them?

484. Sometimes in the course of making your choice, you realize that you need still more information before you can come to a definitive choice. And so, sometimes, your plan is to get more information about the problem, by consulting someone else, by reading about it in a book, by looking

up something on the internet, by doing an experiment to see what seems to work better, or various other means. Deciding to get more information is sometimes the best decision you can make for now.

Getting information was one of the early steps in decision-making, before even listing options or weighing advantages and disadvantages. But this section seems to imply that

A. getting information must come after objective formation and before listing options,
or
B. getting information can come at any or all points of the decision process?

485. Although you may not want to record your internal celebration for going through the decision process in writing, you deserve to congratulate yourself for your efforts. A "Hooray for me, I've done some good work on this! I've turned nonproductive worrying into productive decision-making!" is in order.

The author is advocating a thought that in the twelve-thought exercise was called

A. celebrating your own choice,
or

B. not blaming someone else?

486. Once you've made your choice, then for the time being, you're done with writing. If your worrying had waked you, perhaps now you can go back to sleep! Often returning to sleep is easier, knowing that the thoughts about the decision are stored on paper or electronically so that you don't have to worry about forgetting them!

When you get the chance, you do what you have chosen to do, and you notice very carefully what seems to result from your action. You learn from the experience you have had. When you return to your "decisions" computer file, it's good to write some follow up to your decision, recording your action and its result and your learning from it, for future reference.

This section seems to imply that part of the reason people stay awake in their beds worrying is that

A. thoughts about what they should do come to their minds, and they don't feel comfortable forgetting them,
or
B. night brings out worry because night has for millennia been more dangerous than daytime?

487. Let's look at an example of this process. A teenage girl is lying in bed and waiting to go to sleep and finds

herself worrying. She flashes on the image of a classmate who has been acting unfriendly to her lately. This leads her to think that maybe all her friends are going to join in other cliques and she will be left out. She imagines that maybe this is because she is getting too fat and she worries that she might gain too much weight, even though at present, she is in a good range. When she thinks about eating, she remembers that sometimes when she feels anxious, she feels nauseated at school and worries that she might throw up and be embarrassed. When she tries to tell herself, "At least I make good grades." She then flashes on the fact that there is going to be a big test soon, and she's scheduled to play in a big tournament the night before and won't have time to study. Then her mind flits around among all these uncomfortable images for a while, in the way that we do when we worry.

About how many possible decisions is it possible to break this worry up into?

A. only one,
or
B. at least five?

488. In order to turn her worrying into organized decision making, she gets up out of bed and sits down at a computer. She tries to bring to mind everything that she has been worrying about and summarize this in terms of questions that she can pose to herself. She writes the following on her word processor:

1) What do I want to do about the fact that Rachelle has been acting unfriendly to me lately?
2) What if my friends join other cliques and I'm left out?
3) What do I want to do about feeling nauseated sometimes and feeling scared I'll throw up?
4) What do I want to do about the World History test that's the day after I have to play in the basketball tournament?
5) What do I want to do about my weight?

After writing each of these, she sits back and purposefully tries to bring another worry to her mind. As soon as another worry pops in, she translates it into a question and writes it down. She keeps going until no more worries pop into her mind.

Why does the person in this example try to bring worries into her mind?

A. she has a streak that wants to punish herself,
or

B. she wants to get all the questions that she needs to deal with down into writing, so that she can deal with them systematically?

489. Now she scrolls back up, and under each question that she has posed, she writes an analysis of the situation, how high the stakes are, what her objectives are, what information she can get or needs, what options she can list, the advantages and disadvantages of the best options, and her choice. Then she celebrates making the choice.

What the person does is to

A. write out the steps of decision-making, for each of the choices she has put on her list,
or
B. goes back to bed and thinks about the questions she has posed to herself?

490. She starts with the problem "What do I want to do about the World History test that's the day after I have to play in the basketball tournament?" She writes the following:

Situation: The World History test counts for 200 points toward the grade. It makes a lot of difference in what grade I get in this course. I want to get good grades because I am interested in scholarship money for college. The World History test is much more important to me than the basketball tournament, because I'm not one of the best players and I probably won't play all that long a time in the game. But the games end up taking quite a long time and I know I won't have much time to study that evening.

How high are the stakes? It is important for me to get a good grade on the test, even though it isn't anywhere close to life and death. There will be other tests, and a pretty good number of them. Still, it's important for me to keep my momentum up. It's sort of important for me to be at the basketball game and to support my friends on the team, but they will have plenty of people to play even without me, so it's not as important.

This section gave an example of the person

A. going through all the steps of decision-making,
or
B. just writing about the situation?

491. The person continues as follows: Objectives: I want to not let this upset me and bother me a lot. I want to do well on the World History test. If

possible, in second priority, I want to be seen as not letting the team down.

Information: I think I have all the information I need for this decision.

Options:
- I could just quit the basketball team.
- I could try to take the World History test later
- I could try to study ahead of time so that I'm ready for the World History test a day early.
- I could try to get to the game just when it starts and leave as soon as it ends so I'll have more time to study.

The three steps the person illustrated in this section are

A. objectives, information, and listing options,
or
B. options, inference, and learning from the experience?

492. Now that she's listed some options, she scrolls back up with her word processor and writes some advantages and disadvantages under the ones that she thinks are the best. She picks two options to write advantages and disadvantages for, as follows:

- I could try to study ahead of time so that I'm ready for the World History test a day early. Disadvantage: It could be that without the pressure, I don't do this. I won't have as much time to relax between now and then. Advantage: This would totally solve the problem if I can pull it off. Since I still have a few days before the test, I've got enough time to work my studying in, if I schedule it carefully.

- I could try to get to the game just when it starts and leave as soon as it ends so I'll have more time to study. Advantage: This gets me some more time to study. Disadvantage: This kind of defeats the purpose of basketball for me, which is to be able to hang out with my friends before and after. Plus this won't make enough difference in time saved to be worth it.

Choice: I'm going to look at my scheduling book and schedule in my study time for the World History test so I'll be ready a day ahead of time. I'm going to try really hard to use self-discipline and stick to my schedule.

Then she thinks: Celebration! I think this is a good choice! Hooray!

The person

A. listed advantages and disadvantages for all the options,
or
B. listed advantages and disadvantages for just those options that were the top candidates for the choice?

493. Now, having made a systematic decision on this question, she tackles each of the others in turn.

Regarding the unfriendly friend, she guesses that the friend may be angry about a time she had to cancel an appointment with the friend. She decides to have a conversation with the friend and apologize for this and explain it. She had a good reason for having to cancel, that she never really communicated to the friend. She will try talking about this, and if that doesn't work, she will ask the friend if there is any other problem. If this doesn't work, she'll try not to worry about it and try to pay more attention to other friends for a while.

What she decided to do first for this problem was to

A. talk with her friend about an issue her friend could possibly feel resentful about,

or
B. cultivate relationships with other friends, and avoid the one who is being less friendly?

494. Regarding the problem of what if her friends join other cliques, she decides to get her friends together as a group to do something fun together. She also decides to be friendly to people outside her group and to make as many connections as she can.

Her decision about the worry of losing her friends was a strategy to

A. be happy by herself, without friends,
or
B. strengthen her relationships with friends?

495. Regarding her worry about throwing up, she decides to habituate to images of throwing up by prolonged exposure to pictures on the internet, and then parts of movies showing people throwing up. She also decides to carry around with her a little plastic bag, which will remind her that even if she does throw up, it won't be horrible; she can just throw up into the bag and not have to worry about the embarrassment of getting vomit all over the place.

Her decision about the worry of vomiting was to

A. avoid the places where throwing up would be embarrassing,
or
B. habituate to images of people vomiting, and carry a plastic bag just in case?

496. Regarding the problem of gaining too much weight, she decides to look up on the Internet the tables of body mass index, see what the good range for her weight is, and to weigh herself and see where in the range of body mass index she falls. If, as she suspects, she weighs too much, she plans to eat much less junk food, bread, fat, and sugar, and to exercise more. She also resolves always to get adequate nutrition so she won't get an eating disorder. She plans to get lots of exercise by walking with a friend while chatting.

Her plan for her weight involved

A. going on a very low salt diet,
or
B. first checking her body mass index, and if she needed to lose weight, cutting back on the high calorie foods and exercising by walking?

497. Now she has a plan for each of the things that she was worried about.

She saves everything that she has written in a file called "decisions." She takes a look at her schedule book and writes in when she is going to do the things that she has planned to do.

Now, knowing that she has concrete plans and she has a schedule of when she is going to carry them out, she goes back to bed and now she finds that she can fall asleep.

The author is justified in ending this story with the main character's being able to sleep better mainly because

A. she has now completed decision-making about several things that were bothering her, rather than leaving them unfinished;
or
B. she has now been up for a while and has probably gotten sleepier?

Suggestions on where to channel your self-care motivation

498. The thesis of this chapter is that worrying is a product of the urge to use your brain to protect yourself and the people you love; furthermore, such urges can be very useful if you can harness your self-care motivation in useful ways.

Where many people go wrong is in wasting their self-care effort on the wrong questions. For example:

A woman spends lots of time worrying that her clothes don't look good. Meanwhile, her son is getting involved in dealing drugs, and she is not expending effort trying to solve this problem.

A high school boy worries about his social standing, and he spends huge hours practicing sports in order to make himself more popular. Meanwhile, he wants to go to college but does not have money to do so, and he is not spending time in either earning money or getting the higher test scores that would allow him to get scholarships.

The people in these examples

A. spent their time worrying about things of low priority, while neglecting things of higher priority, or
B. used various relaxation techniques to reduce their worry?

499. Here are some more examples of people worrying about low priorities and neglecting the higher priorities.

An eight year old boy worries that bad people will come out of his closet at night. However, he does not worry about the fact that he often rides a bicycle fast without a helmet.

A ten year old girl worries that she will look silly in martial arts class if she doesn't learn her moves well enough; she spends hours practicing. Meanwhile, she is falling farther and farther behind in math.

A man spends lots of time worrying about the impression he makes on strangers. Meanwhile, he is in the habit of acting very irritable and grumpy with his own family members, and he doesn't worry about the effects of this.

One of the examples in this section had to do with

A. worrying about an imaginary danger but neglecting a real danger, or
B. worrying about what goes on in the news but neglecting what is going on in carrying out your job?

500. If you have a tendency to worry, you can look at this as having a lot of self-care motivation – a tendency to put lots effort into protecting yourself and/or the ones you love. The main idea is to think carefully, and decide where you want to put your effort. If you have a checklist of self-care items that you need to pay attention to, and if you are careful to devote to these items all the attention and effort they need, you may feel less need to worry,

because you have systematically dealt with the highest priority items.

The strategy the author is talking about for dealing with worry is

A. saying the word "stop" to yourself when worries come into mind,
or
B. putting your energy into taking care of yourself in systematic ways, using checklists to help you cover the most important areas?

501. Do you remember the types of danger we talked about in the first chapter? These were:

1. physical danger
2. economic danger
3. social danger
4. the danger of failure to achieve goals

Doing self-care well means looking after four sets of needs: your physical health and safety, your economic security, your social support network, and your achievement of meaningful goals – as well as helping to look after all of these for your family members and those you love. These needs, and the priority order in which they are presented, borrow from Abraham Maslow, who introduced the idea of a "hierarchy of needs." Let's look at each of these in turn.

In this section, the author advises you

A. to imagine yourself in a protective bubble that wards off all dangers,
or
B. to channel your effort that would be spent worrying into making specific plans to take care of four sets of needs: physical, economic, social, and achievement?

Physical needs

502. Here are some sample items for a checklist on physical health and safety. There are surely important items left out – a complete list would be quite long. But if everyone followed the suggestions on this fairly short list, the number of deaths and suffering prevented would be vast. We will break the list up into several sections.

Sample items for a checklist for physical health and safety

1. Do you avoid dangerous activities such as motorcycle riding, cutting through traffic on a bicycle, speeding in a car or riding with speeding drivers, diving into underwater caves, diving into untested waters, hang

gliding, experimenting with explosives, and the like?

2. Do you use precautions such as helmets when you bike or skate or ski, seat belts when you ride in a car, and so forth?

3. If you live in, or have to be in, dangerous neighborhoods with lots of "human predators," gun battles, etc. – do you take whatever precautions you can, for example not traveling alone, picking the safest times of day, picking the safest routes, etc.?

What is one of the items listed in this section?

A. staying away from chemical toxins, or
B. wearing a helmet when you should do so?

503. Our checklist on physical safety continues.

4. Do you go inside during lightning storms?

5. Do you avoid drinking alcohol, and especially doing anything dangerous under the influence of alcohol, such as driving, swimming, using guns, and using power tools? Do you avoid other people who are doing these things under the influence of alcohol?

6. Do you and all the people you share living space with avoid smoking tobacco?

7. Do you see a doctor often enough, and follow any directions you are given about immunizations and any special procedures you need to do for your health?

8. Do you avoid exposing yourself to infectious diseases that others have, as much as possible? Do you wash your hands not too much, not too little, but a rational amount to prevent the spread of infections?

Which was one of the items listed in this section?

A. being familiar with which snakes are poisonous and which are safe, or
B. avoiding situations where danger is increased by the drinking of alcohol?

504. The checklist on physical safety continues.

9. Do you have a healthy diet? Do you keep your weight in the range that is not too much, not too little, but in just the right range?

10. Do you get a reasonably high amount of exercise?

11. Do you protect your hearing by avoiding loud noises or using ear protection when around loud noises?

12. Do you protect your skin by avoiding tanning?

13. Do you avoid exposure to toxins such as pesticides, herbicides, organic solvents, paint chips from old houses (that may contain lead) and so forth?

What was an item listed in this section?

A. using ear protection,
or
B. staying out of places where people get into fights?

505. Let's finish the checklist on physical safety in this section.

14. Do you avoid all "recreational drugs" – cocaine, heroin, marijuana, methamphetamine, LSD, "ecstasy," and so forth ?

15. Do you see a dentist regularly and follow directions to take care of your teeth and gums daily?

16. Do you take care, when there are young children around, that the environment is child-proofed, including without heavy things that can be pulled over, high places from which there can be falls, unprotected electrical outlets, knives or other weapons, and so forth?

17. Do you use good judgment about "contact" sports, violent sports, and dangerous sports?

What's an item that was NOT mentioned in this section?

A. using good dental care,
or
B. making sure that your clothes are not so tight that they cut off your blood circulation?

506. A particular type of worry, called *hypochondriasis*, is worrying about your health. Does this sensation in my body mean that I'm coming down with a dreaded disease? Do I have some illness that I'm unaware of? Should I be getting urgent medical care right now? Sometimes people worry about their health so much that they make themselves very unhappy.

The purpose of this section was to

A. explain what is meant by *hypochondriasis*,
or

B. tell you a fool-proof way of getting over hypochondriasis?

507. It is true that sometimes people harm their health by avoiding going to doctors and by ignoring signs that they have an illness. People who worry too much about their health often try very hard to avoid such errors. However, there's a second type of error that they often make: people sometimes harm their health by going to doctors too much! People have gotten unnecessary surgery, unnecessary medications, and unnecessary tests, simply because doctors are human, and if you keep bugging them enough, many of them will try treatments that are not necessary. Many people have suffered complications of medical procedures when they would have been better off ignoring their ailments and staying away from doctors!

This section

A. advises that you never go to a doctor,
or
B. points out some possible dangers of being too worried about your health?

508. How do you tell the difference between a symptom that needs urgent attention and one that is best to ignore? Accurate knowledge and accurate information are key.

Fortunately, we live in a world where huge amounts of information are available over the Internet. Although some of the medical information on the Internet is inaccurate, with enough work and good judgment you can learn a lot about any symptom you have, and check the information with your doctor. I recommend putting some of the energy that would otherwise be spent in nonproductive worry into looking up good information and reading and pondering it.

The author recommends

A. focusing mainly on getting enough exercise,
or
B. diverting energy that would have been spent worrying, into learning about the symptoms you have?

509. Although it's sometimes true that people owe their lives to early diagnosis and treatment of an illness, a much larger portion of people's health is determined by how much they follow the 17 health rules I listed above. If you devote a good part of your energy that would have been spent worrying, into making sure you are doing the things that prevent illness from occurring, you will probably end up healthier.

In this section, the author recommends

A. putting energy into making "healthy life style choices" that would otherwise be put into worrying about illness,
or
B. that you altogether avoid the use of alcohol?

Economic needs

510. Now let's turn to economic health. What does money have to do with taking care of yourself and your loved ones? If a dire need of any sort comes up, you can hire people to help you, if you have the money. If someone needs medical care, assistance in education, a place to live, legal help, you can supply it, but it costs money. You can take off time from work to put time into some important goal, but only if you have enough money saved that you can afford not to work every day.

The author's attitude toward money appears to be that it

A. is the root of all evil,
or
B. is very helpful in protecting yourself and your loved ones, and therefore good to accumulate?

511. How do you make sure you will have enough money to take care of your needs, and those of the ones you love? Again, let's study a checklist.

Checklist on economic health

1. Are you continually working to acquire or improve your marketable skills? This means, are you continually trying to get better and better at some set of skills that fills a need for others, and that people are willing to pay money for?

2. If you are of school age, are you putting enough effort into academic skills, i.e. reading, writing, and math, so as to reach the height of your potential? Are you avoiding letting sports or jobs crowd out academics?

3. If you are of school age, are you thinking rationally about careers that will bring you a reasonable income? Are you getting information on what careers exist, and which will fit the best with your skills and interests and tastes?

Which of the following has appeared on the economic needs checklist in this section?

A. turning out lights to save money on electricity,

or

B. working to improve the sorts of skills people are willing to pay money for?

512. Let's continue the economic needs checklist.

4. Are you avoiding pinning your plans for earning a living on becoming a sports star, a music star, or an acting star? Do you have a "plan B" just in case you don't become a star?

5. How is your work capacity? Can you keep working for a good number of hours without feeling terribly depleted or needing lots of breaks?

6. How are your dependability and responsibility skills? Are you in the habit of coming through with any sort of work you have promised to do? Do you have great "appointmentology" skills – an organized system that keeps you from missing appointments?

7. Do you have good ways of finding out what sorts of credentials you need in order to be in certain careers – what degrees, what licenses, and so forth?

What's an item that was mentioned in the economic needs checklist in this section?

A. cultivating great skills of appointment-keeping, or
B. getting to know people who have power?

513. The economic needs checklist continues.

8. How well organized are you in your decision-making about work? Do you keep track really well of the tasks you have to do? Do you avoid committing yourself to more than you can do? Do you do the highest priority things? Do you make to-do lists, and refer often to these lists as you check off the tasks?

9. When you earn money, how able are you to save a high fraction of it?

10. How well can you resist temptations to spend money on expensive things, expensive trips, expensive entertainment, and so forth?

11. To what extent do you have fun things to do that are not at all expensive – for example taking walks with friends or family, singing, writing, cooking, having homework parties, etc.?

12. How much do you know about investing money, i.e. putting your money into assets that will probably in turn make more money for you?

232

What's an item that was mentioned in this section?

A. not spending lots of time and money on pets,
or
B. saving a high fraction of the money you earn?

514. The checklist on economic needs continues.

13. How much pleasure do you take in investing in stocks or bonds or other money-producing assets?

14. When you invest, do you get a "diversified portfolio" – do you avoid putting "all your eggs in one basket?" In other words, do you spread out your investments so that you'll still have money if some of the investments become worthless?

15. How good are your financial organization skills – keeping track of income, expenditures, budgets, taxes, and so forth? Do you know something about accounting? Do you consult with whatever experts you need help from?

16. Do you totally avoid wasting money on the interest you have to pay if you don't pay credit card bills right away?

An item that is mentioned in this section is

A. take pleasure in buying stocks and bonds,
or
B. stay out of gambling casinos?

515. This section concludes the economic needs checklist.

17. Do you from time to time calculate your "financial net worth," which means the total of how much you could sell everything you own for, minus how much you owe to anyone? (In other words, your assets minus your liabilities?)

18. Do you feel determined to make your financial net worth grow to the point where you could live off the income from your assets?

19. Do you make good decisions about insurance?

The items on the economic needs checklist in the several sections above have to do with broad categories of

A. evaluating economic equations, knowing what hedge funds are, and understanding mortgages,
or

B. learning marketable skills, finding a rewarding career, keeping your finances organized, and saving and investing?

Social needs

516. The next category of needs is to be part of a good social support system, to have good relationships. What is a good relationship? It's one marked by kindness, respectful talk, nonviolence, fortitude and emotional control, reasonable conflict-resolution, and loyalty. It's one where people enjoy being with each other, help each other, and don't exploit each other. It's one where you hear more approval than disapproval. It's one where the criteria for the positive emotional climate described in the emotional climate scales at the end of this book are often met. The following is a checklist on your social support system.

Checklist on social support and positive relationships

1. Do you have at least one person with whom you have a very positive, satisfying relationship?

2. How good is your relationship with each of the members of your "nuclear"

family, the family members you are closest to and/or live with?

3. How good are your relationships with extended family members -- for example, family members you don't live with?

What's an item that has been mentioned in this section?

A. having a really good relationship with at least one person,
or
B. being able to entertain other people well?

517. The checklist on social support continues.

4. How good are your relationships with friends?

5. Are there several people whom you enjoy, whom you would feel comfortable inviting to get together with you?

6. Are there several people you would feel comfortable calling up to chat with?

7. Are there several people you would feel comfortable calling upon for help if you needed it?

8. Do you feel good about your social conversation skills? Is social conversation a source of great enjoyment for you?

What's an item mentioned in the last section?

A. having a Facebook account,
or
B. being good at social conversation?

518. The checklist on social support concludes in this section.

9. Do you feel confident about any other skills that make you desirable to have as a friend?

10. Is loneliness not a problem for you?

11. Is shyness not a problem for you?

12. Are there relationships you are in where your prevailing feeling is definitely neither scared nor angry?

13. Do you spend very little if any time worrying that your appearance makes you undesirable for relationships?

14. Do you have the feeling every day that you have made someone else happy?

15. Overall, does it make you happy to think about the relationships you are in?

The entire social support checklist could probably be boiled down to which of the following:

A. having at least 20 people whom you see socially at least once every six months,
or
B. having several people whom you are very nice to, and who are very nice to you?

519. Some people are lucky enough to have family members who are easy to get along with and pleasant to be with, and/or skilled enough to create a family with a positive emotional climate. Other people need to work harder to find a core of friends who will be kind and loyal to one another, because they can not at present find the positive relationships they need within their families.

The author has the attitude that

A. to be happy, you must have good relationships with family members,
or
B. if good relationships with family members can't be had, good friends can make up for them?

520. I believe that not feeling "social support," not being in relationships with a "positive emotional climate," is responsible for a great deal of anxiety. I also believe that people who want to improve their relationships with other human beings can do so if they are willing to work hard enough at it. My book entitled *A Programmed Course in Friendship Building and Social Skills* goes into the art of friendship-building in more detail.

The author believes that the art of building friendships

A. is something you are born with, or not;
or
B. is a skill you can cultivate by working on it?

Achievement needs

521. So far we have discussed taking care of your physical, economic, and social needs. If each of these is in very good shape, you can celebrate. You probably feel much more secure and safe than you would if these were not in a good state. Yet even someone who has each of these needs met can still reasonably feel uneasy, if something else is missing. That something else is the need to achieve some worthy goal, to do something

worthwhile, to have a positive impact on the world.

The fourth type of need that the author discusses is

A. the need to have a social support system and friends,
or
B. the need to achieve something worthwhile?

522. What sorts of achievement are worthwhile? Which are not worthwhile? The answers to these questions depend upon your value system. I believe that certain achievements are definitely more worthwhile than others, and there are some goals that are wasteful and unworthy of our best selves.

Some achievements are simply frivolous and wasteful. If you set the world record for the number of grapes stuffed into your mouth, or the longest time spent in a tree, or if you walk on a cable over Niagara Falls, according to my personal value system you are not accomplishing anything worthwhile. But even these are better than accomplishing harmful goals – for example, launching a successful advertising campaign that persuades millions of young people to start smoking a certain cigarette.

The author feels that

A. as long as a goal is something you deeply desire, for you, it's worthwhile;
or
B. some goals are more worthwhile than others, and some are even harmful?

523. What constitutes worthy goals? After you've taken care of your own physical, economic, and social needs, and those of your family members, the most worthy goals are those that would better the lot of humanity – improve the human condition – make people happier, in the long run; or do the same thing for the other animals who inhabit the earth with us. Helping even one person improves the condition of humanity. Reducing violence, poverty, disease, ignorance, environmental destruction, and hatred among people appears to me to be top priority goals. In my opinion worthy goals include supplying food, shelter, energy, health care, education, peaceful conflict-resolution, and other really useful things to people. This is particularly true when this is done in ways so that some people don't get too much and others too little. Creating arts including drama, fiction, and music that bring out the best in people rather than appealing to the baser elements of human nature can be an extremely high calling. Discovering or

transmitting scientific truths that can benefit humanity is another.

The author feels that worthy goals

A. are too complicated to be defined,
or
B. are those which when accomplished, better the condition of humanity, in at least some small way?

524. What does this have to do with anxiety? I believe that a real sense of security comes from dedicating oneself to a cause greater than oneself. The thought, "No matter what befalls me, at least I have the satisfaction of knowing I have tried to make a worthy contribution to a very worthwhile cause," is one that has given comfort and courage to countless people throughout history.

The point of this section is that

A. it's important to make goals specific,
or
B. working for a cause you deeply believe to be worthwhile can give people comfort and courage?

525. What are the biggest obstacles to sustaining progress on very worthwhile goals? One is a failure to set those goals in the first place. For many people, the question, "How

would you like to make a positive impact upon the world?" does not "compute." The question, "What sort of accomplishment could you imagine making, that would give you a peaceful feeling of having bettered the world at least a little bit," often is one that people don't even raise with themselves. And sometimes the goals for work or school are not explored beyond the question of "What would I get into trouble for not doing?"

The point of this section is that

A. a big obstacle to accomplishing worthy goals is the failure to set those goals to begin with,
or
B. a big obstacle to accomplishing worthy goals is setting goals that are beyond our capabilities and aptitudes?

526. Another huge obstacle to achieving worthy goals is that it's hard to make yourself do tedious, boring, frustrating work. Almost every worthy project involves getting some big ideas, making some lofty plans, and having some real pleasure in starting toward the goal. But sooner or later, a logjam of tedium stands in the way. You have to fill out a bunch of forms. You have to keep reading something you're tired of reading. You have to look up a bunch of information and organize it. You have to make sure

that the references at the end of your article have the right page numbers on them. You have to make sure that you're not breaking the tax laws. You have to practice something over and over until proficient performance becomes automatic, not just until you can do it fairly well. It's at the point of tedious work that most people drop out of the game. Keeping on working toward the goal, even when the work has become boring, is perhaps what most often separates success from failure.

This section speculates that perhaps the biggest reason people fail is

A. not being able to make themselves do the boring part of the project,
or
B. not setting goals in the first place?

527. The following checklist goes over many techniques for attaining your goals. For a detailed discussion of how to use these techniques, please refer to my book, *A Programmed Course in Self-Discipline*.

This is the fourth and final in the checklists to make sure you are adequately taking care of yourself and those of others.

Checklist of techniques for meeting goals

How much do you use each of these, for each particular goal?

1. Careful goal selection. Did you select the goal carefully, thinking about what is most ethical and worthy of your effort?

2. Goal written, specifically. Have you written the goal, describing specifically what achieving it would be like? Do you read those words often?

3. Internal sales pitch. Have you written an internal sales pitch, and do you read those words often? (The internal sales pitch is the list of reasons you want to achieve the goal.)

Which of the following items on meeting goals was mentioned in this section?

A. writing down the reasons for wanting to accomplish the goal, or
B. making sure you have enough money to accomplish the goal?

528. The checklist on meeting goals continues.

4. Plans. Do you write overall plans and daily plans for how you will achieve your goals?

5. Hierarchy of difficulty. Do you make resolutions that are neither too hard nor too easy for your current skill?

6. List of choice points. Have you listed the most important self-discipline choice points?

7. Decisions. Have you decided clearly what you would like to do, think, and feel in those choice point situations?

8. Rehearsals. Do you often do fantasy rehearsals of triumphing in those choice points? Do you frequently practice the skills you need?

Which item having to do with achieving goals was mentioned in this section?

A. fantasy rehearsing what you'll do in the important choice points, or

B. using meditation to "recharge your batteries" while working toward your goal?

529. The checklist on achieving goals continues.

9. Self-reinforcement. Do you use self-reinforcement for bits of progress toward your goal, immediately after such successes?

10. Celebrations exercise. Do you think back and recall your triumphs, and feel good about them?

11. External reinforcement. Do you use external rewards for your triumphs?

12. Self-monitoring. Do you frequently monitor your progress toward your goal, using numbers?

13. Advanced self-discipline. Do you try to learn to *enjoy* your work toward the goal?

What's an item mentioned in this section?

A. to congratulate yourself for your successes,
or
B. to read lots of instructions on how to accomplish the goal well?

530. The checklist on achieving goals continues.

14. Work capacity. Do you use "exposure" and "habituation" to increase your work capacity? Do you believe in the effort-payoff connection?

15. Stimulus control. Do you avoid situations that tempt you to do the wrong things, and put yourself into situations that tempt you to do the right things, to accomplish the goal?

16. Routines and momentum. Do you try to stay in habits that will help you?

17. Organization. Are you staying as organized as you can?

18. Twelve thoughts. Do you choose consciously among twelve types of thoughts?

Which of the following is an item mentioned in this section?

A. putting your written goal on the wall,
or
B. choosing among the twelve thoughts, so as to help you accomplish your goal?

531. This section concludes the checklist on achieving goals.

19. Modeling. Do you collect positive models, and avoid negative ones?

20. Frequently reading instructions. Do you keep reading about how to accomplish this goal?

21. Time on task. Are you devoting enough time to get the job done?

22. Restoring persistence power. Do you use techniques to restore your persistence power? (Restoring your persistence power means being able to refresh yourself after you've used up some of your energy or motivation, and re-energize yourself to keep working.)

Which of the following was an item mentioned in this section?

A. collecting positive models of the patterns of behavior you need to succeed at your goal,
or
B. making sure you get enough sleep to energize yourself to work on your goal?

532. So let's remind ourselves again – what do all these checklists have to do with avoiding worrying? The idea is to devote productive thought to the items on these checklists, in an organized and systematic way. That way, you can create confidence in yourself that your plans for looking after your needs are under control. The organized thought and the confidence tend to replace worry. Rather than trying to stop thinking about what to do, the idea is to do this thinking in a very organized and systematic fashion. Hopefully the thinking you do in this way is both more effective and more pleasant than worrying.

What is the point of this section?

A. Worrying can create stress that can be harmful to your health.
Or
B. The idea behind the checklists in this chapter is to think about taking care of your needs in an organized and systematic way that you will enjoy, and that will let you not need to worry.

Chapter 14: Memories and Images as Resources to Reduce Anxiety

533. The sorts of "resources" we will be talking about in this chapter are not natural resources such as iron or silver deposits, nor are they financial resources such as money in the bank. Rather, they are resources of memories or images in your memory bank, stored away in your brain, or possibly even stored in writing. Specifically, you can use as anti-anxiety resources the memories of yourself thinking, feeling, and acting in ways that are confident, brave, relaxed, bold, spontaneous, nonchalant, competitive, assertive, loving, friendly, cool and calculating, or any other way that you would prefer to anxiety or aversion! If you are running short on images of yourself behaving in these ways, you can also use as resources the images of other people behaving in these ways.

An example of the sort of "resource" the author is talking about in this chapter would be

A. a clean water supply, which is a natural resource,
or
B. a memory of oneself meeting new people, feeling confident and friendly, which is a resource held in the memory bank?

534. The sorts of resources and memories we are talking about are meant to help you create really useful positive fantasy rehearsals. If the thoughts, feelings, or behaviors you are rehearsing are ones that you have actually done before, then your task is easier. Rather than creating new patterns for your brain, you simply reactivate old patterns that are already stored in your brain.

The resources the author speaks of are

A. memories of ways of positive ways of behaving, stored in your brain, that you can activate for use in a certain situation,
or
B. memories of things that happened that teach you a lesson about what not to do the next time?

535. In drawing upon your resources and using them, here are some questions to ask yourself:

1. What is the situation I am wanting to handle without so much anxiety or aversion?

2. How would I like to act in this situation: confident, focused, determined, relaxed, brave, fun-loving, humorous, calm...?

3. Can I retrieve from memory a time when I acted in just the way that I want to act?

4. Can I relive this memory as vividly as possible, so as to activate the pattern fully in my brain?

5. Can I now visualize myself in the situation I'm working on, thinking, feeling, and behaving in the same way? (In other words, can I do vivid fantasy rehearsals of handling the situation well?)

6. Can I now step into the situation in real life, and act in the way I recalled and imagined?

7. If I am successful in this situation, can I be sure to store away in memory this new success experience as a resource for use in the future?

The purpose of going through these seven steps is to

A. transfer positive ways of acting from old situations to new ones, or

B. make sure that unpleasant memories have been dealt with effectively?

536. Here's an example of using these steps. Years ago I got a call from a woman who was suffering from a sudden bout of anxiety. She had been a teacher for many years, and was retiring. There was a dinner to be given, that very night, in her honor, and she would be expected to say a few words to the assembled group. This image filled her with fear.

I explained that I wanted to go through several steps with her. She had already done the first, in describing the feared situation. How would she like to feel in this situation? This was easy: she would like to feel relaxed and confident and to enjoy the situation, and to feel grateful for being honored.

I asked if she could retrieve memories of feeling confident and relaxed, perhaps even in situations like this one. Immediately she replied that she had spent thousands of hours in front of students in her classrooms, and she would like to have the same feeling she had then. I asked her to pick out some specific memories in which her teaching was most pleasant, enjoyable, and confident, and to run these memories through her mind as vividly as possible. She did so. Then I asked her if she could imagine herself feeling, thinking, and acting in the same general way at the dinner in her honor to take place tonight. She vividly imagined it as we both held the phone, silently. She was able to transfer that mental pattern into the target situation and make a big success of it, as she told me the next day.

The main purpose of this section is to

A. convince the reader that people can handle situations well, even if they had been afraid of them,
or
B. give an example of how the steps listed in the previous section can be used?

537. I knew that this method worked, because I had used it myself. I was scheduled for a speech before a large number of people, and I felt nervous. I wanted to feel energized and joyous, happy with the opportunity to "show off" in front of people. The resource I hit upon was a memory of myself as a young teenager, on a camp-out with a bunch of other boys. We were around the campfire, and groups of us would put on skits for the rest. Some of my friends and I would think of funny jokes that we had all heard, and we would simply act them out for the other boys, mostly younger ones. A great time was had by all, and this served as a wonderful resource for the

pattern of joyous and confident public performance. I visualized myself giving the speech with the same joyousness and confidence, and then "stepped into the role" in real life. I would guess that some of the same patterns of firing of brain cells happened during my speech that happened during the skits around the campfire.

The main point of this section is to

A. explain that brain cells either "fire" or "don't fire," in an all-or-nothing setup, and when they fire, electric potentials change,
or
B. give another example of using resources of past memories to create positive fantasy rehearsals of present situations?

538. What if you can't recall a time when you thought, felt, and acted in the way you'd like to? Then a vivid image of someone else, or a "conjured up" image of yourself, can do as well. Images of characters in books or movies can also work well. Every image that goes into your memory bank, or that you purposely import into it as a model, is a resource that can potentially help you handle a certain situation.

If you've read *To Kill a Mockingbird*, for example, the

character Atticus Finch is a southern lawyer who bucks the social pressure of his racist community to defend an African-American man accused wrongly of a crime. This image can be used as a "courage resource" for anyone who incurs the disapproval of others as a result of making an ethical choice.

The author mentions the book *To Kill a Mockingbird* because

A. it is a pleasant and entertaining book to read,
or
B. it is a source of models that can be courage resources?

539. What if you have stored in your brain a bunch of images of ways that you DON'T want to think, feel, and behave? For example, some people have many images stored in memory of very critical talk from people who criticized them at every move. It is often difficult for such people to avoid activating these mental patterns and criticizing themselves for nearly everything they do. Sometimes the fear of their own disapproval contributes greatly to anxiety.

The great thing about mental resources is that the majority doesn't necessarily rule. You can have many undesirable images stored away, and many fewer desirable images, but if you wish very strongly to choose one of the better ones, and make a conscious effort to activate that pattern, that pattern may prevail.

The main point of this section is that

A. even if you have lots of undesirable patterns in your memory, you can retrieve and activate desirable patterns if you do it purposely,
or
B. people should not criticize other people too much?

540. We've spoken about vicious cycles of anxiety, where bad things cause other bad things which make the first bad things worse, and the cycle causes things to get worse and worse. But with mental resources, it's possible to have a "virtuous cycle," where a feedback loop makes things better and better.

Here's the way the loop goes. Someone gets some positive patterns into the brain to use as resources. The person is able to use those resources to handle situations well. Then, the memories of handling those situations well become more resources, which can be drawn upon in the future. Positive courage triumphs create memories that are resources you can use to create more courage triumphs.

The "virtuous cycle" described in this section is that

A. when you get more friends, you feel more confident, which helps you meet more people,
or
B. when you have courage triumphs, you create memories of yourself acting courageously, and you can then use these as resources for future situations?

541. I've advised people to use the "celebrations exercise" and the "celebrations diary" in many of these books on psychological skills. In the celebrations exercise, people tell each other things they're proud that they have done. In the celebrations diary, they write down those things. These exercises are meant to strengthen your mental resources – your memories of positive patterns. It's all too easy to forget the things we do that are courageous, self-disciplined, kind, or examples of other psychological skills. But if we recount them and write them, we are able to remember them more easily. These resources are more available to us when we search through our memories for the resources we need.

The main purpose of this section was to

A. mention self-discipline as a skill that is also important,
or
B. explain why the celebrations exercise and the celebrations diary tend to strengthen your storehouse of mental resources?

Chapter 15: Compulsions

542. Everything in this book that tells about how to reduce fears or aversions also tells how to reduce compulsions. Why? Because a compulsion is a behavior that temporarily relieves a fear or aversion, by providing escape from the situation. The compulsive behavior reduces the fear or aversion in the short run, but does not get rid of it in the long run. A compulsion is something that someone does over and over again, even though it doesn't seem like a good idea.

One of the points made in this section is that

A. it's good to resist compulsions, or
B. compulsions are behaviors that we do to try to reduce fears and aversions?

543. Here's an example of a compulsion. Someone feels that he might have touched something with germs on it, so he washes his hands. So far, this is a very rational thing to do. Hand washing is an effective means of reducing the chances of the spread of infection. However, let's imagine that this particular person has a very strong negative emotion connected with the feeling that his hands are contaminated. When he washes his hands, that negative emotion is relieved. The relief provides negative reinforcement, or the reward of stopping something unpleasant. The man has been rewarded very strongly for washing his hands, because of the relief of negative emotion that occurred during the hand washing.

Negative reinforcement means

A. the same thing as punishment, or
B. the stopping of something unpleasant, which is a reward?

544. Now suppose the man has a certain amount of "free floating anxiety." If his brain somehow interprets his anxiety as a contaminated feeling on the hands, then there is a way for him to get relief. He can wash his hands again. He does this, and again there is momentary relief.

Each time this sequence of events occurs, he is learning two things: First, he is learning that washing the hands brings powerful relief of bad feelings, even though the relief doesn't last long. Thus he is being reinforced for hand washing.

Second, he is learning to interpret otherwise unidentified negative feelings as a feeling of his hands' being contaminated; it's rewarding to do this, because those feelings can be momentarily relieved by the hand washing.

The point of this section is that

A. over and over, the person gets rewarded both for handwashing and for interpreting bad feelings as contamination on the hands,
or
B. compulsive hand-washing can chafe the skin of the hands, plus waste a lot of time?

545. As the habit of hand washing becomes more and more strengthened by the repetition of this pattern, the man gradually may realize that he is not washing his hands to reduce the chance of getting sick. He is now washing his hands to reduce his feeling of dread or aversion. The compulsion now does not serve an external purpose; it's meant to change the way he feels. This realization would sound something like, "I'm not so worried about getting sick. I'm washing my hands to reduce this awful contaminated feeling that I have."

The point of this section is that

A. At some point the motive of the handwashing becomes reducing bad feelings, not prevention of infectious illness,
or
B. there are many other compulsions that are reinforced in the same way hand washing compulsions are?

546. Throughout this book, we've looked at examples where people get used to a "scary situation" or an "aversive situation," so that they respond to the situation with much less distress than before. What is the "aversive situation" for the person with the hand-washing compulsion? It's having touched something, like a table top, a chair, or any other object, if that touching gives the feeling that the hands have been contaminated. The person's goal is to learn to handle this situation in a different way: with thoughts of "Who cares," emotions of indifference or calmness, and behaviors of going on about his business without washing his hands.

The point where the person has touched a computer keyboard, but has not washed his hands, is most likely the

A. emotion of calmness,
or
B. aversive situation?

547. Here's another example of a compulsion. This is a member of a set of "symmetry" compulsions. In all the symmetry compulsions, you have the feeling that "If I do it on one side, I have to do it on the other side." Or, "If I do it a certain way the first time, I have to do it the same way the second time." Kyle looks at a corner of the room; he feels very uncomfortable if he doesn't also look at the other three corners of the room. So he makes sure to look at the other three corners.

What is the aversive situation here? It's the situation of having looked at one corner, without having looked at the other corner. This is that situation that Kyle wants to practice handling in a different way. He wants to practice the thought, "This is no big deal," the emotions of being calm and relaxed, and the behavior of doing anything but looking at the other three corners.

In this example, having looked at one corner of the room without looking at the other corners was the

A. compulsion,
or
B. the aversive situation?

548. Here's another example of a symmetry compulsion. Someone touches one side of his desk. He feels the need to touch the other side of the desk, the same distance from the far edge of the desk. He feels a distress level of 8 on a scale of 10 if he doesn't let himself touch the other side of the desk.

The aversive situation this time is

A. having touched one side of the desk and not the other,
or
B. having touched both sides of the desk, symmetrically?

Many repeated behaviors are "good ideas" to do

549. Not everything that we get the urge to do over and over is a compulsion. For example, in the winter when I go out to shovel snow, I get a strong urge to put on a coat and some gloves. I do this over and over, each time I go out. So there's "something I feel a strong urge to do, over an over." The situation where I go out for a good while, without gloves, causes me distress; it's an aversive situation. Do I have a compulsion? Of course not, because my behavior serves a purpose other than reducing temporarily an unrealistic aversion. The aversion to being in cold weather with no coat or gloves is a very realistic aversion!

The point of this section is that

A. many people have compulsions about clothing, such as making sure socks are pulled up to the same length or not feeling "right" in certain clothes,
or
B. not all behaviors that we have a strong urge to do over and over are compulsions?

550. Here's another example of a "good idea" in contrast to a compulsion. A speaker often gives speeches after eating supper. Before he gives each speech, he checks carefully to make sure that he doesn't have any bits of food on his face before he stands up in front of everyone to talk. Is this checking ritual a compulsion, or a good idea? It serves a useful purpose, and in my opinion, it's a good idea. The aversion to having someone tell him that he had spinach on his chin while was giving his talk is a realistic aversion. So with compulsions, as well as with fears, the first step is to decide whether an aversion is realistic or unrealistic, and whether the urge to do something is a compulsion or a good idea.

The main idea of this section is that

A. you should rate how strong any unrealistic aversions are, and monitor them over time,
or
B. you should figure out whether aversions are realistic or unrealistic, and whether urges are compulsions or good ideas?

Exposure and ritual prevention as a strategy in getting over compulsions

551. Do you remember our discussion of the avoidance learning training that psychologists did with rats? To review: The rat was in a cage and a light came on, and a couple of seconds later the bottom of the cage shocked the rat's feet. But the rat found that if he jumped over a barrier, he could escape the shock. Very soon he learned to jump over the barrier before the shock even started, as soon as the light came on. Thus he was able to avoid the shock altogether. Now the experimenters turned off the electricity so that there was no chance of shock to the rat. But they kept turning on the light. The rat kept jumping over the barrier, without getting the chance to learn that the shock had been turned off. We can call jumping over the barrier an "avoidance maneuver." It was a way for the rat to avoid the feared

consequence. Because the rat did the avoidance maneuver, he never had the chance to find out what the feared consequence wouldn't really occur. So he continued with the avoidance maneuver indefinitely.

The rat failed to learn that there is no need to escape because

A. unlike humans, the rat's memory was not good enough,
or
B. the rat didn't stick around long enough to find out that the shock would not have come on?

552. The "cure" for the rat's unnecessary avoidance maneuver was exposure. When he was physically prevented from jumping over the barrier, he looked for ways to escape when the light came on. But as the light came on more and more times, without his getting the shock, he gradually seemed to learn that the light was no longer the signal that something bad was about to happen. He learned not to do the avoidance maneuver anymore.

The message this section suggests to people is that

A. if you want to quit avoiding a situation that isn't really dangerous,

the thing to do is to expose yourself to that situation,
or
B. what you say to yourself during your exposure to unrealistically aversive situations makes a lot of difference?

553. Exactly the same exposure strategy has been used with compulsions in human beings. For example, someone with a hand washing compulsion gets a strong feeling of contamination and a strong urge to wash the hands, but simply does not permit himself to wash. He notices that his SUD rating (rating of Subjective Units of Distress) is close to 10 on a scale of 10. But as he continues to expose himself to the aversive situation (having touched but not having washed), his feeling of aversion and dread gradually goes down. His brain gets to discover that nothing awful happens. He habituates to the situation. Within a few minutes, his SUD level has gone down to 6, and after a while, it goes down to 2 or 3. The more exposure he does, the more he habituates.

The point of this section is that

A. exposure can lead to habituation with a compulsion, just as it can with a conditioned fear,
or

B. compulsions usually refer to behavior, whereas obsessions usually refer to thoughts?

554. Thus the same strategy, and the same reasoning, are used with compulsions as with other unrealistic fears and aversions. There are two pathways to feeling better when you have an unrealistic aversion: avoidance, and mastery through exposure. Avoidance tends to reinforce or maintain the unrealistic aversion in the long run, while making you feel safer in the short run. Achieving mastery through exposure does just the opposite: it feels worse in the short run, but reduces or eliminates the aversion in the long run. To get rid of a compulsion, you expose yourself to the aversive situation, but you don't let yourself perform the compulsion. You practice thoughts, emotions, and behaviors compatible with feeling good in that aversive situation.

The point of this section is that

A. compulsions can be very unpleasant, especially when someone is doing them many hours a day, or
B. you get rid of compulsions just as you get rid of unrealistic aversions: expose yourself to the situation and don't let yourself escape it by doing the compulsion?

555. Let's look at another example of a compulsion. This one is called a "checking compulsion." A woman is about to leave her house. She stops and thinks, "Could I have left the stove burner on?" She gets out of her car, goes back into the house, and checks the stove. So far we are talking about rational decision making. But suppose the woman has a huge dread of the house burning down and checking the stove produces a feeling of intense relief from that dread. Now she gets back into her car and notices the anxious feeling returning. She wants the relief she could feel by checking again. To justify this, she thinks "I just paid attention to the one burner. Perhaps I left a different burner on." So she gets out and checks one more time; as she predicted, the anxious feeling is momentarily reduced. This quick fear reduction again reinforces the checking behavior. Like other behaviors that are powerfully reinforced, the frequency of checking goes up and up, to the point where the woman finds it hard to get out of her house.

In this example with the checking compulsion, as in the hand-washing example, the author makes the point that

A. doing the compulsion, in this case checking, is reinforced by a brief reduction in anxiety,
or
B. mastery fantasy rehearsals are very useful in overcoming compulsions?

556. As with the hand washing compulsion, the "cure" for the woman's checking compulsion is for her to check one time before leaving the house, not permit herself to check anymore, watch her SUD level rise when she does not permit herself to check again, and then gradually habituate to the situation of having left the house with only one check. She exposes herself to that situation, and doesn't permit herself to use escape or avoidance by going back to check again.

In the way the author uses the word *avoidance* in connection with aversions and compulsions, the woman discussed in this section would have used avoidance if she had

A. gone back and checked the stove again, thus avoiding the scary situation of leaving with only one check,
or
B. stayed away from checking, thus avoiding giving in to the unrealistic fear?

557. The phrase "exposure and response prevention," or "exposure and ritual prevention," has been used to describe what people do in getting over compulsions. Ritual prevention or response prevention simply means that you don't let yourself do the compulsion. Exposure means that you put yourself in the aversive situation, the one that tends to trigger the compulsion. Exposure and ritual prevention is just another phrase for getting over fears by practicing dealing with the unpleasant situation rather than trying to use avoidance and escape.

The "ritual" referred to in the phrase "exposure and ritual prevention" is

A. the ritual of checking, or hand-washing, or whatever avoidance maneuver the compulsion is,
or
B. the ritual of fantasy rehearsing braver self-talk?

558. Obviously, if you are going to use exposure strategies with compulsions, you need to muster a lot of self-discipline. The easy thing to do is just to give in and do the compulsion one more time. The hard thing to do is to keep yourself from doing the compulsion long enough to get used to the aversive situation. This is the same self-discipline challenge

that's necessary in using any of the other exposure and practice techniques we've talked about in this book. This, as always, is the big "catch" for exposure-based ways of getting over fears and aversions and compulsions.

The main point of this section is that

A. before doing exposure, you should make sure that the repeated behavior is not a "good idea" instead of a compulsion,
or
B. it takes lots of self-discipline to use exposure to reduce compulsions?

559. As we have said before, human beings are more complex than rats. There are a variety of other things you can do to reduce unrealistic aversions in addition to simply throwing yourself into the aversive situation and waiting until habituation takes place. You can set up a gradual hierarchy. You can pay conscious attention to using the best self-talk. You can use any of a variety of relaxation techniques to turn down your level of arousal. You can use fantasy rehearsals. You use all the techniques we discussed before to permit yourself to use exposure rather than avoidance and escape.

The main idea of this section is that

A. you can use any of the techniques we discussed before regarding anxiety and aversions, to make exposure easier and more effective with compulsions,
or
B. practicing doing exposure joyously, if you can do it, gets you farther than practicing exposure painfully?

Exposure through fantasy rehearsals

560. One of the main techniques for making exposure easier is mastery fantasy rehearsals. The person with the checking compulsion, for example, imagines herself checking one time before leaving the house and then leaving, feeling no anxiety whatsoever, and going happily about her business. She imagines the "miracle story": What would it be like if by some miracle she were totally delivered from her compulsion? The more she imagines this miracle story, the easier it is for her to enact it, because she is practicing the brain activity that she will use when doing it.

The person with the hand-washing compulsion imagines a day in which he washes his hands after trips to the rest room and before meals and so forth, a reasonable number of times and no more. He imagines himself not getting the urge to wash when he doesn't need it and imagines himself feeling no distress over the whole issue of contamination.

This section gives examples of people

A. just "gutting it out" so as to do exposure,
or
B. making it easier for themselves to do exposure by first doing mastery fantasy rehearsals?

561. Sometimes people find it difficult to do mastery fantasy rehearsals. They just can't imagine themselves feeling nonchalant and un-anxious about these situations. In this case, sometimes it's easier to start imagining someone else doing the desired pattern. You imagine someone you know or a generic imaginary person, handling the situation just exactly as you would like to handle it. Gradually you have the person come to resemble yourself more and more. Then you see yourself doing it, as though you were looking at yourself on a television screen or in a movie or seeing yourself as a spectator. Finally, you imagine yourself doing it as though you're seeing the world through your own eyes.

In this section the author gives an example of how someone can use the technique of

A. gradual hierarchy: moving in steps from imagining someone else doing the desired pattern, to seeing oneself from a distance, to seeing oneself through one's own eyes,
or
B. probabilities and utilities: deciding that the probability of bad outcomes from doing the brave thing is very low?

562. As you do fantasy rehearsals, you can also practice the type of self-talk that will make this situation less painful. For example, when the person with the stove checking ritual finds herself flashing upon the image of the house burning down, she thinks to herself, "This is an image that I need to habituate to. The more I can get used to this without having to do anything about it, the better off I'll be. It's a very improbable image, but even if it happened, I could handle it. I'm being very brave by continuing to do exposure without escaping. Hooray for me for that!"

The type of self-talk that this calm and self-reinforcing self-talk is likely replacing is

A. Oh my gosh! Oh no! That would be terrible!

or

B. Let's see, I want to remember to pick up some potatoes while I'm out?

563. In addition, the person who is preparing for exposure methods with compulsions can do lots of practice in turning up and down his or her own sympathetic nervous system tone. Using relaxation and biofeedback can give the person control of their autonomic nervous system that will make the time of exposure while waiting for habituation much less painful. You can, and should, use relaxation techniques not just in the real situation, but while doing fantasy rehearsals as well.

The main point of this section is that

A. the more you arrange to be rewarded for exposure, and get support from your friendly allies, the easier it will be,

or

B. the more you practice relaxing and calming yourself during exposures or fantasy rehearsals of them, the easier exposure will be?

Nipping new compulsions in the bud

564. If you have experienced unrealistic fears and aversions or compulsions, it's likely that after you conquer them by exposure and habituation, another will pop up for no particular reason, every now and then. It's usually not a realistic goal that no compulsion will ever again appear. However, it is a realistic goal that when a compulsion does appear, you can start the exposure and habituation process so quickly and so automatically that you habituate to the compulsion almost before it has even had a chance to become a compulsion.

The author feels that it's a realistic goal that

A. all compulsions and unrealistic fears will be forever eliminated,

or

B. you automatically start exposure and habituation so quickly that no compulsion or unrealistic fear has a chance to get very far?

565. Here's an example. An elementary school age boy has had various compulsions having to do with his clothing: it feels too tight, it just doesn't feel right, and so forth. He has

successfully reduced these compulsions and then eliminated them by exposure methods. One day he notices that he is spending lots of time making sure that the buttons on his shirt are lined up vertically rather than getting out of a straight line. He notices the distress he feels when the buttons are zig-zaggy. (Having the buttons out of line is the aversive situation for him.) As soon as he realizes this, he evaluates whether his aversion is realistic or unrealistic, and immediately decides that it is unrealistic. He decides to go through the same set of steps he's used in the past to undo unrealistic or useless aversions.

The aversive situation in this case is

A. having the buttons out of line,
or
B. being embarrassed by people's noticing when he makes sure the buttons are straight?

566. The boy in the previous example immediately deliberately adjusts his shirt so that the buttons do not make a vertical line. He relaxes. He pays attention to his self-talk, and he says to himself, "Hurray! I think I'm going to nip this compulsion in the bud! I'm so glad I got on it so quickly! There's no realistic danger in this situation at all. I'm using my muscle relaxation skills." He notices that his SUD level is going down fairly rapidly. His attention drifts off onto the tasks that he has to do that day. When he notices his buttons again, there's very little distress. He deliberately makes the buttons go out of a vertical line for a few days after that, even though the SUD level has gone down to zero. The total time that this compulsion eats up before it is ended by habituation is just a few minutes. The boy found it easy partly because he refused to practice avoidance or escape through repetition of the compulsion. That way, he started exposure before getting a "reinforcement history," an experience of having the compulsion reduce his anxiety a little in the short run many times.

In the example of this section, the boy had an advantage that lots of people who have had compulsions for a while don't have that advantage was that

A. he started doing exposure before he had been reinforced many times for doing the compulsion,
or
B. he used his allies?

567. Here's another example. Ingrid has gotten over various compulsions by exposure and practice. She notices that as she walks along the sidewalk, she is avoiding stepping on the lines

that divide the panels of the sidewalk from each other, and the little cracks in the concrete. She knows that nothing bad will happen bad if she does step on these, but doing so would cause her distress at maybe a 5 on a scale of 10 level. She decides that she's developing a new compulsion.

The moment when she has stepped on a line or a crack in the sidewalk is called the

A. aversive situation,
or
B. compulsion?

568. Ingrid realizes this just as she has arrived at school. Throughout the school day, when she gets a spare moment, she does some mastery fantasy rehearsals of walking along the sidewalk, stepping on the lines and cracks, feeling no distress whatsoever. She does some coping rehearsals, imagining that stepping on the lines and cracks is aversive, but becomes less aversive over time. After school, she walks in exactly the same way that she has rehearsed. She feels a little distress, but it rapidly goes down. She greatly celebrates that she has nipped the compulsion in the bud.

When she walks on the sidewalk without avoiding the cracks and lines, she is doing

A. a compulsion,
or
B. exposure?

Identifying the aversive situations to practice with

569. Let's practice identifying the aversive situations associated with compulsions. Humphrey has a counting compulsion – he finds himself counting, and he feels that he can't stop unless he lands on a multiple of 10. But then he needs to keep going until he's stopped on a multiple of 10, a multiple of 10 times. If he loses track of how many, he has to start over. What's the aversive situation for Humphrey?

A. the moment of having counted and having stopped before landing on the right number,
or
B. a high SUD level?

570. Angelina feels she has to tap on her desk in a certain rhythm and a certain spatial pattern at the beginning of a certain class at school. If she doesn't start the tapping, or if she has to stop in the middle, she feels very upset.

The two aversive situations in this example are

A. having classmates be annoyed by the tapping, and getting in trouble with the teacher,
or
B. having started the class without tapping, and starting the tapping pattern but stopping before it is finished?

571. Brad has a compulsion that interferes with his handwriting. When he puts dots over i's, if the dot is not directly over the rest of the i, he has to erase the letter and do it over again. What is the aversive situation?

A. having made a dot over an i that is to one side or the other rather than directly above,
or
B. having to write an essay and knowing he might get a bad grade?

572. Why am I asking you to practice identifying the aversive situations that trigger compulsions? Because, as I've said before, if you have a compulsion, once you identify the aversive situation, the steps you go through and the methods you use to get over that compulsion are just the same as in getting over any other fear or aversion. You practice getting used to stepping on a crack or leaving the house without checking the burners or counting to 13 and stopping, just the same way you would get used to being on an elevator, being on an airplane, or being around dogs if you had a phobia of any of those things. If you have a phobia, you avoid escaping by not running away from the scary situation. If you have a compulsion, you avoid escaping from the aversive situation by not doing the compulsion. (Not doing the compulsion is called "ritual prevention.")

The point the author is making in this section implies that

A. everything in this book is relevant to getting over compulsions, and you don't need another whole book devoted to compulsions,
or
B. you need to practice at least 13 times if you want to get over compulsions such as not stopping counting on certain numbers?

Chapter 16: Obsessions

Obsessions are unwanted thoughts

573. In the previous chapter we spoke of compulsions, which are actions that people feel that they need to do over and over again, even though these actions are not warranted or not useful. An obsession is similar, only rather than an observable action, it's a thought that someone finds himself doing over and over, even though he wishes he could stop it. Thus someone can be troubled by obsessions without anyone seeing this.

Compulsions are to behaviors as obsessions are to

A. thoughts
or
B. feelings?

574. Obsessions are not just any old type of thought. Obsessions tend to be thoughts that are so repugnant or against the person's ethical system or scary that the person very much wishes not to have this thought go through the mind.

For example, a new mother is involved in taking care of her infant. When she passes a kitchen knife in the kitchen, she has the image go through her mind of hurting her infant with the knife. This image seems so horrible to her that she feels very guilty about even having the thought. She strongly wishes never to think such a thought again.

However, the more she tries not to think this thought, the more it seems to pop into her head. The more she thinks it, the worse she feels about herself, and the more strongly she wishes to banish this thought from her head.

In the example given in this section, the thought that kept popping into the person's mind was

A. a thought the person found mildly annoying,
or
B. a thought the person found shockingly revolting?

The white bear problem

575. Now the mother in this example has run into what has been called the

260

"white bear problem." In a story written by Leo Tolstoy, someone challenged someone else to try very hard not to think about a white bear. (They referred to the animal as a white bear rather than a polar bear, and I'll continue that tradition.) The person who tried this had to admit that the image popped into his head repeatedly while he was trying not to think about it. You might try this yourself. Take a minute and try as hard as you can not to think about a white bear. If you're like most people, the image of the white bear will go through your mind on several occasions, if not almost constantly!

The point of the "white bear" story is that

A. if certain thoughts seem very bad to you, then of course you should try not to think them,
or
B. trying very hard not to think certain thoughts often makes those thoughts pop into your head more often, not less often?

576. Why does the white bear problem take place? Whenever we set a goal that is very strongly desired, we automatically tend to check and see whether we are attaining that goal. If I am running a foot race, for example, I will automatically check and see

where I am relative to my fellow competitors. If I am trying very hard to get home by six o'clock, I will repeatedly look at my watch and see if I'm going to be on time or not. Now, how do I check to see if I'm successfully performing the task of not thinking about a white bear? To monitor your success in this goal, you become aware of what you are thinking of, and then you check to see how those thoughts compare with the thought of a white bear. But to do that, you must bring the thought of the white bear into your mind. So, to check and see if you are successful, you must make yourself unsuccessful.

The purpose of this section was to

A. explain why the white bear problem takes place,
or
B. make clear that the people who get obsessions tend to have strong value systems, so that they view certain thoughts as unacceptable?

577. I have mentioned this white bear problem to many, many people in my life, but I have never once had one report to me that he or she kept on thinking about the white bear for days or hours or even more than a few minutes.

Why is this? Because after the point has been made, people quit trying not to think about the white bear, and most importantly, even if the white bear does pop back into consciousness every now and then, people tend to react to this event with the thought that it's no big deal. Having the image of a white bear go through your mind every once in a while does not make you a bad person or signify any danger or bring up any fears or revulsion or anything else very interesting or exciting. For this reason, the person forgets about the white bear issue and the thought recedes from consciousness.

The point of this section is that

A. because the thought of a white bear is not threatening or forbidden, people don't keep trying not to think of it, and for that reason, it doesn't become an obsession,
or
B. people try hard enough not to think of a white bear that they eventually succeed?

578. However, our young mother who has the image of stabbing her baby is not so fortunate. She's not easily able to say to herself, "It's no big deal." She is thinking something much more like, "This is terrible that this thought goes through my mind! I desperately wish for it to disappear!" The desperate need for the thought to go away paradoxically keeps it recurring.

Various other obsessions are like this in that they seem to be perpetuated by the desire not to think them. Here's another example. A very religious person has the thought come into his head that "God is evil." He immediately feels very guilty, because he feels he is committing blasphemy against the Holy Spirit. These thoughts are very upsetting, and the more the person tries to banish them from consciousness, the more they return to consciousness.

In the example of the young mother and the very religious person, the thoughts that intruded repeatedly caused them

A. great guilt,
or
B. mostly pleasure?

579. A father of two children parks on the top floor of a big parking garage in a city and the image comes to his mind of jumping off the building to his death. He pictures his children left without a father. He feels great grief and guilt just from the image. He is so repulsed by this idea that he tries very hard to banish it from his mind and it becomes an obsession.

The emotional reaction the father had to his thoughts was

A. similar to that of the young mother and the very religious person,
or
B. very different from that of the young mother and the very religious person?

580. Why do some people get obsessions like these and others not? The easiest explanation for all individual differences is that they are genetic. Some people do seem to be born with more of a tendency to develop obsessions than others.

Another idea is that the people who develop obsessions seem to have a stronger sense of morality and a stronger sense of shame and guilt, particularly over the content of thought, than other people do. In other words, it could be that most of humanity has "forbidden" or "taboo" thoughts flip through their minds from time to time. Those who tend to accept this as "no big deal" tend to not get obsessions, and those who are shocked and horrified by their own thoughts tend to get obsessions more.

One of the theories this section mentions is that

A. people who are frightened or repelled by taboo thoughts may get obsessions more than those who are not fazed by having those thoughts,
or
B. acceptance of your own thoughts may be increased by doing the "observing what the mind does" exercise?

The thought–behavior barrier

581. In dealing with obsessions, one of the most useful thoughts is as follows: "Just imagining this behavior does not mean that I will do it." For example, imagining a violent or immoral act does not mean that I will actually do it.

The white bear problem does not exist for behaviors as it does for thoughts. For example, the mother has to think about stabbing her child in order to check whether she is thinking about that. But obviously she does not have to do it in order to check whether she has done it.

So behaviors are very different from thoughts with respect to the white bear problem.

The main point of this section is that

A. some people think that you should focus your attention on obsessive thoughts purposely; the author doesn't agree;

or
B. imagining something doesn't mean you have to do it?

582. Someone may say, "But doesn't the fact that fantasy rehearsal helps people to do things in real life mean that it is not good to fantasy rehearse violent acts?" As a therapist, I've observed something that may be comforting to the person with obsessions: fantasy rehearsal in the absence of any motivation to change one's behavior seems not to work well.

For example, suppose someone has a habit of bullying others. A therapist prevails upon the bully to do lots of fantasy rehearsals of being kind and compassionate to those less powerful than he is. But suppose that this particular bully does not really want to become more kind and compassionate. He really enjoys dominating those less powerful. As soon as he completes the requisite number of fantasy rehearsals, he tends to go back to bullying with full force.

In like manner, the person who has the image of hurting someone go through her head many times but strongly desires not to do this is very unlikely to actually carry out the behavior.

The point of this section is that

A. fantasy rehearsals in the absence of motivation to change often don't work well in changing behavior,
or
B. fantasy rehearsals of positive behavior are often overridden by negative models on television and in movies?

583. When we do fantasy rehearsals for the purpose of building up the strength of a behavior in our repertoire, we always try to imagine feeling good about doing the behavior. This is the celebration part of fantasy rehearsal. The person who has an obsession with a taboo or unacceptable act typically does not celebrate that act, but is horrified by it. And in fact, the fear and the wish to avoid the thought really supply the emotional energy that sustains the obsession.

This section made the point that

A. an obsession of a forbidden action usually does not include the celebration part of the fantasy rehearsal,
or
B. the author recommends doing the "celebrations exercise" at least once a day?

584. When overcoming obsessions, it is extremely useful to have as much

confidence as possible in the distinction and the barrier between thought and behavior. It is also important to have behavior rather than thought as the criteria for success or for goodness of one's conduct. If I am an excellent parent, have a great relationship with my child, and am careful for that child's health and safety, I deserve to feel good about myself, even if I happen to have the propensity to obsessions and have violent images flitting through my mind frequently. Similarly, if I act very cheerful, take care of myself and others, and intend to continue taking good care of myself well, then I don't want to let it worry me too much if the image of suicide flits through my imagination. Paradoxically, the less bothered I can be by these thoughts, the less they will tend to recur.

This section has to do with

A. the increase in the vividness of imagination that you can bring about with conscious practice,
or
B. using behavior, not thought, as the main criterion for goodness or morality?

The strategy of "let them run their course" while using your time well

585. So if trying very hard to push obsessional thoughts out of the mind doesn't work well, what should someone do about such thoughts? A good phrase to keep in mind regarding obsessional thoughts is to let them *run their course.* This means to let them continue without trying either to make them stop or to make them come more frequently. Letting them run their course means not trying to control these thoughts. It is either observing or ignoring them, without getting too upset about them.

In this section the author advises

A. purposely thinking obsessive thoughts over and over,
or
B. letting obsessive thoughts run their course, without trying to control them?

586. But, one may ask, what do you do while the thoughts are running their course? One of the best answers I can give is "Do the next good thing." In other words, you figure out what is the best use of your time, or at least a good used of your time, and do it, obsessions or no obsessions. Do you need to organize your desk? Do you

want to call someone and arrange a social event? Do you need to do homework? Then do it. You can do any of these things, even with some obsessive thoughts running their course in the background. Do you need to childproof your house so that your toddler will be safer? Do you need to go for a run to practice for the track meet? Do you need to sit down and organize your to-do lists? The simple strategy I advise is to figure out what you would do if you didn't have obsessions and to do that "best use of your time" anyway.

The author advises that when obsessions pop into your head, you

A. stop what you're doing and focus on the obsessive thought until you habituate to it,
or
B. choose the behavior that's your best use of time and do it, while the obsessions run their course?

Using fantasy rehearsals with obsessions

587. The desired sequence for someone who has obsessions is that when the forbidden or taboo thought comes to mind, you

1. not get too upset about it;

2. relax;

3. remind yourself that imagination and behavior are not the same thing;

4. figure out your best use of time;

5. do that behavior, letting the obsessive thoughts run their course in the background;

6. celebrate and feel good about handling the situation well.

You can practice this sequence in your imagination; such practice constitutes a coping fantasy rehearsal.

The main point of this section is that

A. the most important step in responding to obsessions is to figure out your best use of time,
or
B. you can practice the steps in dealing with obsessions by fantasy rehearsals?

588. Here's an example. A teenage boy has an obsessive image of walking into a girls' rest room at school. His fantasy rehearsal sounds like this: "I'm at school and I pass the girls' restroom. The obsessive thought of walking into the girls' restroom pops into my head. Well, I wish this

thought didn't occur to me, but it's not so horrible. At least I can control my behavior, and I'm confident that I would not actually do that behavior. The thought is irritating, but I can put up with it and let it run in the background while I go about my business. What is that business? I'm on my way to the library. I'm continuing and focusing on what I need to look up when I get there. I'm relaxing my muscles as I do so. I'm feeling relaxed and calm and not scared that I'll do something unacceptable. Now I'm in the library and I'm looking up what I need to find. The obsessive thoughts are still going in and out of my mind, but that's OK; I'm accomplishing what I need to accomplish and I'm feeling good about that. And I feel good about the overall way in which I've handled this challenge."

The purpose of this section was to

A. give an example of a coping fantasy rehearsal of handling obsessive thoughts,
or
B. explain several ways in which obsessions are different from compulsions?

589. Here's an example of what a mastery fantasy rehearsal would sound like: "I'm at school, and the image of walking into the girl's bathroom comes to mind again, but it doesn't bother me at all. I keep on with what I'm doing; I don't get distracted. I feel fine. It's no big deal. Now it's an hour or two later and I realize that it just came into my mind and went out quickly, without distracting me at all! This experience was just like those that many people often have, where taboo thoughts come and go without attracting much notice. I celebrate that."

In this mastery fantasy rehearsal, the person imagined

A. not having any taboo thoughts at all, ever,
or
B. having a taboo thought come and go without getting worried about it?

Obsessions and the fear of losing control

590. What's the connection between obsessions and compulsions, on the one hand, and anxiety and aversions, on the other? First, people who get anxiety also tend to get obsessions or compulsions. Second, obsessions and compulsions very much depend, for their existence, on anxiety and aversions. People do compulsions in order to reduce the pain of a fear or aversion that they feel. For example,

someone does a hand washing compulsion to reduce an unrealistic aversion to the possibility of contamination. With obsessions, the unrealistic fear or the very large aversion is often an aversion to the obsessive thought itself.

This section seeks to explain

A. how trouble getting work done is sometimes due to a work aversion,
or
B. why anxiety and aversions are connected with obsessions and compulsions?

591. Sometimes the unrealistic fear that energizes obsessions is the fear of "Losing control." Or this fear may be expressed as the fear of "going crazy." The person fears that a forbidden thought's popping into the mind is a signal that he or she is "losing control." The lack of control over one's thoughts is seen as evidence for this. Loss of control is particularly scary because it brings up the fear of doing the forbidden act that's the subject of the obsession.

This section says that

A. some thoughts that keep recurring have a pleasant aspect as well as a fearful aspect,
or

B. obsessions are scary because it's hard to control them, and a "loss of control" brings up the fear of going crazy and doing something crazy?

592. Fortunately, most of the people who have big fears of going out of control or going crazy have never once in their lives gone out of control or gone crazy, and the best predictor of future behavior is past behavior.

In addition, people with the "cautiousness genes" responsible for anxiety and obsessive-compulsive problems very seldom carry out one of the forbidden behaviors that they are obsessing about, partly because of that innate caution.

Thus in almost all cases, fortunately, the fear of losing control and doing the horrible act that is obsessed about is an unrealistic fear.

The author states in this section that

A. the people who are cautious enough to be greatly troubled by their taboo thoughts are almost always cautious enough not to enact them,
or
B. not all unwanted recurrent thoughts are obsessions?

593. Sometimes people with obsessions think to themselves, "I have thoughts that pop into my head, without my being able to control them.

Therefore, I don't have control of myself, and therefore there's great danger that I'll lose control of my behavior and do something crazy!"

Fortunately, and reassuringly, there's a flaw in this reasoning. Our brains are constructed so that we have less control over our thoughts than our behaviors. We are built to have random thoughts pop into our heads lots of the time. We have many, many more options pop into our minds than we ultimately act on. The fact that we can't keep certain thoughts from popping into our heads does NOT imply that we can't control what deliberate acts we do with our muscles.

What's the point of this section?

A. People who have used exposure and ritual prevention have successfully made their brain scans look like those of people without compulsions.

or

B. The fact that we can't tightly control our thoughts does not imply that we need to fear losing control of our behaviors.

Varieties of recurrent thoughts

594. The distinction between obsessions and compulsions is not as clear-cut as we might hope it would be. It would be simple if we could say that a compulsion is something you act out with your muscles and an obsession is something that you think without someone being able to see you. However, there are some invisible actions that are more like compulsions than obsessions. An example of these "invisible compulsions" is counting compulsions. For example, someone gets the urge to keep counting until a multiple of 50 has been reached. When the multiple of 50 is reached, there is some short-term relief. But then the discomfort starts back again, and the person thinks that maybe a multiple of 100 will better get rid of the uncomfortable feeling. Again, the short-term relief reinforces not only the counting, but also the channeling of "free floating anxiety" into the idea that "I haven't counted to the right number yet." Thus the counting is repeated.

The thing that, according to this section, keeps the counting going is

A. the attempt to stop counting, as in the white bear problem,

or

B. the relief that reaching the right number gives, thus reinforcing the counting?

269

595. Even though the counting may be totally silent and invisible, this fits the pattern of compulsions more than the one we just talked about for obsessions. The emotional engine supplying the energy for the counting compulsion is the relief that the counting gives, whereas the source of energy for the obsessions with forbidden thoughts is the horror and repulsion that the thoughts provoke.

With invisible compulsions such as this one, the usual best strategy is to use exposure and ritual prevention just as with visible compulsions. In other words, the person purposefully stops counting, even though he has ended up on an unfavorable number. He notes his SUD level and relaxes while waiting for the SUD level to go down and for habituation to occur. He practices self-talk along the lines of "Hooray, I'm doing exposure; this is an example of self-discipline and courage."

In this section the author advises the person with a counting compulsion to

A. let the counting run its course, or
B. purposely stop counting on an unfavorable number, and wait for the SUD level to decrease?

596. Another variety of recurrent thoughts is fantasies that are pleasurable, though somewhat taboo. The engine driving these thoughts is the pleasure they afford, although the wish to drive them out of the mind and the white bear problem may be mixed in also.

For example: a boy encounters bullies, critical teachers, and miscellaneous rude people, and has violent or destructive revenge fantasies. In fantasy, the offending people get what the boy feels they deserve, and the fear of their future actions is relieved. Thus two sources of pleasure reinforce the fantasies: the delight in revenge and the relief of fear.

The revenge fantasies discussed in this section are driven by

A. the white bear problem (i.e. the wish to get them out of mind is so strong that they are brought to mind), or
B. the pleasure of revenge and the relief of fear?

597. For revenge fantasies, I recommend trying to substitute "prosocial power fantasies." For example: rather than imagining myself burning down the house of the boy who offended me, I imagine that it is years from now and I am a great surgeon, and he comes to me to get an operation for a family member, and he

apologizes for bullying me. Or I imagine that I get one hundred percent correct on a big test, and he looks at me with envy. Or I imagine that I am hugely wealthy and am funding a new school for kids that have problems with bullies, and I speak about how I was once bullied in school. In each of these fantasies there is an element of revenge, but also positive, prosocial action.

In this section the author advises that

A. people with revenge fantasies try to get rid of the revenge motive altogether,
or
B. people with revenge fantasies try the alternative of "prosocial power fantasies?"

598. What if unwanted thoughts are complex mixtures of these? What if you can't figure out whether they recur because of an element of pleasure, or because of the white bear problem?

     In that case, it makes sense to first do an experiment, and try to stop thinking the thoughts (and think something else instead, including prosocial power fantasies). If that doesn't work, and trying to stop the thoughts only makes them come back with greater frequency, then it makes sense to let the thoughts "run their

course in the background" while doing the best use of time you can think of.

The author advises that if you can't tell whether unwanted thoughts keep coming because of some pleasure or because of the white bear problem,

A. you keep analyzing and looking inside yourself until you find the answer,
or
B. you do an experiment to see whether it's possible to stop thinking the thoughts and think something else; if that doesn't work, let the thoughts run their course while doing your best use of time?

Two very different ways of using fantasy rehearsal with obsessions

599. When obsessions consist of forbidden thoughts, some therapists advise prolonged exposure to the images in those forbidden thoughts in order to desensitize oneself to them – to make them less scary. For example, a person who has an obsession about doing something violent would do prolonged exposure to the forbidden violent fantasy, using very graphic images. This is often very painful. Some people flee from therapy when they are asked to do this.

My preferred strategy is different. I believe that the aversive situation to practice with is not "I am doing or have done something violent." The aversive situation is, "The image of doing something violent has come into my mind." The two situations are very different. Practice handling the second one is less painful and more in keeping with one's value system than practicing the first one.

The way in which the author's preferred practice with obsessions differs from some others is that he

A. advises more prolonged exposure, or
B. advises fantasy rehearsal not of committing the violent or sexual or otherwise forbidden acts themselves, but of dealing with the situation, "I have had unwanted images go through my mind."

600. Let's look at an example of the very important distinction I'm making. Suppose that someone has obsessive thought where the image of suicide comes into his mind. This is very scary to him. The strategy I don't like would be to ask him to imagine himself committing suicide, to try to make this image less threatening. But what's the point of practicing with the image of actually harming oneself, if

he is never going to deal with that situation? And the principle of fantasy rehearsal is to practice desirable behaviors, not undesirable behaviors.

For someone with an obsession with a suicidal image, the author feels that

A. you have to get used to the forbidden images in all their graphic detail, to turn down the engine that drives the obsession, or
B. it doesn't make sense to fantasy rehearse doing actions that you think are very bad to do?

601. The strategy I do like is where the person fantasy rehearses handling precisely the situation he is dealing with, that is the situation where the thought of suicide has come into his mind. He starts his fantasy rehearsal by describing the situation: "I'm feeling lonely, and the thought of suicide passes through my mind." Then he practices thinking desirable thoughts: "This is not awful, because I have the power to choose. My goal is not to let it distract me much from what I want to do. I think I'll choose to invite someone to get together with me, because I'm feeling lonely. If that doesn't work out, I'll get some work done." Then he practices the desired feelings: "I feel annoyed by this image, but I also feel determined to

make a success experience of this. And I feel proud of the plans I've made." Then he rehearses the behaviors: "I'm letting the thoughts run in the background while I extend an invitation and get some work done." Finally, he celebrates: "I feel proud of myself for not letting this get me down, and for doing useful things despite having this thought!"

In using fantasy rehearsal with obsessions in this way, the way the author likes, the person is practicing handling the situation of

A. committing suicide,
or
B. having the thought of suicide go through his mind?

602. In dealing with obsessions, you want to aim toward responding to unwanted thoughts the way non-obsessive people do. That non-obsessive response to mental images of forbidden behaviors is not to stop everything and focus on them (an action consistent with their being a "big deal") but simply to keep going about your business (an action consistent with their being "no big deal.")

It's good to keep in mind that you're trying to reduce the aversion to having forbidden images go through your mind, not your aversion to

committing a violent or destructive or otherwise unwise act.

What's the main point of this section?

A. The eventual goal is to handle unwanted thoughts by not letting them distract you too much from your goal-directed activity.
or
B. Ethics is the study of what sorts of actions are right and good, and the study of how to make good choices.

603. Despite the fact that your goal is not to let obsessive thoughts pull you away from doing good and wise behaviors, it is wise to invest time into fantasy rehearsals of handling obsessions.

So I recommend logging in a fair amount of time imagining that an obsessive thought has come to mind, and then imagining yourself going about your business of doing the next wise thing while the obsessive thought either goes away or runs its course in the background. I think that this is likely to be a better use of time than purposely running the obsessive thought through your mind over and over in graphic detail. It is surely a better use of time than trying hard, and failing, to keep the obsessive thought out of your mind!

The author feels that the most useful
anti-obsession strategy is

A. imagining getting the obsessive
thought, not letting it bother you, and
doing the next wise thing while the
obsessive thought runs its course in
the background,
or
B. purposely imagining in graphic
detail the worst example of the
obsessive thought that you possibly
can, at great length, so as to habituate
to the image?

Chapter 17: Getting Sleep and Rest

604. If you have trouble getting to sleep, staying asleep, and/or waking up and staying awake, you're not alone. Difficulty sleeping is one of the most common complaints which people present to doctors.

Trouble sleeping is also often a contributor to other problems people have: irritability, bad moods, lower mental efficiency, and even, according to some studies, overeating.

This section makes the point that

A. some sleeping pills can cause problems with memory,
or
B. trouble sleeping is an extremely common problem?

605. Many people want a pill that will solve their sleeping problems. In this book, I don't want to go into all of what could be said about various sleeping pills and their possible risks and benefits. To make a long story short, however, lots of research indicates that most sleeping pills don't help very much, and they also can create either physical or psychological dependency. Dependency means that someone becomes unable to sleep well without the pill. Physical dependency occurs when the withdrawal from the pill results in effects on the brain that keep someone awake. Psychological dependency means, for example, that people think that they can't sleep without the pill, and this belief makes them nervous when they go to bed without having taken it.

Despite these risks, there are circumstances when sleeping pills are useful. But in my opinion, they should be a last resort, after the non-pharmacological techniques of this chapter have gotten a thorough try.

One of the points of this section is that

A. watching television while in bed is a bad idea,
or
B. people should try the nonpharmacological methods of this chapter before trying sleeping pills?

606. For many people, the bed becomes a scary place to be, because they have come to associate it with tossing and turning and worrying. Sometimes these worries are about life problems, and sometimes the worries are about the specific problem of "Oh no, I can't get to sleep."

Life is too short to spend much of it in this way. That's why the first rule is: if being in bed remains unpleasant for you for several minutes, get out of bed. If there are worries, I recommend writing about them and letting writing assist you in decision-making, as was discussed in the chapter on worrying. If there are not worries, but just a feeling of being wide awake, I recommend doing some not-very-exciting work, such as cleaning up one's room, organizing a closet, organizing papers, reading a school textbook, or perhaps reading one of the books I've written!

The advice in this section is that if you are not enjoying being in bed,

A. you should not allow yourself to get out, so that you will habituate to the situation,
or
B. you should get out bed and do some writing on decisions or some not-very-exciting work?

607. Why is it better to do some not-very-exciting work rather than something really fun and interesting, such as watching a great movie? One reason is that you don't want your brain to be very greatly reinforced for waking up or failing to get to sleep. If your habitual thought is, "If I can't find myself spending unpleasant time in bed, I have some boring work to look forward to," your brain might decide to put you back to sleep or let

you enjoy your waking time in bed, just to avoid having to do the work.

This section tells you that it's good to do unexciting things when you wake up because

A. you don't want to mess up your circadian rhythm much by getting too excited,
or
B. you don't want to reward yourself too much for finding it unpleasant to lie in bed awake?

608. We've just reviewed the advice of getting out of bed if you find it unpleasant to lie in bed awake. However, a second piece of advice is to learn to enjoy lying in bed awake, having pleasant, calming fantasies and being deeply relaxed. One way to do this is to use the relaxation techniques discussed in the chapter on relaxation, especially the "pleasant dreams exercise." The pleasant dreams exercise consists in making up pleasant fantasies of calmness, kindness, beauty, and security, which can spin on without end.

The advice in this section is to

A. get out of bed if you're not sleeping, whether you're enjoying it or not,
or

276

B. learn to spend very enjoyable time in bed in a half-awake, drifty, relaxed state?

609. There are several reasons for learning to enjoy lying awake in bed. First, it's normal for everyone to take a while to fall asleep, and to wake up occasionally during a night's sleep; if you can enjoy that waking time, rather than fearing it, you'll be much more likely to drift off to sleep. Second, even if you spend a fair amount of time in bed awake during the time you're in bed, if you can get deeply relaxed and peaceful, you'll still be fairly refreshed when the morning comes. Third, since everyone spends some time lying awake in bed, it's better to enjoy it than to hate it!

The purpose of this section is to give you

A. step-by-step instructions on how to learn to enjoy lying in bed awake,
or
B. three reasons why it's good to learn to enjoy lying in bed awake?

610. Many, many people find themselves in vicious cycle that goes like this. They find themselves lying in bed awake, not enjoying the time. They come to dread more time of lying awake in bed. The fear and dread of such time causes arousal, which works against both falling asleep and getting good rest. Thus they spend more time awake in bed, which increases their dread, and so on.

Eliminating the fear of sleeplessness is thus one very important goal in improving the quality of your time in bed. If you go to bed knowing that when you are not asleep, you can either get up and do something useful or spend enjoyable and restful time relaxing in bed, you have reason not to fear sleeplessness. You are freed from the vicious cycle of the fear of sleeplessness.

The main point of this section is to

A. explain why the two tips given previously can help you stay out of a vicious cycle,
or
B. introduce a new tip on how to improve your sleep and rest?

611. For anyone with difficulties sleeping, the relaxation techniques described in the chapter on relaxation become doubly important. I would recommend practicing each of these techniques that appeals to you both during the day, while sitting in a chair and remaining awake, and while lying in bed at night.

The main advice of this section is

A. be aware of whether you are clenching your jaw while lying in bed, or

B. practice the relaxation techniques described in a previous chapter, both during the day and while lying in bed at night?

612. The next important tip is to monitor your self-talk while you are lying in bed. If you are saying things to yourself that would be expected to make you upset, worried, excited, or scared, be aware of these thoughts, and consider revising them. For example: someone notices herself thinking, "Oh my gosh. I'm still awake. What if I can't get to sleep? I'm going to be a wreck tomorrow. This is awful." It's very hard to either get to sleep or get some peaceful rest while thinking things like this. She'll feel better if she can switch to thinking things like, "People have worked all night and all the next day, and have been OK. If I relax deeply, I'll be more refreshed than those people, even if I don't get to sleep at all. I know I can put myself into a state of deep relaxation, because I've done it many times before. It will feel very pleasant to lie here relaxed."

The main point of this section is

A. get lots of exercise during the day, or

B. monitor your self-talk while you are lying in bed, and change it if that's a good idea?

613. The next important tip on sleep and rest is to try to stay in a steady rhythm, where you go to sleep and wake up at about the same time, day after day.

Why is this important? Because your brain contains some cells that act like a clock. This clock-like part of your brain causes you to get sleepy and to wake up around a certain set time. How does the brain know what time to get sleepy and to wake up, on any given day? It knows this largely by a pattern's having been set up in the previous days.

Suppose someone goes to bed night after night at 2 in the morning and wakes up at 11 a.m. He sleeps very well on this schedule. Then suppose he wants to wake up at 6:45 a.m., because of a test at 8 a.m. He goes to bed at 9:45 p.m. What's likely to happen? He is likely to lie in bed, wide awake, for a long time. Then he finally falls asleep, and in the midst of a deep sleep, the alarm rings. It is extremely difficult and unpleasant for him to get out of bed, and he feels like a "walking zombie" for most of the morning.

The person in this example

A. couldn't get to sleep well, and also woke up early without getting back to sleep,
or
B. had trouble falling asleep, but then had trouble waking up from a deep sleep the following morning?

614. What's the matter with this person? Does he have an illness that causes a sleep disorder? No – his sleep clock is working just fine; the problem is that it's set at the wrong times (or that he's taking the test at the wrong time, however you want to look at it.)

Let's imagine that he's going to have several 8 a.m. tests. If he wants to be at best performance for the next one, he needs to reset his sleep rhythm for at least several days, if not several weeks, before the test. He needs to start going to bed earlier and getting up earlier, until the clock inside his brain has been reset to the 9:45 pm to 6:45 schedule.

The person in the example above

A. has something wrong with the clock in his brain that makes him sleep at the wrong time,
or
B. has a clock that works well, but needs to be gradually reset?

615. The rhythms set by the clock in your brain that make sleep and waking recur about every 24 hours are called circadian rhythms. The word *circadian* means about daily.

There are four "clock-resetters," or stimuli that tend to change circadian rhythms. We've already talked about a very important one: getting out of bed, or going to bed. The other three are bright light, exercise, and eating. Each of these three, plus being out of bed, tell the brain, "It's daytime! It's time to be awake!" Bright light, exercise, eating as soon as you get up, and getting up earlier, tend to set the sleep clock earlier. Bright light, exercise, and eating later in the evening, and going to bed later, tend to set the sleep clock later.

If you know these four things that make sleep rhythms get set earlier or later, you can use them to get your sleep rhythm set where you want it. But it takes time and some self-discipline to move your sleep rhythm.

The stimuli that set sleep rhythms earlier or later are

A. cold, heat, and mental calculation,
or
B. bright light, exercise, eating, and being out of bed?

616. Our prehistoric ancestors didn't have so much temptation to disrupt their sleep rhythms. When night came,

and only torches or fires or the moon could give light, there was not much to do but sleep. But with the invention of candles and lanterns, and especially with the invention of electric lights, a social "night life," where the action is only beginning at 10 pm and lasts sometimes till 2 am or later, became possible. Late-night television, sleepovers that don't feature sleep, all-nighters when big papers are due, all night conversations, and even all night parties for children, are now temptations that are very difficult to resist. If people want to keep a steady sleep rhythm in our age, they need to use a great deal of self-discipline to do so.

The author's main point in this section is that

A. it's wonderful that we are freed from the restrictions on our activity that occurred before electric lights, or
B. since the invention of the electric light, keeping a steady sleep rhythm requires self-discipline?

617. For most people with sleep problems, the unfortunate news is that you can't have your cake and eat it too. You can't often do lots of things that keep you up late, and expect to be able to shift your sleep rhythm several hours earlier whenever you feel like it.

You have to choose: do you want the late night activities, or do you want the morning activities? When do you want your standard bedtime and wake-up time to be? A large portion of sleep difficulties comes from our wish to have it both ways, to be able to sleep just fine without *any* standard bedtime and wake-up time.

The message of this section is

A. if you want the soundest sleep, you have to pick a standard bedtime and an awakening time, and give up most of what goes on between those times, or
B. it is easier to reset your sleep clock to be later than to reset it to be earlier?

618. If you're trying to reset your sleep rhythm earlier, and there's not very bright sunlight out when you wake up, you might consider investing in an electric light bright enough to reset your sleep rhythm. Several companies, among them the Sun Box Company, Uplift Technologies, and Northern Lighting, market lights bright enough to reset circadian rhythms but not harmful to the eyes. When setting your sleep rhythm earlier, you can expose yourself to bright light as soon as you get out of bed, while you are eating breakfast, getting your things together, getting dressed, and/or exercising. Half an

hour of bright light in the morning, especially combined with some aerobic exercise and breakfast, moves the sleep rhythm earlier faster than just rolling out of bed and trying to be about your business.

The main point of this section is

A. if sleep rhythms are a problem for you, you probably should invest in a bright light and use it first thing in the morning,
or
B. it's important not to use bright light late at night if you're wanting to set your sleep rhythm earlier?

619. Here's the next tip for good sleep: try to get so much exercise during the day that you are really tired when bedtime comes. For most people this will require an hour or more of moving vigorously. It's good not to do this just before going to bed, because many people find that exercise late at night can activate them and interfere with going to sleep.

Again, our prehistoric ancestors didn't have the same problem most of us do. In prehistoric times, life probably consisted of foraging for food most of people's waking hours. Only relatively recently in human history have people begun to sit in chairs for most of the day and manipulate information rather than

walking around and moving things. The sleep mechanisms of most people haven't evolved enough yet that we can sit around all day and sleep really well all night.

The tip given in this section is

A. avoiding the exercise that comes from football, boxing, or hockey may be helpful to your brain, because your head doesn't get knocked around so much,
or
B. getting more exercise improves sleep quality for most people?

620. Here's the next tip. This one is connected to choosing a standard bedtime and wake-up time. Do some experimenting to find out how many hours of sleep and rest lead to your best functioning, and set your standard times accordingly.

People vary in their sleep requirements. Some adults need 10 hours of sleep to be at their best, whereas a few seem to do fine on 6 hours. How do you tell whether you are getting enough? If you are not falling asleep or sleepy during the day, that's a sign you're sleeping enough at night. If you find that your brain seems to work as well and you are not more irritable on days after sleeping less than others, that's a sign that the reduced sleep may be just fine for you.

If you spend lots of time in bed not sleeping, despite having a regular rhythm and no fear of sleeplessness, that may be a clue that you can cut down your time in bed. The opposite of all these may be clues that more time in bed may make your daytime functioning better. If getting out of bed is one of the most unpleasant and difficult things you do, that's a sign that either resetting your sleep rhythm or spending more time in bed is clearly in order.

In this section the author advises choosing your standard bedtime and wake-up time

A. by looking up the number in a table,
or
B. by experimenting to see how many hours in bed let you function best?

621. Let's talk for a minute about conditioning, and conditioned associations. If you feed a hungry dog, the dog will produce saliva. If you ring a bell just before you feed the dog, after a few trials the bell will start the dog's saliva flowing, before the dog even sees or smells the food. The bell is called a conditioned stimulus, and the salivation is called a conditioned response. There is a conditioned association between the bell and salivation.

In trying to improve your sleep and rest, you want to build up a conditioned association between the situation of lying in bed in your dark room, and the response of falling asleep or at least getting pleasantly deeply relaxed.

The author feels that a goal is to build up a conditioned association between

A. ringing a bell and salivating,
or
B. lying down in your bed in the dark, and going to sleep?

622. People who are trying to overcome the fear of sleeplessness and the habit of tossing and turning in wakeful distress whenever they go to bed often benefit from setting the standard bedtime and wake-up time to a short enough interval that they are *very* sleepy when bedtime comes. When they have more of a conditioned association between the bed and resting/sleeping, they can lengthen their time in bed if they wish.

This section advises that people who are reducing a habit of tossing and turning unpleasantly should

A. increase their time in bed, so they get enough hours of sleep,
or

B. decrease their time in bed, so that they will be very sleepy when in bed and get more of an association between the bed and sleep or rest?

623. Speaking of conditioned associations between the bed and sleeping or resting, here's another important tip for those who want to sleep better. Don't spend time in or on the bed doing activities like reading, doing homework, listening to music, talking on the phone, and so forth. Don't argue with anyone with whom you share your bed or bedroom. You want lying on the bed to be a signal to you to relax and sleep. The more time you spend doing these other activities in or on the bed, the more you break up that association.

The author feels that spending lots of time talking on the phone in bed

A. is a good idea, because it makes the bed a comfortable place to be,
or
B. is a bad idea, because it breaks up the association between the bed and sleeping?

624. In the above list of things not to do in bed, I left out one of the biggest. If you want to sleep well, don't spend time in bed watching television! In fact, I believe that it is a very bad idea to have a television in a bedroom.

Producers of television shows employ very smart people who all have the goal of producing programs that a) capture your attention, and b) do not put you to sleep. Television is made for excitement and not relaxation.

The point of this section is

A. spouses should not argue with each other in bed,
or
B. it's not a good idea to watch television in bed?

625. While we're on the subject of television: scary movies and television shows can create images that interfere with getting to sleep. Many adults, as well as many more children, become afraid of predators – animals, monsters, or bad humans – as soon as they go to bed. Restricting your intake, via television, movies, and videogames, of horrible murders and assaults can reduce your brain's expectation and fear of being murdered.

The author feels that horror movies

A. are useful in exposing and habituating you to violence,
or
B. should be avoided, especially if the fear of predators tends to keep you awake at night?

626. The fear of someone attacking, kidnapping, or murdering you while you sleep is probably not just due to scary movies, but also to an evolutionary past in which murdering someone in his sleep was perhaps a convenient way to resolve conflict and dispose of enemies. However, in contemporary society, it is fortunately a very rare occurrence that someone is attacked by a stranger while sleeping. It's good to keep in mind how improbable that event is.

The author feels that the fear of being attacked while sleeping

A. was more realistic early in human history, and less often realistic now,
or
B. has never been a realistic fear?

627. The next tip is to experiment with eliminating or reducing or timing the intake of caffeine. Caffeine is present in coffee, tea, some sodas (read the labels or check the Internet to find out how much), and chocolate. One of its effects is to interfere with sleep, and it's very often used just for this reason.

If you search for the half-life of caffeine, which means the time required to eliminate half of what's in the body, you find a range of about 2.5 hours to 10 hours in healthy people.

This is a big range. For those with a 2.5 hour half-life for caffeine, if they drank a cup of coffee at 7 a.m., half of the caffeine would be left at 9:30 a.m., one-fourth left at 12 noon, one-eighth left at 2:30 p.m., and so forth, so that by 10 pm only one-sixty-fourth of the original dose would be left. However, for someone with a half-life for caffeine of 10 hours, after the same 7 a.m. dose, half would be left at 5 p.m., and one-fourth would still be left at 3 a.m.!

According to this section, if two people have a drink containing caffeine at the same time,

A. it should affect the sleep of both of them about the same,
or
B. it may affect the sleep of one of them much more than the other?

628. It's unlikely that you'll get a test to see what the half-life of caffeine is for you. But the best way to see whether controlling or eliminating the intake of caffeine will help your sleep is to do an experiment. The first step is to measure how much caffeine you've been taking in to start with. If you've been using a lot, you can't just stop using it suddenly without having some withdrawal symptoms. You gradually reduce the dose over a week or more. When you are off caffeine, you take at

least a week to see how much better you sleep.

For those who have been drinking several cups of caffeinated coffee each day, the author advises

A. immediately stopping all caffeine, or
B. tapering off caffeine gradually?

629. While we are speaking of caffeine, all people with anxiety problems should assess their caffeine intake. Too much caffeine can produce a jittery, trembling, and nervous feeling indistinguishable from anxiety. Reducing or eliminating caffeine intake can sometimes do great things for anxious feelings.

The point of this section is that

A. if you need caffeine to stay awake during the day, you're probably not sleeping enough at night, or
B. too much caffeine can cause anxiety?

630. Nightmares, or scary dreams, can greatly disrupt sleep. The subject of reducing or eliminating nightmares is big enough for its own chapter. The next chapter in this book will cover this subject in detail. But to preview, the most effective techniques for

nightmares simply represent a version of fantasy rehearsal. You rehearse, while awake, the direction you'd like your dreams to take when they start to get scary. You practice making the plots go in directions that are compatible with peaceful sleep. And the key plot turn is usually not killing your enemies, but turning them into friends – magically reforming the personality of any would-be predator. After enough practice with this during full wakefulness, you also practice it during the fantasies you have when you are half-asleep. With enough fantasy rehearsal of the desired plot lines, the plot lines of your dreams can be altered accordingly. However, this procedure only works well if you are not simultaneously importing a lot of fantasy models from scary movies and TV shows and video games.

The essential principle that will underlie the program for nightmares described in the next chapter is

A. breathing slowly enough, or
B. fantasy rehearsal?

631. Before finishing our discussion of sleeping, it's necessary to mention one other common problem. Some people don't sleep well because of sleep apnea. The word apnea means "not breathing." People with sleep

apnea often stop breathing for 15 seconds or more on several occasions during the night. After a short episode of not breathing, people tend to wake up and breathe. But the episodes of not breathing, if they occur often, can interfere greatly with the quality and quantity of sleep.

Sleep apnea means

A. breathing too fast during sleep,
or
B. not breathing for an episode during sleep?

632. There are two types of sleep apnea, called central and obstructive. Central means that the brain doesn't do a good enough job of telling the person to keep breathing. Obstructive means that some tissues in the throat obstruct the flow of air into the lungs. The second type is more common. Lots of people with obstructive sleep apnea snore very loudly. Loud snoring, particularly if other people hear the snoring stop for periods of 15 seconds or more, followed by loud catch-up breathing, may be a sign that the person should see a doctor and be evaluated in a sleep laboratory for obstructive sleep apnea.

According to this section, loud snoring, particularly if people hear it

stop for periods of time, may be a reason to get evaluated for

A. anxiety,
or
B. sleep apnea?

633. This chapter contains lots of recommendations for improving sleep. My guess is that if everyone with sleep difficulties followed each of them, a very large fraction would attain satisfactory rest on most nights, without sleeping pills. However, to follow each of these suggestions requires a great deal of self-discipline.

The author's attitude is that

A. the suggestions of this chapter are quick, easy, and sure to work fast,
or
B. the suggestions of this chapter require enough self-discipline that only a distinguished minority of people can follow them?

634. The following checklist summarizes what we've gone over in this chapter.

Checklist for improving sleep

1. If you spend more than about 20 minutes lying in bed awake in an

unpleasant way, do you get out of bed?

2. When you get out of bed because it's unpleasant to lie in bed awake, do you either write about the decision you're trying to make, or do some not-very-exciting work?

3. Are you very proficient in the relaxation techniques described in a previous chapter?

4. Can you use those relaxation techniques, especially the pleasant dreams exercise, to enjoy your time lying in bed awake?

5. Do you quickly become aware of the type of self-talk that promotes the fear of sleeplessness? Are you able to change that self-talk?

6. Do you get so much exercise during the day (not just before bed) that you are really tired by bedtime?

Which of the following has appeared on our checklist so far?

A. get proficient at relaxation techniques,
or
B. talk with your doctor if you are prescribed any medicines containing amphetamine?

635. The sleep checklist continues.

7. Have you decided upon a standard bedtime and a standard wake-up time that you would like to stick to, with few exceptions?

8. Do you have the self-discipline to avoid many of the late-night activities that would mess up your circadian rhythm?

9. If you are trying to reset your circadian rhythm, are you making best use of bright light, exercise, and eating, as well as going to bed and getting out of bed?

10. If you're trying to reset your circadian rhythm, do you have access to a light bright enough to reset your rhythm but not so bright as to hurt your eyes?

11. If you're trying to set up a conditioned association between the bed and sleeping, do you temporarily shorten your total time in bed so as to make this easier?

Which of the following was listed in this section?

A. not playing video games in bed,
or
B. sticking to a standard bedtime and wake-up time?

636. The sleep checklist continues.

12. Do you avoid reading, doing homework, arguing, talking on the phone, watching TV, and the like, while in or on your bed, so as not to break up the association between the bed and sleep?

13. Have you tried reducing or eliminating violent movies and television and video games?

14. Are you aware of the statistics on how infrequently people are attacked, kidnapped, or murdered by strangers while sleeping?

15. Are you aware of how much caffeine you typically take in?

16. If you use caffeine every day, have you tried tapering off caffeine and seeing how much your sleep is improved with no caffeine?

17. If you have nightmares, have you used the fantasy-rehearsal based methods of reducing them described in the next chapter?

18. Have you considered an evaluation for sleep apnea, especially if you snore loudly with periodic long silences?

Which of the following was included in this section?

A. Avoid napping for long periods during the day.
or
B. Don't watch TV in bed.

Chapter 18: Nightmares

637. A monster chases you; you are in a car or plane seconds before a crash; someone you loves falls from a high place; you find yourself looking at the wrong end of a loaded gun barrel with a very bad person at the other end; you are trapped in a small cave and can't get out; you are in an earthquake; a bomb is headed your direction; you are rejected and taunted by everyone you know. These are the sorts of experiences that most of us, fortunately, do not experience very often. However, some of us are unfortunate enough to experience these things vividly, and often, in our nightmares.

The main purpose of this section is to

A. furnish some examples of nightmares,
or
B. make the point that people with anxiety tend to have nightmares more often?

638. We spend a very substantial part of our lives sleeping, and a fair fraction of that sleep time is spent dreaming. Even people who don't often remember dreams usually spend time dreaming. Using an electroencephalogram, which measures the electrical activity of the brain, scientists can tell when someone is dreaming. If we don't wake up during the dream stage of sleep, we usually can't remember our dreams. Most people can report dreams if they are awakened while dreaming.

Because we spend so much of our lives dreaming, it makes sense to try to make our dream lives as pleasant as possible. Experiencing horrible things while dreaming is something we should want to change, for that reason alone.

One of the points of this section is that

A. since we spend so much time dreaming, it's worthwhile to try to make our dream lives pleasant,
or
B. although people in the past felt that dreams could foretell the future, there's no evidence of that?

639. In addition to being unpleasant, nightmares can sometimes make it harder for people to go to sleep, because they consciously or unconsciously anticipate having scary dreams. Nightmares also often wake

people up from sleep and make it hard to get back to sleep. Thus they are a cause of sleep difficulties.

This section makes the point that

A. if people dream about tense situations, they may grind their teeth more,
or
B. nightmares can be a problem by interfering with sleep?

640. People have debated for a long time about what causes dreams, and what, if anything, dreams mean. How useful is it to try to remember your dreams, and to try to figure out whether they give you any messages about yourself that you didn't already know? These are questions that this book won't tackle.

The author's point of view is that

A. dreams aren't as useful to analyze as some people think they are,
or
B. the author doesn't take on the question of how useful it is to analyze dreams?

641. But in order to reduce or eliminate nightmares, we don't need to know what, if anything, dreams mean. For our purposes, one fact about dreams is very important: they are very much influenced by what you think about and imagine during the day. If you are very worried about bad things happening, or if you see scary movies, television shows, or video games, or if scary things happen to you in real life, you are more likely to get nightmares. If you imagine very scary things, you are more likely to dream about those things.

The fact about dreams that is presented in this section is that

A. we only remember our dreams if we wake up from the dreaming state,
or
B. the content of our dreams is influenced by what we have been imagining and thinking about during the day?

Reducing or eliminating unnecessarily scary books, movies, and TV shows

642. The first tip for reducing nightmares is to reduce or eliminate whatever we can of scary experiences while awake. Most of the time real-life experiences like being in earthquakes or having someone hold you at gunpoint are not the type that you need someone to advise you to stay away from!

However, huge numbers of people subject themselves to horrible vicarious experiences through movies, television shows, video games, as well as books. The brain experiences these imaginary events in similar ways to the experience of real-life events. The horrors experienced in movies can become embedded in the memory bank and re-experienced many times during dreaming. In the interest of reducing nightmares, it makes sense to reduce the exposure to horrors through movies to a minimum.

In this section the author advises

A. reducing your exposure to horrible scenes in movies as much as possible,
or
B. making sure your house is safe, so as to protect yourself from danger?

643. The decision about whether to stay away from scary movies can be a difficult one. Often friends will provide lots of social pressure to join them at very violent movies. Often violent and frightening movies are fun, as a direct result of the excitement and arousal caused by the scary situations. Often scary situations in movies allow the characters to model courage skills, and can provide some very positive models. Sometimes scary or unpleasant scenes in movies can be very helpful to some people in habituating to the images contained in them. Sometimes the depiction of violence in movies is necessary for the anti-violence message of the author to come through.

The main point of this section is that

A. there are no good reasons to go to a scary or violent movie or read a scary or violent book,
or
B. sometimes there are good reasons to experience violent images through books or movies, and the decision about whether to avoid them can be difficult?

644. Despite the fact that there are often good reasons to experience scary stories, in today's world we tend to see many more violent or scary images than most human beings have ever seen before the invention of movies and television, even given the large amount of real-life violence that prevailed. The average child today sees thousands and thousands of murders on TV before reaching adulthood. If we were to restrict our viewing of scary and violent images to those where there is a really good reason to experience them, we would experience far fewer of these images.

The author believes that the number of scary and violent images that people watch in today's society is

A. excessive,
or
B. just about right?

645. Much of this book has promoted exposure rather than avoidance. Why do I recommend avoiding most scary images in movies, rather than exposure to them?

      The first question about a fear or aversion is, do you *want* to become desensitized to this situation? Do you want to be able to experience this with little or no negative emotion? If the experience is public speaking or taking a test or meeting strangers or being on a high floor of a building, there's no question that you would want to handle that situation comfortably. However, if the experience is seeing someone stabbed or shot or some other violent act, fear and revulsion is normal, natural, and desirable. Too many people have gotten to the point where they can see other people hurt and killed without feeling much of anything.

The reason the author doesn't advocate prolonged exposure to violence in movies is that

A. it doesn't work in eventually making people get desensitized to the image of violence,
or
B. we shouldn't want to become desensitized to violence?

646. This is an important point in dealing with nightmares. The goal is not to be able to dream about death and threats of death and experience such content as pleasant, peaceful images. The goal is to change the actual content of dreams so that you are not dreaming about murders and death and threats of death, but dreaming about kindness, calm, and beauty instead.

According to the author, the goal with nightmares is to

A. be able to visualize any image, no matter how gory or terrible, with calm and with absence of fear,
or
B. to be able to substitute images of kindness, beauty, and calm for images of death and threats of death?

The fantasy rehearsal strategy for nightmares

647. Here's how to get rid of nightmares, in a nutshell. You do fantasy rehearsals, while awake, of

creating pleasant dreams. Part of this is done with any setting or characters you want, and is the "pleasant dreams exercise" we've referred to before. Part of this is done with the settings and characters that have led to scary dreams for you in the past. But in your fantasy rehearsals, you create pleasant dreams with those settings and characters. You take control of the direction your fantasies take. You do the same thing when you are lying in bed half-asleep, having emerged from a dream. With enough practice, your dreams will go in the pleasant direction when you are asleep.

A one-sentence summary of how to get rid of nightmares is to

A. do fantasy rehearsals of pleasant dreams,
or
B. try to increase your intake of omega-3 fatty acids from foods?

648. Here's an example of someone's transforming a nightmare into a fantasy rehearsal of a pleasant dream.

Bob has had scary dreams of a big scary angry-looking person chasing him through a rocky canyon. In his fantasy rehearsal, he goes to the same rocky canyon. This time, however, he has a magical power to stop the person in his tracks, simply by pointing a finger at him. He calls the person to come and talk with him, and the person comes and sits down, knowing that Bob can stop him whenever he wants. Bob asks the person why he has been chasing him. The person replies that he can't help it; he just gets an irresistible urge to chase and try to hurt people. Bob replies that he has a magical power to cure that, and the person is very happy to take the cure. Bob points his finger, and the person is cured. The person is so grateful to Bob that he wants to help him out in any way possible. They walk around the canyon together and talk pleasantly. At the end of their time together, the person gives a gift to Bob: a magical canteen that will never run out of cool, clean water.

In this fantasy rehearsal, Bob dealt with the bad character of the dream by

A. killing him,
or
B. changing him to a good character?

649. Why is it good to change scary characters of dreams rather than to kill them, in fantasy rehearsals? One reason is that you want to eliminate killing from your dream plots. Killing should be an unpleasant event in a dream, even if you're the one doing it rather than having it done to you. Second, if you kill a bad character, the bad character's friends and relatives

will logically want to take revenge on you – the same way things are in real life! On the other hand, if you change the scary character to one who is both better and happier, you incur gratitude. Third, the strategy of learning to live in at least peaceful coexistence with one's enemies, rather than destroying them, seems to work better in real life, most of the time, for people in civilized societies.

One of the reasons given in this section for changing bad characters to good ones rather than killing them in fantasy rehearsals is that

A. having to kill someone should be a nightmare, and thus a fantasy rehearsal of killing doesn't solve the problem,
or
B. people with cautiousness genes tend to worry if they've killed the wrong person, if in their dreams they kill someone?

650. Here's another example. Joe has a dream where his daughter falls off a cliff. He wakes up from the nightmare in fear, and feels relief to find that he was only dreaming. As he settles down to go back to sleep, he revises the nightmare, in several ways. The first time the daughter goes near the cliff, but as soon as she starts to get too close to the edge, a magnet gently

pulls her back and keeps her a safe distance from the edge. The second time, he imagines that she can fly, and she has a very pleasant time flying all around.

In this example, Joe visualized pleasant alternatives to a horrible scene

A. during the day,
or
B. during the night, in bed, just after having a nightmare?

651. Here's another example. Jean dreams that she has just eaten poison, and there is no way that the poison can be removed from her body. She awakes from this nightmare. As she lies in bed, she fantasy rehearses transforming the dream. In one version, she puts her hand on her belly, and magically transforms anything harmful inside her to pure water. In another version, as soon as there is an unpleasant realization, she can reverse the course of the dream, and make the "movie" of the dream run backwards. Once it has backed up to the point where she is safe, she decides on a different course, one that is very safe and pleasant, and runs the movie forward from there.

In both of these fantasy rehearsals, as with many of the other examples of transformed nightmares the author has given so far, there is an element of

A. magic,
or
B. violence?

Why include magic in re-fantasy of nightmare situations?

652. Why do I advise creating magical solutions to problems in dream situations, when those solutions won't work in real life? Because the goal of these particular fantasy rehearsals is not so much to prepare you for real life, as to make your dream life more pleasant. With magical powers, you can rapidly get yourself out of any danger you find yourself in during the dream. Magic wouldn't be used in so many works of literature if it weren't such fun to imagine.

The purpose of this section is for the author to explain why many of the fantasy rehearsals of nightmare revisions involve

A. an exchange of gifts or kind acts,
or
B. magical powers?

653. However, I also recommend that in fantasy rehearsals of revisions of

nightmares, you use your magical powers only to help people, and not as a method of combat, deceit, exploitation, or bullying domination. With a little creativity, you can make any situation come out to a desirable ending, while still sticking to the highest principles. If there are enemies, you can either cure your enemy of an irrational wish to harm you, or you can find a mutually acceptable solution to the problem, or you can put up a magic wall that separates you from your enemy, or turn yourself invisible to your enemy. There's no need, in the dream world, to harm enemies. I think that the best solution is to turn them into friends and allies.

The author recommends using magical powers in fantasy rehearsals of revisions of nightmares

A. to get rid of one's enemies in whatever way you want,
or
B. to make yourself safe without harming anyone?

654. Here is another example. Tonya has bad dreams of bullies who corner her and intimidate her and are about to do some unknown horrible act to her, just before she wakes up.

In her fantasy rehearsal of a revision of the dream, Tonya

magically stops the bullies in their tracks. While they are frozen, as if in a video that is paused, Tonya summons lots of allies. Lots of friends, relatives, characters from novels she's read, and other powerful and good supporters magically appear at the scene. Now the action starts back again, but the bullies clearly recognize they are outnumbered. They realize that their best strategy is to be nice. They do so, and Tonya magically reinforces those nice patterns in their minds so that they become permanent.

  The general strategy, when dealing with bullies in real life, of getting as many other people on your side as possible, is often one of the most useful ones that someone can pick. It's nice when the fantasy rehearsal of the revision of the nightmare is analogous to real-life positive strategies.

The strategy that Tonya rehearsed in this fantasy rehearsal of a nightmare revision was

A. getting allies,
or
B. appealing to the rule of law?

655. What if your nightmares are reenactments of horrific things that actually did happen to you in real life? My recommendation is to use the same strategy, and to create fantasies of happier versions of the events that give you nightmares. If it's important to you not to forget which is fantasy and which is real, then write down the real version of what happened. But then you can start visualizing the same scene and the same characters, but with things happening much differently.

If someone has nightmares because of a traumatic event that happened in real life, the author advises

A. a totally different strategy,
or
B. the same strategy?

656. Here's an example. Kenneth was in an auto accident, where his dad was driving. In real life, Kenneth experienced horror at seeing a car approach them from the side he was sitting on, and pain when broken glass cut him in the face, and a great deal of fear after that before he could finish getting the medical attention he received. He often has nightmares of this event.

  After writing down exactly what happened, Kenneth starts to fantasy rehearse revisions of this scary memory. In the first version, the car that is approaching him has a big spring on the front of it; the spring compresses and expands, with the result that the oncoming car safely bounces off with a sound of "boing." There are other similar versions with Styrofoam and foam rubber rather than a spring.

This section presents an example of

A. refantasy of a nightmare caused by a movie,
or
B. refantasy of a nightmare caused by a memory of a real-life traumatic event?

657. Then Kenneth fantasy rehearses another version: the car approaches, but Kenneth has the magical power to make the oncoming car go up into the air. The car sails over them, lands safely on the other side, and both cars go on their way.

In a third version, the car approaches, but Kenneth has the magical power to make the brakes on the other car work super-well. The car screeches to a halt and stops 6 inches from the side of Kenneth's car.

This section gives examples of

A. refantasy of a nightmare, making magical changes so that a happy ending takes place,
or
B. increasing self-discipline by staying in the habit of keeping resolutions one has made?

658. In a fourth version, Kenneth has himself driving the car, and he is able to notice the other car coming from the side, stop, and wait to let the car pass by. The traumatic event in this version becomes a non-event because of his anticipation of the other driver's move.

In a fifth version, Kenneth envisions that the same thing happened that happened in real life. Only this time, everything from the wreck until the total healing of his cuts is run in a super-fast video that takes less than a second; the video is then run backwards and forwards a few times.

Kenneth experiments with all these different versions. He finds that all of them are much more pleasant than the original memory. He also finds that the original memory loses the power to make him feel so bad as he fantasizes more revisions of it. And finally, he finds that the nightmares of the wreck become fewer and father between.

The main point of this section, and the previous two, is that

A. you can use the same technique, of fantasy rehearsal of revisions of nightmares, when you are reacting to a real-life traumatic event,
or

B. one type of revision suggests another, as for example when a "spring" revision suggests a "foam rubber" revision?

659. If you want the most effective strategy for nightmares, you won't just wait for nightmares and revise them. Instead, you'll fantasy rehearse the types of images you would like to dream about, in large number and wide variety. In other words: you'll do the following strategies, which were described in the chapter on relaxation and meditation:

the pleasant dreams exercise,
visualizing relaxing scenes,
visualizing acts of kindness,
the good will meditation,
and the psychological skills meditation.

This section advises

A. lots of practice revising nightmares,
or
B. lots of practice with pleasant dreamlike images that were not derived from nightmares?

660. If you need to "prime the pump" with some examples of kind acts and psychologically skilled acts, the vignettes in my book *Illustrated Stories That Model Psychological Skills* and the stories at the beginning of *Programmed Readings for Psychological Skills* may fill the bill. Images of kindness, relaxation, and beauty seem to be more abundant in literature written for children than that written for adults. (Very scary and violent images are also present in lots of children's books!) If you search for pleasant images and purposely import them into your memory bank, you stand to make your dream world a more pleasant place to spend a good part of your life!

The point of this section is to advise that the reader

A. make up fantasies of kindness, beauty, and calm,
or
B. read fantasies of kindness, beauty, and calm that other people have written, especially in children's literature?

Chapter 19: Work Block and Procrastination

661. A student has worked very hard and has paid thousands of dollars to go to school, but in order to get her degree, she has to write a long paper. She puts off the writing, and she just can't bring herself to write it. She fails to get her diploma.

A housing remodeler gets a contract to go to someone's house and do some repairs. But he starts putting off doing the work, and after a while he just can't bring himself to go. The job goes to someone else, and the remodeler makes no money.

A person has a pile of papers on her desk, with bills mixed in. But she puts off tackling this paperwork. Eventually she gets charged large penalties for failing to pay her bills on time.

Procrastination is a very large problem for many, many people. It not only results in work not being done. The conflict people feel between the wish to get work done and a very strong aversion to doing the work is very painful.

This section

A. explains why procrastination and work block take place,

or

B. gives some examples of procrastination and work block?

662. We've talked about vicious cycles several times. Here's how the vicious cycle of procrastination and work block goes:

1. Someone has some work that needs to be done.
2. The person considers doing the work, or resolves to do the work.
3. The resulting feeling is so unpleasant that the person decides to put off the work to a later time.
4. The next time the person thinks about doing the work, the resulting feeling is even more unpleasant, and it gets put off again.

What's a major idea of this section?

A. The more times a job is put off till later, the harder it is to get started on it.
or
B. What you say to yourself when you are trying to get work done is very important.

663. Why does the job get more unpleasant the more times you put it off? Do you remember our very important principle that brief exposure

299

followed by escape from a unpleasant situation tends to increase the fear or aversion connected with that situation? Let's review this idea a bit.

We used the example of a fear of being on elevators. Suppose someone gets on the elevator; then the fear becomes very unpleasant; then the person rushes off the elevator, and the fear goes way down. The part where "the fear goes way down" is a powerful reinforcer, or reward. (It's an example of "negative reinforcement.") What behavior does it follow, result from, and reinforce? It powerfully reinforces escape from the elevator. And since the emotion we call fear is very much the same as a strong urge to escape, the fear is higher next time.

What's the purpose of this section?

A. To explain how relaxation can help overcome work block.
or
B. To review how escapes from unrealistically feared situations can cause fears to grow.

664. What happens with procrastination and work block is much the same. Reaching the time when "I am supposed to do the work now" is an exposure. The strong negative feelings one has at that time are an aversion. Changing the mind and thinking, "I'll do it later," is an escape from the exposure. There is usually a great deal of relief that one feels after this escape; this reinforces the escape and makes the urge to escape even stronger the next time. In other words, the aversion to the work grows with each repetition of exposure followed by escape.

What's the purpose of this section?

A. To point out how the familiar idea, that exposure followed by escape increases aversions, applies to the procrastination problem?
or
B. To point out how important self-reinforcement is in overcoming work block?

665. How do you prevent this cycle? If you realize how each procrastination increases the degree of aversion, and how important it is not to put off unpleasant tasks in response to the unpleasantness, you can aim for the goal of avoiding the very first instance of procrastination. If you can start working on the task the very first time you are scheduled to do so, the snowball of procrastination and work block can not start rolling.

What's a summary of this section?

A. Getting very skilled at writing tends to make work block on writing tasks less likely.

or

B. If you're very aware of the vicious cycle we've been talking about, you can prevent it's getting started by working hard the very first time you've scheduled yourself to start.

666. What if you're already in the midst of work block? Then the central principle of prolonged exposure applies. You simply make a reasonable goal and get to work, noting how high your SUD level is. (SUD level is "subjective units of distress," or how bad you feel on a 0 to 10 scale.) An example of a "reasonable goal" is, "I will work for one hour, or until I finish the next section, whichever comes first." Keep working, and see if your SUD level falls. Quit working based on goal achievement, not based on how good or bad you feel.

Why do you think the author advises quitting work when you've achieved a goal rather than quitting when you feel very tired of working?

A. Because quitting working is a reinforcer, and you want it to reinforce goal achievement rather than reinforcing work aversion.

or

B. Because it's a good idea to speak to yourself with calm, but determined, tones of voice while you are working?

667. The other principles that we've discussed in overcoming fears and aversions also apply to work block and procrastination. The following sections give some examples.

Jean is trying to work on a homework assignment, in which she is supposed to write a short paper. She finds herself stopped by this scary image that she will get the paper back from her teacher with a big F written at the top and some very insulting comments on the low quality of the paper. But then she thinks to herself, "How likely is that to happen?" She decides that the chances are fairly small. Then she thinks, "How terrible would it be, even if that did happen?" She decides that although the score would bring her grade down somewhat, it would not be devastating, and even if she failed the whole course, she would still have a good chance to live a happy and productive life.

In this example, Jean is probably reducing her fear by thinking about

A. Skill-building strategies

or

B. Probabilities and utilities?

668. As Jean sits down to write her paper, she becomes conscious of what she is saying to herself. She finds herself saying things like "That sentence is terribly awkward!" and, "That's really bad writing!" She catches herself imagining the disapproving faces of people who have read her paper. She decides to change these thoughts. She starts saying to herself things like, "Good for you! You've gotten going; that's the hardest part!" She also says things like, "Even though that sentence will need to be revised, it gets me closer to my goal!" She imagines people approving and cheering her on for the good work that she is doing. These changes make it much easier for her to get her work done.

She is now using the technique of

A. Information gathering,
or
B. Self talk and imagery?

669. Alan has some school work that he is finding himself blocked on. Alan calls up his friend Fred, who is a very serious hard worker. Allen explains his work block problem. Alan arranges to have a "work party" with Fred, in which Alan will sit silently and work on the project that he has been putting off. With the support of his friend, Alan finds it much easier to get his work done.

Alan was using the technique of

A. Getting help from one of his "allies,"
or
B. Making sure that he isn't breathing too fast?

670. Lucinda has a lump in her body that she fears could be cancer. She has the urge to procrastinate in calling to make an appointment with her doctor. The very idea of calling for an appointment makes her feel quite scared. However, she picks up the phone and calls and makes the appointment. The whole time, she feels scared, and she even feels scared after she made the appointment. But she thinks to herself, "What's important is not whether I feel scared. What's important is that I make the appointment and that I keep it, and that I get an answer to the question of how serious this problem is."

In this example Lucinda is considering

A. Probabilities and utilities
or
B. Doing, rather than feeling, as the criterion for success?

671. During her first year of high school, Teresa experiences a great deal of work block on written assignments. In the summer between freshman and sophomore year, she decides that she will help herself by becoming a much better writer. She devises a course for herself wherein she gets lots of practice writing. She also reads several books on how to be a good writer, and does the exercises in them.

The technique that Teresa is using to reduce her fear and aversion is

A. Skill-building,
or
B. Relaxation techniques?

672. In the course that Teresa teaches herself, she starts out with "free writing." This means that she simply writes whatever comes to her mind without worrying about the quality of what she is writing. Next, she practices writing journal entries, where she simply talks about what she has experienced during the day. Both of these are quite easy for her. She gradually works her way up to more difficult writing, where she is writing a story as well as she can write it, or an article to submit for publication. She devises a series of steps from easiest to hardest, and if the going gets too unpleasant, she drops back to a slightly easier task.

This section illustrates the technique of

A. Moving gradually along the hierarchy of difficulty,
or
B. Paying attention to self-talk and imagery?

673. Jane has to look through a bunch of records in order to prepare a tax return. She has to dig up lots of financial information that isn't stored in a very organized way. She makes an appointment with herself to start this task at a certain time. As she is riding the bus home, she closes her eyes and relaxes, and that visualizes herself doing this task. She visualizes it in two ways. First, she visualizes that she gets to work and accomplishes a lot and feels very good from start to finish about what she's doing. In the second fantasy, she imagines that it is hard to get herself to work and the task is not very pleasant, but she continues it with self-discipline anyway. Finally, when she gets home, she enacts the patterns that she had rehearsed in her imagination.

Jane used the technique of

A. Getting allies,

or
B. Fantasy rehearsal?

674. Frank intends to do a lot of studying for an exam at home. But when he gets home, he enjoys hanging out with his housemates. His housemates turn on the television, and he gets hooked into watching a show, and then another. His housemates sit around the table eating and talking for a while after that, and he joins them just to be sociable. He realizes that he is using these activities to procrastinate instead of studying for his exam.

The next day, he decides that he will try a new environment. He goes to the library, and sits down at a table where a bunch of other students are studying quietly. He joins them with the same activity, and gets lots accomplished. He decides to go to the library often, to do his work.

The idea that Frank used in this situation was

A. Fantasy rehearsal (or practicing things in your mind)
or
B. Stimulus control (or arranging the environment so as to bring out the behaviors you want to do more of.)

675. Jack runs his own business. He tends to procrastinate on billing and bill collecting and writing down financial records. He decides that part of his problem is that he does not have a regular time scheduled for doing this financial work. He figures out how much total time the task needs. He decides to enter the records of each day's financial activity before he goes home from work. He marks in his schedule one hour each week, the same time each week, to do his billing.

Jack is taking advantage of a special case of stimulus control, which is called

A. establishing a regular routine,
or
B. using a hierarchy of difficulty?

Chapter 20: The Stress of Time Pressure

676. Time pressure is a major source of stress and anxiety.

A student in high school is taking lots of very demanding courses, with lots of homework. The student also feels the need to do lots of extracurricular activities, to impress college admissions people. As a result, life becomes a constant struggle to finish one assignment after another, to work faster and more accurately, and to try to get by on as little sleep as possible. There is a backdrop of anxiety almost all the time. In my opinion, life is too short to choose this sort of life style when there is an alternative.

The author's apparent attitude toward the life style where a student is struggling with constant time pressure is that

A. this is exactly what we need if our students are going to compete in the global work force,
or
B. this is a life style that is unnecessarily stressful?

677. But sometimes the stress of too much to do in too little time is unavoidable. For example, someone searches for months to find a job, and she is overjoyed to finally find one.

But then the person finds that once on the job, she has to meet with one person after another, fill out all sorts of forms and write reports on each meeting she has, and answer phone calls with more people wanting her to do things. Meanwhile her supervisors are constantly pressing for more "productivity" and are very angry if any of the forms or reports is not done exactly right.

The purpose of this section was to

A. give another example of a situation that causes stress from time pressure, or
B. tell one solution to the problem of stress from time pressure?

678. There are a few possible solutions to the problem of time pressure. They are:

1. Take on fewer commitments (also known as, "Don't bite off more than you can chew.")
2. Cut out some activities that are relative time-wasters.
3. Learn to work faster or more efficiently.
4. Learn to relax more and worry less while working and in between working times.

5. Accept lower quality in certain parts of your work.

The purpose of this section is to

A. present possible solutions to the problem of time pressure,
or
B. try to understand why schools and workplaces create such time pressure?

679. Frida recognizes that she is feeling so much stress from time pressure that she doesn't enjoy life much. She makes a list of all the courses that she is taking and the musical activities she is doing and sports she is playing. She numbers them in order from most valuable to least valuable. She simply resigns from the least valuable activities so that she can relax more and have more time for the other activities.

The solution Frida uses is to

A. reduce commitments,
or
B. accept lower quality in certain areas of her work?

680. Benny, a student, loses lots of sleep because writing assignments take him a very long time to complete. When he gets a vacation from school, he spends some concentrated time working on writing. He practices typing, grammar, organizing thoughts, and coming up with compositions quickly. He gradually gets faster and faster at writing. He finds that when he goes back to school, he is under less stress.

The strategy Benny used was

A. to learn to work faster or more efficiently at something,
or
B. to cut out some activities that are relative time-wasters?

681. Agnetha is under lots of time pressure. She makes a record for a few days of how she is spending her time. She finds that she is spending a good amount of time on Facebook. She decides that even though this is fun and it connects her with friends, she would rather spend time actually doing things with friends, like going for walks, rather than sitting and writing. So she removes herself from Facebook, spends more time in person with friends, and still has saves some time to relax and relieve the time pressure.

Agnetha used the strategy of

A. learning to relax more and worry less while working,
or

B. cutting out an activity she decided was, relatively speaking, a time-waster?

682. Pierce, a student, is in the habit of studying for each test until he is almost sure he can get 100% correct. When he writes an essay, he revises it many, many times, deliberating over the right word and the right way to express each sentence. He gets very good grades, but he decides that the quality of his life is suffering greatly. He decides not to be so perfectionistic. He studies less for tests and sometimes turns in an essay after just proofreading it once. He finds that his grades are almost as high, and that he has much more time to have fun and enjoy life.

Pierce used the strategy of

A. learning to accept lower quality in certain parts of his work,
or
B. learning to relax more and worry less while working and in between working times?

683. Amanda finds that she spends a lot of time when she isn't working, feeling tense and worried about the work she has to do. She also finds that while she is working, she worries about whether the job she is doing will be good enough. This tension and worry is sapping her of energy.

She reads what someone wrote about Gandhi, a man who led India to independence. The writer said that Gandhi worked 15 hours a day, 7 days a week, for more than 30 years, but showed no trace of being driven. He had gaiety in his eyes, and a lighthearted mood even when dealing with very difficult problems.

Amanda forms a vivid image of doing lots of work, but remaining relaxed and lighthearted while doing it and while taking any breaks from it. She gradually does more and more of what she fantasy rehearses, and is able to relieve much of the stress she feels.

Amanda used the strategy of

A. learning to relax more and worry less while working and between work times,
or
B. not biting off more than she can chew?

684. Bjorn is a college student who is playing in a band, taking a full course load, working at a store to make some money, and playing on a sports team. He decides to cut out the sports team and the work at the store, so that he can do his college work and band work well.

He also notices that he is doing a lot of awfulizing: thinking, "What if I don't finish this?" "What if this is not good enough?" "That will be terrible if that happens!" He decides to shift his thinking to less awfulizing and more goal-setting and celebrating his own choices. He thinks more thoughts like, "I want to do this well enough." "I want to work fast enough to be able to get to bed early." And, "Hooray, I did a good job on that!" "Yay, I made a good decision on how to use my time!"

What two strategies has Bjorn used?

A. learning to relax more and worry less, and reducing the number of commitments,
or
B. learning to work faster, and accepting lower quality of work?

Chapter 21: Test Anxiety

685. Some people study hard for tests, until they feel they know the subject matter thoroughly. But when the test comes, they get nervous, or freeze up, or otherwise fail to achieve peak performance. They walk out of tests feeling disappointed, and later they grimace to find that they have missed test questions that would have been easy for them at any time other than in the performance pressure situation.

This section is referring to people who

A. have simply not put in enough time studying,
or
B. have studied for enough time, but can't perform well enough during the test itself?

686. Excitement can sometimes be pleasant, and it can sometimes help you achieve your best score. It's possible to be too relaxed, not excited enough, when taking a test. But it's also possible to be too excited. The mental state you are in when you are ready to sprint away from a predator is not necessarily the mental state that will most help you come up with answers to math problems! You are seeking a level of excitement that is not too high, not too low, but just right for the particular task you are doing.

This section implies that

A. the more psyched up and excited you are, the worse will be your performance on a test,
or
B. there is a certain level of excitement that will help you do best on a test – not too high, not too low, but just the right level?

687. What do we mean by peak performance? We mean that in the situation where your performance "counts," for example the real test, you do about as well as, or better than, you have done in your best practice performances. We mean that the excitement of knowing that this is the "real thing" does not hurt your performance, and even helps it.

The main purpose of this section was to

A. define what is meant by peak performance,
or
B. make the point that too much excitement and arousal can reduce the quality of your performance?

688. The guidelines I'll present in this chapter are useful for all sorts of performances in addition to tests. Job interviews, music or drama performances, sports contests, and public speaking are all situations calling for peak performance where others are watching or monitoring your performance.

The main idea of this section is that

A. the guidelines in this chapter should help with all sorts of situations where you want peak performance,
or
B. if you want peak performance, you should teach yourself to control your own level of arousal?

689. When you take tests, peak performance means that you perform as well as, or better than, you have on practice tests. In order to do this, you have to have done at least one practice test in the first place!

In your practice tests, you want to practice doing as close as possible to *exactly* what you will be doing on the test itself. If you will be writing several essays with an average of seven minutes allocated to each, you want to practice writing essays at that pace. If you will be solving problems with the help of your calculator, and then picking the correct answer from five choices, at the rate of at least one problem per minute, then you want to practice doing exactly that.

The first guideline, offered in this section, is that you should

A. practice with tasks that resemble the "real performance" as closely as is possible,
or
B. remind yourself that your performance on the test is not a life-or-death matter?

690. When you start doing practice tests, you should take as much time as you need to answer the questions accurately. But it's important that you eventually practice answering questions at the speed that you will have to answer them on the real test. Some students practice test questions without creating time pressure for themselves, and then when they take the real test, they find themselves in a situation that feels totally different. When you're in a situation where every second counts, you want to have practiced performing in this circumstance. If there is a certain watch or timer that you will use during the test, I recommend using that same timer during practice tests.

The main idea of this section is the guideline that

A. you will want to focus on each test question without worrying about the previous or upcoming questions,
or
B. in practice tests, you should practice performing with a time limit?

691. When you do practice tests, it's useful to go, if possible, to the very room where the test will take place and do a practice test there. If this is not possible or convenient, you can still do something that is possibly even better: you use your imagination to take the practice test under the same conditions as the actual test. You imagine the room where you will take the test. You visualize your fellow students around you. You visualize the teacher giving instructions and presenting the test questions to you. You start the clock, and imagine that it is timing the real test.

The guideline spoken about during most of this section was

A. imagine yourself in the actual test conditions while you take your practice test,
or
B. wear the same clothes and use the same pen or pencil that you will use during the actual test?

692. In attempting to duplicate the conditions you will experience during the actual test, the most important, of course, is the test questions. You want to practice with questions that are as similar as possible to the questions you will encounter on the test. Where do you get these? Here are some possibilities:
1. Previous years' tests
2. Test prep books
3. The questions you have been assigned for homework
4. The questions or problems presented in your textbook
5. Types of questions used in previous tests in the same course
6. Questions your teacher has given in anything other than homework, such as study guides
7. Questions you yourself make up
8. Questions you find on the Internet (for standardized tests, upon typing the phrase "released tests" into your search engine)

This section presented a list of

A. different ways to prepare yourself to achieve the right degree of excitement,
or
B. different sources for practice test questions?

693. What's the point of making your practice test experience resemble as

311

closely as possible the actual test? One reason has to do with skill-building: you want to practice just the skills you will need on the test. But the second reason has to do with reducing anxiety. As we know well by now, three of the most important words about reducing anxiety are *prolonged exposure* and *habituation.* Exposure means that you put yourself into, or expose yourself to, the scary situation. That is, if you want to get over being anxious about tests, you put yourself into the test situation. With prolonged exposure, you stay in the situation for a long time, not just a brief exposure. And habituation is what happens after prolonged exposure: you get used to the scary situation, and you can handle it in a more relaxed way. Habituation means "getting used to it."

So if you want to get over anxiety about tests, you will want prolonged exposure and habituation to just the sort of test conditions that make you anxious.

This section makes the main point that

A. you get over anxiety by prolonged exposure and habituation,
or
B. practicing relaxation can not only reduce anxiety, but also be a pleasant way to spend time?

694. Each time you do a practice test, you vividly imagine yourself taking the real test. You notice whether your level of excitement is

very much too high
somewhat too high
just right
somewhat too low
very much too low.

Over time, excitement and anxiety that are too high should become lower, because with prolonged exposure comes habituation. It helps to notice the anxiety level go down as you practice more.

This section contains advice about

A. what to do during the real test
or
B. what to do during practice tests?

695. How do you know how much excitement is "just right?" You try to remember, or write down, how much excitement you were feeling, and grade your own practice tests. You see how much excitement seems to lead to the highest scores on the practice tests. This is the level that is the "just right" level you want to shoot for on the real test.

The purpose of this section was to

A. remind you that you should try for the "just right" level of excitement,
or
B. help you figure out what the "just right" level of excitement is?

696. Some students find that there's a part of them that resists going to the "just right" level of excitement when the stakes of the test are high. It's as though a part of them is saying, "What are you doing relaxing? Don't you know this is so important? This is an emergency—you need to act and feel like it!"

It's good to recognize that inner voice, if it does exist, and calmly to reply to it. An example of the reply might be, "But I've already figured out that more excitement is not necessarily helpful and can take away from my performance. I want to work close to the 'just right' level of excitement that I've already discovered."

The main advice given in this section is to

A. recognize and reassure any part of yourself that seems to feel that you *should* feel extremely excited and scared,
or
B. speak calmly to yourself when emergencies happen?

697. As you take your practice tests, (and as you take real tests) regularly take just a fraction of a second to use "self-reinforcement." That is, when you feel sure you have gotten a question right, you don't just go on to the next one. You say to yourself something like, "Yes! I got it!" and you try to feel good about that success.

Why do this? First, when you're feeling proud of yourself and excited about your successes, it's hard to feel a great deal of fear at the same time. The feelings of celebration are not compatible with a high degree of test anxiety. If you can practice associating positive feelings with test-taking, this is one of the most important things you can do to make success more likely.

Second, taking practice tests is something you'll want to do a lot. The more you celebrate your successes, the more you will enjoy your practice tests, and the more you enjoy them, the more often you'll be able to do them.

This section offers two reasons why

A. you should celebrate and feel good about your successes as you take tests,
or
B. you should take a large number of practice tests?

698. As you take tests, here's a thought to flash upon that might help you celebrate and feel good about your successes in answering questions: "How long ago was it that I would have had no idea how to answer this question? And now I can answer it perfectly! That's progress!" You don't want to go into great detail about this, because you don't have time – you want to practice just an instantaneous awareness that the fact that you can answer the question you just answered is a sign that you're growing and improving and getting more skilled.

Another way of expressing the thought that this section advises flashing upon is

A. "I'll be able to use this knowledge to help people!"
or
B. "I've come a long way!"

699. The next guideline is to make use of the principles of the chapter on success memories as "resources" you can use to reduce your fear of any situation. Before going into the situation, you ask yourself, "How would I *like* to feel in that situation?" For example, instead of scared, you may want to feel determined, focused, excited, confident, or proud of yourself. Then, you recall or imagine situations in which you've felt just the

way you want to feel, and you picture those scenes vividly. You then visualize yourself going into the new situation, feeling the same way you felt before. Finally, you actually go into the new situation, bringing into it the feelings you've decided you want to have.

In the technique this section describes, you

A. relax your muscles to turn down your level of excitement,
or
B. recall or imagine situations when you felt the way you want to feel, so as to bring those feelings into the new situation?

700. Let's go through an example of how to use this technique for a situation other than test-taking. Suppose someone is set to put on a musical performance, and is nervous. The person asks, "How would I like to feel?" The answer is, "I'd like to have fun, feel excited, and enjoy the way the music sounds." Then he searches his memory for times when he's felt this way. He remembers a time recently when he had a jam session with some friends, and he had a great time making music that came out sounding good. He vividly recalls this experience, and how he felt. Then he imagines himself performing, feeling

much the same way. Finally he actually performs, bringing those feelings with him.

The purpose of this section was to

A. present a new guideline for overcoming test anxiety,
or
B. to give an example of the technique that was described in the previous section?

701. If you are searching your memory for times when you felt the way you want to feel while taking a test, hopefully you won't have to search very long. Hopefully your practice tests will provide just those memories – especially those practice tests where you have performed and felt the best. If, during those practice tests, you have felt excited but not too excited, proud of yourself for the answers you are getting right, and totally focused on the question you are answering, then it's good to relive those memories just before the actual test. You visualize yourself feeling the same way while taking the actual test. Then you do take the actual test, bringing those feelings with you.

What does this section advise you to do just before the actual test?

A. remind yourself that the test is not a life-or-death matter,
or
B. recall how you felt taking your most successful practice tests, and visualize yourself feeling the same way while taking the real test?

702. Thus just before you are taking your practice tests, you vividly imagine that you are taking the real test. Just before you take the real test, you vividly recall taking a practice test. After you've done this for a while, your images of taking the real test will include images of recalling the practice tests. And your memories of practice tests will include imagining that you are taking the real test. Thus your images of the real test and practice tests will become more and more intertwined with one another. That's a good thing – you want to import into the practice tests the energy and excitement of the real tests, and you want to import into the real tests the relative calm and feeling of safety you have during practice tests.

This section describes

A. something good that might happen after you've used these imagination techniques for a while,
or

B. several reasons why you should focus completely on the question you are answering at that moment?

Don't waste energy during the test on painful emotion

703. Suppose you come across a test question on a subject you neglected to study. Many people would think, "Why did I not study that? I blew it. I could have had a much higher grade if I had studied. I was too lazy!" But thinking thoughts such as these wastes precious seconds that one could be using on another question. These thoughts also tend to create negative emotions that distract from the next task.

So you need to rehearse before the test, that if there is something you do not know, you will calmly take your best guess and then move on to the next question without fretting at all about the previous one. If anything else unwanted happens, you take it in stride and concentrate on getting the next question right. This advice is overridden if you need to help put out a fire, resuscitate a fellow test-taker, pull yourself out of the rubble of an earthquake, and so forth. But for the more ordinary bad things, you don't have time to worry about them!

The author advises

A. preparing so thoroughly that you know the answers to all the questions,
or
B. preparing not to distress yourself when you don't know the answer to a question or when other bad things happen?

704. While the test timer is running, you don't have time for awfulizing, getting down on yourself, and blaming someone else. You need to spend your time loading test questions into your memory, processing the question, and outputting answers. You do have time, however, for some celebration. You should take a split second to say "Yay!" or something synonymous very often when you think you've gotten an answer right. Internal celebration energizes you and reinforces you for the effort you are putting out.

The author advises

A. avoiding all emotion while taking a test,
or
B. avoiding the thoughts that produce painful emotion, but doing the sort of celebration that reinforces and energizes you?

Blunder control

705. Even someone who is at the ideal level of arousal can make costly blunders on tests, particularly science and math tests. How do you reduce them? Checking your work is one traditional way. But many test-takers do well to finish a test, and it's out of the question to go over every question a second time for checking.

The strategy I recommend, after you've gotten fast enough at answering questions that you have some time for checking, is to check each problem immediately after solving it. In complicated multi-step problems, I recommend checking each step immediately after carrying it out.

The strategy the author recommends is

A to finish all the questions before doing any checking, and then go back and check the ones that you are uncertain about,
or
B. to check each question or step as you do it?

706. Why do I recommend this strategy? Because if you finish all questions and then go back to check, you will spend lots of time rereading questions, re-loading the question into your memory. But if you check while the question is still in memory, you can save lots of time. The checking can be very fast.

Why do I recommend quickly checking after every step of a multi-step problem? Because if you make a blunder early on, all your work after that will be wasted. By catching blunders early in the process, you can save yourself the frustration of having to go through all the steps over again.

The purpose of this section was to

A. explain why checking as you go along is a good strategy,
or
B. describe exactly how you check?

707. If you are going to check as you go along, you should definitely use this strategy in your practice tests. You want to make sure that you will have time to check as you go along and still finish the test. You may need to increase the speed of your checking, if you find that you run out of time. If you can't get fast enough to check every question as you go along, you will have to figure out from practice tests how much checking to eliminate.

The author feels that

A. you should check every question as you go along, no matter how long it takes,
or

B. you should use practice tests to improve your checking speed and to figure out how much checking you should take the time for?

The error-reduction checklist

708. When you check, you don't want to simply go through the same mental processes that you used in solving the problem the first time. You want to have a mental list of possible blunders, and you rapidly search for each one of them, mentally crossing it off the list if you fail to find it and correcting it if you do find it.

The list of possible blunders has been called the "error-reduction checklist." Every time you make a blunder on a practice test, you classify it. What sort of blunder was this? You make a list of every type of mistake you are likely to make, and check for the most likely ones.

The main point of this section is that

A. when you check your work, you go through a mental checklist of possible errors,
or
B. pilots and surgeons and others who do high-stakes work should also have error-reduction checklists?

709. Here's an example of an error-reduction checklist for a math student.

1. Did I copy numbers correctly?
2. Did I keep straight what each number represented?
3. Did I do all calculations accurately?
4. Did I make sure any conversions of measurement units were done right?
5. Did I make sure I answered the question that was actually asked, and not some other question that could have been asked?
6. Did I pay particular attention to crucial words in the directions the question gives? (For example, did I notice the word *not* in the question "Which of the following is *not* true?")
7. Does the answer make sense, estimating from the original question?
8. Once I found the answer, did I enter it correctly on the answer sheet?

Of course, the error reduction checklist you will want to use depends on what types of questions you are answering, and what sorts of mistakes you make if you're not careful.

The author believes that

A. the error-reduction checklist you just read is the one you should use on all tests,
or
B. you should make your own error-reduction checklist, listing the types of

errors you have made on practice
tests?

Chapter 22: Picky Eating

710. Picky eating, which is also called food neophobia, is another type of problem which has fears and aversions at its root. Some people actually fear that the food will poison them or make them sick. Others simply fear that the food will taste bad. Picky eaters avoid all foods except a small set of foods that they find acceptable. These foods vary from person to person. Foods that seem to appear often on the acceptable list include macaroni and cheese, grilled cheese sandwiches, chicken nuggets, chocolate milk, and pizza. Green vegetables and salads very frequently show up on the unacceptable list. Many picky eaters have strong aversions to foods getting mixed with one another. If one food on a plate touches another, the food at the points of contact is treated as if it is contaminated. Picky eaters also tend to be very suspicious of little specks or irregularities in food.

What's the purpose of this section?

A. To explain how to get rid of picky eating problems,
or
B. To describe what picky eating problems are like?

711. Picky eating is more common among children than adults, and many children find themselves growing out of this sort of problem as they become bigger and older. Evolution may explain this. Picky eating represents too much of a good thing, something that had some survival value. There are many plants that are poisonous, and many of those poisonous plants are bitter tasting. Children with an aversion to these plants would have a better chance of survival. When you are a child, and your body is not very big, you don't have to eat as much of a poisonous plant to be killed by it as you do when you're an adult. When you're an adult, your caloric needs are greater, and it becomes more important for you to eat a larger volume of food. Thus it makes evolutionary sense for genes to develop that made people picky eaters as children but not so picky as adults.

A summary of this section is that

A. There's a theory that evolution selected for children to be picky or eaters and become less picky as they grow up.
Or
B. The bitter taste and/or poisonous chemicals that some plant species

have developed were probably selected for in order to keep the plant from being eaten by animals.

712. Picky eaters as a group tend to consider the "disutility" of chewing on a disliked food to be extremely high, probably much higher than non-picky eaters do. As an example, I do not like shredded coconut. But if I were offered money to eat shredded coconut, it wouldn't take much to get me to do it. For many picky eaters, in contrast, the price would have to become very high before they would be willing to eat a disliked food.

The point of this section is that

A. relaxing the muscles while doing an exposure to an unacceptable food can be useful,
or
B. picky eaters tend to regard the "disutility" of eating a disliked food as very high?

713. Picky eaters may be able to use the principle of probability and utility by indoctrinating themselves into the idea that although it is not pleasant to eat something one doesn't like, it is not horrible and it is not torture. I have mentioned earlier that I have gotten several wisdom teeth pulled and have had a couple of other minor surgical operations carried out without

anesthesia, but with the use of relaxation and fantasy rehearsal to reduce or eliminate the fear. My conclusion from these experiences is that the actual pain involved in the procedures, while significant, is not enough to make them horribly unpleasant, if the fear is very low. It could be that the same is true for eating a disliked food.

The main idea of this section is that

A. extreme restriction of the diet can result in major health problems,
or
B. picky eaters may benefit from the idea that eating a disliked food is not so horrible, if one can greatly reduce the fear?

Using exposure and practice with food aversions

714. Does the very high aversion that picky eaters have to eating a disliked food obey the rules of exposure and habituation that other aversions do? More research is necessary before we can make very definitive statements about picky eating, but at least some evidence points to the conclusion that prolonged exposure, practice, and habituation work the same way with

food aversions as with other sorts of aversions.

This section implies that

A. you can use the same principles with the fear of eating disliked foods that you use with other unrealistic fears and aversions,
or
B. carefully observing, and paying attention to, other people's eating and enjoying the foods you dislike can furnish models that are beneficial to you?

715. Our principle that prolonged exposure tends to reduce aversion whereas short exposure followed by escape tends to increase it is probably also true for picky eating. This would suggest that if one is trying to eat a food that one does not like, putting it in the mouth, holding the nose, and gulping it down as quickly as possible will not help the aversion. Putting it in for a brief time and then spitting it out would be even less useful. Rather, our principal of prolonged exposure would suggest that the picky eater would do better to put a bite of the food in the mouth and to chew it as long as possible before swallowing.

This section's main idea is in turn based on the idea that

A. you don't want the relief of getting disliked food out of the mouth to reinforce the aversion to the food,
or
B. the foods you most want to become able to eat are the most nutritious ones?

716. Does it make sense that it would be advantageous to do such exposures when hungry rather than when satiated? Since most people enjoy eating a much wider range of food when they are hungry rather than full, it would seem logical for the picky eater to take advantage of this principle and to schedule exposures while hungry. As a proverb states, "Hunger is the best sauce."

This section implies that it is better to use a disliked food as an

A. appetizer,
or
B. dessert?

717. It would also make sense that mastery fantasy rehearsals would be quite useful for the picky eater. In such rehearsals, the picky eater first becomes relaxed and then vividly imagines eating a food that was previously on the unacceptable list. In order for this to be a useful fantasy rehearsal, you can imagine that the food tastes good, but you do not need

to. You simply imagine that the taste does not cause unpleasant emotion. You can imagine eating the food with the unpleasant taste, but feeling as though "it is no big deal." You also imagine feeling proud of your accomplishment in eating it.

What does the author advise about fantasy rehearsals of eating disliked foods?

A. always imagine that the food tastes just wonderful,
or
B. sometimes you may want to imagine that the food does not taste great, but you do not feel unrealistic fear or aversion?

718. Coping fantasy rehearsals may also be useful for the picky eater. In these, one would imagine putting the unacceptable food in the mouth and feeling some fear or aversion over and above the inherent unpleasantness of the taste. But in the coping fantasy rehearsal, you imagine continuing this exposure and having that unrealistically large negative emotion gradually diminish over time. At the end of the coping rehearsal, you celebrate your self-discipline and the fact that the unrealistic aversion goes down over time.

What's the difference between a mastery and a coping fantasy rehearsal?

A. With mastery, you imagine handling the situation with no unrealistic fear or aversion; with coping, you imagine unrealistic fear and aversion on their way down.
or
B. With a mastery rehearsal, you celebrate your success, whereas you don't with a coping rehearsal.

719. Practicing relaxation strategies very thoroughly, and then using them during exposures may also be quite useful for the picky eater. Muscle relaxation, for example, may be a very useful strategy. It is difficult to feel extremely high anxiety or aversion with totally relaxed muscles. Thus a challenge for the picky eater is to become totally relaxed, and then do a prolonged exposure using a food on the unacceptable list.

The main idea of this section is that

A. The author predicts that exposures to scary foods will be more successful if you thoroughly relax the muscles first.
or
B. The fact that picky eating probably has a genetic cause doesn't mean that

it can't be changed by experience and practice and learning.

720. How would one use the principle of gradual hierarchy in overcoming a picky eating problem? As with other fears and aversions, you rate the unacceptable foods in terms of this SUD level that you project would come from exposure to them. You start with those that are fairly low on the SUD scale. If there is even one food that you can move from the unacceptable list to the acceptable list, this tends to increase the confidence that further movement is possible.

If a person hates broccoli 3 on a scale of 10 and chili 10 on a scale of 10, which of the two would the author recommend that the person start exposures with?

A. broccoli
or
B. chili?

721. Another way to use the concept of hierarchy when working on picky eating is starting with very small bites of the aversive food, and working your way gradually up to larger bites. But even with the small bites, the principle of making the exposure last as long as possible still holds. Chewing the small bite or holding it in the mouth as long

as possible before swallowing makes lots of sense.

The point of this section is that

A. you can use the principle of hierarchy by first practicing in fantasy, then practicing in real life,
or
B. you can use the principle of hierarchy by first practicing with very small bites of food, and working you way up to larger ones?

722. As with other fears and aversions, each success that comes constitutes a "resource" that is useful in bringing about more successes. You vividly bring back to mind the procedure of exposure and relaxation and fantasy rehearsal and so forth that produced the prior success, and then duplicate this to produce the next success.

If someone moves a food to the acceptable list, the author recommends

A. vividly reviewing in memory how this was done, so as to use this memory as a resource with other foods and other situations,
or
B. putting it out of mind without getting overconfident, and going on to the next challenge?

723. For most picky eaters, the choice point of avoidance versus mastery that we spoke about in an earlier chapter is the main sticking point. Continued avoidance of all the unacceptable foods is sometimes compatible not only with continued life, but with a fair degree of health. The picky eater's diet is seldom that which is recommended for ideal health, in which fruits and vegetables form the large majority of what is eaten. Nonetheless, continuing with avoidance rather than mastery is very much possible for many picky eaters.

The author makes the point that picky eaters

A. sometimes can use the avoidance strategy for years,
or
B. sometimes are reinforced by the power they gain over other people from picky eating?

724. In making the choice between avoidance and mastery, it is often useful to make a list of pros and cons, or advantages and disadvantages. There are major social advantages in being able to eat a fair fraction of what is served at social gatherings. There are major health advantages in being able to have a high vegetable and fruit intake. Counterbalanced against these is the major disadvantage, that using

exposure and working toward mastery requires self-discipline and time and effort. However, countering this is the fact that if the attempts at mastery are successful, these will be major resources that can be used in the solving of many other problems.

In this section the author recommends

A. overcoming picky eating as early in life as possible,
or
B. making a list of advantages and disadvantages of going for mastery versus avoidance with picky eating?

725. In my experience, picky eaters usually have one or more other anxiety related problems. The process of exposure and habituation that probably can be successful in overcoming picky eating is the same process that is used for other anxiety problems. Successes in the picky eating arena can become resources that can be applied to the fear of perfection in work, the fear of negative social judgments, the fear of intruders, or of any other unrealistic fear or aversion.

In this section the author makes the point that

A. A major advantage of overcoming picky eating is that it gives good experience that can be used in overcoming other anxiety-related problems, which picky eaters tend to have.

or

B. If picky eating is reinforced by someone, it is good if that person will try to figure out how not to reinforce the picky eating.

Chapter 23: Return to the Courage Skills Workout

726. At the beginning of this book, I mentioned a courage skills workout to do daily. Let's return to this idea. For those who have had significant anxiety or aversion problems, I recommend a workout time of 10 minutes to half an hour that you devote solely to doing the activities and exercises you have learned about in this book.

If you plan to do positive fantasy rehearsals during the commercials while you're watching TV, you may be successful. If you plan to do a few seconds of relaxation at random times during the day, this may help you a lot. But the advantage of having a time of total focus on courage skill activities is that it's easier to be accountable to yourself. It's easier not to tell yourself that you are logging in time working, when you actually are doing next to nothing.

One of the reasons, mentioned in this section, for having an anti-anxiety workout of a few minutes every day is that

A. if you do it at the same time each day, you'll have the power of habit working with you,
or

B. it's easier for you to be honest with yourself about whether you are logging in the time necessary to solve the anxiety problem, or not?

727. For many, many people, there is a very big gap between how important they consider it to accomplish something, and how many minutes they actually devote to working toward the goal. We can call this the problem of "time on task." For many people, the following dialogue applies:

Question 1: How much do you want to reduce the anxieties or aversions that are bothering you?

Answer 1: It is of very high priority, it is of greater importance than almost anything else.

Question 2: How many minutes, total, have you devoted to reducing those anxieties or aversions, in the last week?

Answer 2: Zero.

The point of this section is that

A. how much we think we want something, and how much we are willing to work at it, are often very different,
or

B. a good fraction of this book has been devoted to explaining how to do the work that is necessary to accomplish the goal?

728. It is very difficult for most people to get themselves to work on anything for a few minutes every day. If you can do this, you deserve to feel very, very good about yourself. If you have difficulty doing this, you might pick up some tips from reading another book I wrote, called *A Programmed Course in Self-Discipline*. One thing I *don't* recommend is a lot of getting down on yourself if at a certain time, you can't get yourself to do a daily workout. Just stick with an awareness of the difference between how important the goal is to you, and how much time you are putting in, and wish for the self-discipline to put the time in, without self-punishment. This is one case where wishing may eventually make something come true!

In this section the author recommends

A. keeping written records of how much time you log in, and reporting those records to someone else,
or
B. being gentle with yourself, keeping aware of the gap between importance of the goal and the time spent working on it, and wishing for the self-discipline to do the work?

729. Now let's make a menu of activities to include in your daily workout.

Menu of activities for the daily workout

1. Hold your breath and correct
2. Hyperventilate and correct
3. Listing situations that are important to practice with
4. Re-deciding, what thoughts, emotions, or behaviors you want to respond to those situations with
5. The twelve-thought exercise
6. The four-thought exercise
7. Doing the STEBC of fantasy rehearsal
8. Writing out fantasy rehearsals
9. Reading, silently or aloud, the fantasy rehearsals you've written out
10. Doing real-life exposure and practice with the situations on your list
11. Reading this book or other ones to review important principles
12. Refantasy of nightmares

Which of the following has been listed so far?

A. writing out fantasy rehearsals,
or
B. muscle relaxation

730. Let's continue the menu by listing each of the relaxation/meditation activities.

13. Physical exercise
14. Muscle relaxation
15. Breathe and relax
16. Observing what comes to mind
17. Meditation with a word-mantra
18. Meditation with movement
19. Visualizing relaxing scenes
20. Biofeedback
21. Imagining acts of kindness
22. The good will meditation
23. The psychological skills meditation
24. The pleasant dreams exercise
25. Reading inspiring quotations
26. Simple rest

Which of the following was included in the above list?

A. the celebrations exercise,
or
B. biofeedback?

731. Let's continue the menu just a little further.

27. The celebrations exercise (telling someone the positive examples you've done)
28. Recalling the "resources" of positive examples you've done in the past

29. Keeping a celebrations diary of positive examples
30. Filling out the questionnaires at the end of this book, or others, to self-monitor how you are doing
31. Doing the morning activities of physical exercise, bright light, and breakfast, to set your circadian rhythm well.
32. Writing questions to yourself and writing out decisions (in place of worrying)
33. Using the checklists on physical, economic, social, and achievement needs as a guide to productive use of energy (instead of worrying)
34. Fantasy rehearsing saying the things on the Emotional Climate Act Frequency Scale
35. Practicing the social conversation role play
36. Deciding which of the five strategies listed in the chapter on time pressure you want to use, and rehearsing using them

Which of the following is listed in this section?

A. Wishing for self-discipline to do the daily workout,
or
B. Posing questions to yourself and answering them in writing, as an anti-worrying technique?

732. So you decide: which of these activities do I want to include in my daily courage skills workout? (You can rotate some activities off your list, and others on, from time to time, whenever you want.) I would suggest maybe 5 or 6 activities. Then you get into a daily rhythm of doing the exercises you've chosen. Usually it's best to set aside a routine time each day. You want to try to enjoy your courage skills workout, because you want to make it sustainable over a very long time – the rest of your life! Even if you have almost no time, you can do a quick 12 thought exercise, a quick fantasy rehearsal, a quick celebration, and a one-minute meditation in under five minutes. If you have lots of time, you can do many more activities, much more elaborately.

What's a summary of this section?

A. Pick, from the large menu, a few activities for your daily courage skills workout, and do them daily.
or
B. It is probably useful to read this book more than once.

733. If you are able to invest time daily into the courage skills workout, I believe that the benefits will be very great.

If one were to ask many people with anxiety or aversion problems, how much time per day they spend doing these exercises, I feel fairly sure that for over 99% of them, the answer would be, "Zero." Most of them have no idea how to do a daily courage skills workout. Most of the rest who know what sorts of activities help, will not have the self-discipline to carry them out.

But you have the opportunity to be different. You have the opportunity to change your life by your own effort of will.

If you are able to do this, you deserve to feel great about yourself.

Both of the statements below are true. Which is a summary of this section?

A. Few people can improve their lives by doing courage skills exercises daily, but if you can be one of them, you deserve self-reinforcement!
or
B. The author would love to hear from successful users of these methods; you can write to the email address listed on page 2.

Appendix 1: Fear and Aversion Rating Scale

How much fear or aversion is connected with each of the following situations? You can answer this question in any of three ways. First: How much of a problem does the unrealistic fear of this cause you? Second: If you were in this situation, what's your guess as to how much distress you would feel? and Third: If you vividly imagine being in the situation, how much distress or discomfort does it cause you right now?

Your name:_____ Date:_____

Answering in which of the three ways above:

0=None
2=Very little
4=Some but not much
6=Pretty much, moderate amount
8=High amount
10=Very high amount

1. Getting shots or getting blood drawn
2. Speaking or acting to an audience
3. Being criticized
4. Eating or drinking with other people
5. Traveling alone in a bus
6. Getting called upon to answer a question in a class
7. Walking alone in busy streets
8. Having people look at me
9. Going into crowded stores
10. Traveling to school
11. Being at school and participating in school day
12. Being at the school building after school is over
13. Being at the place I live when no one else is there with me

14. Getting disapproval from an authority
15. Seeing someone else who has a small cut and is bleeding
16. Going alone far from home
17. Throwing up, vomiting
18. Feeling that it is possible that I might throw up
19. Feeling that it is possible that someone else will throw up
20. Going to the dentist for a routine visit, to get teeth cleaned and examined
21. Going to the dentist for a procedure such as a filling
22. Being in a large open space
23. Being in a small confined space, such as a small room with the door closed
24. Taking a test
25. Getting back a bad grade on a test or paper
26. Trying to say something but stumbling over some words
27. Staying overnight away from family or home
28. Making a mistake or being wrong in front of people
29. Being around a person who intimidates people with words
30. Being in high places
31. Being put in a leadership position
32. Meeting new people at parties or social gatherings
33. Not being able to come up with an idea when you have to for a project
34. Being in a social situation with someone of the opposite sex
35. Seeing a spider that you know is not dangerous
36. Having your performance measured
37. Trying some sport or game, with the knowledge I could fail
38. Trying some academic task, with the knowledge I could fail
39. Being in a social situation where people could possibly tease or make fun of me
40. Having someone my age get mad at me or not like me
41. Flying on airplanes
42. Riding in a car driven by someone else
43. Driving a car myself
44. Getting rejected by someone my age
45. Thinking thoughts that might be thought sinful or wrong
46. Playing music in front of people
47. Singing in front of people
48. Dancing in front of people
49. Not being able to go to sleep

50. Not being able to think of something good to say in a conversation
51. Looking nervous around people I don't know well
52. Getting lost when I am trying to find my way somewhere
53. Being alone in a certain room or floors of the house, with someone else home but not in the same place
54. Lying in bed with the lights off at night, before going to sleep
55. Having to fall asleep with no one else in my room
56. Being in the dark
57. Touching something that has a chance of having germs on it
58. Being around someone who has an illness that could possibly be contagious
59. Talking with people about disagreements or conflicts I have with them
60. Knowing that a family member could get ill or injured and die
61. Being in my bedroom at night in darkness
62. Anticipating going to sleep, knowing I could have a nightmare
63. Getting ready to go to school or work, anticipating what will happen
64. Being in a situation where I should ask someone to change something they are doing
65. Having someone ask me to do something, where I want to say "no"
66. Being far away from home, with people I know
67. Touching something other people have touched with their hands
68. Walking outside and knowing that there's a small chance that an animal predator could attack me
69. Being outside where there may be bees or wasps
70. Being around insects such as ladybugs or daddy-long-legs
71. Being in my house and knowing there's a small chance that bad people could break in
72. Doing school work, and knowing that it's possible that the work could be unsuccessful or could be criticized or get a bad grade
73. Trying a food I've never eaten before
74. Having to eat a food I don't like very much, for social reasons
75. Being in a close relationship with someone, knowing that it's possible the person could abandon or reject me
76. Having many different things to do, and knowing I should keep straight which I've done and which has highest priority to do next
77. Having a lot of work to do that feels as if it will be boring or tedious
78. Being among people and knowing that it is possible that I will embarrass myself by getting very nervous

79. Being among people and knowing that it is possible that I will embarrass myself by not doing social conversation skillfully (saying the wrong thing, not knowing what to say)
80. Reading out loud where people can hear me
81. Having reading to do for school
82. Having a writing assignment to do
83. Having a physical symptom and worrying about what it could mean
84. Being around a dog
85. Having to use a toilet in a public bathroom
86. Noticing that I have gained some weight
87. Having a lot of work to do
88. Having the feeling I get when I take several rapid deep breaths (the feeling of CO_2 deficit)
89. Having the feeling I get when I hold my breath (the feeling of CO_2 excess)
90. Feeling dizzy
91. Having to take orders; having someone tell me what to do
92. Having someone point out that I was wrong or disagree with me
93. Having the idea of suicide pop into your head
94. Seeing things that are unbalanced or asymmetrical or not even or that should be straightened.
95. Having a certain pattern or rhythm created, but not being able to complete it. (For example, touching three corners of a desk but not being able to touch the fourth.)

96. Other:

Appendix 2: Emotional Climate Scale, Form A

Your name: _____

Date:_____

Please rate the following interpersonal environment:

_____

10=Strongly Agree
8= Agree
6=Slightly Agree
5=Neutral
4=Slightly Disagree
2=Disagree
0=Strongly Disagree

_____ 1. People often give approval to one another.
_____ 2. It is easy to talk to other people about things on your mind in this environment.
_____ 3. People often interrupt each other instead of listening.
_____ 4. People often use pleasant and enthusiastic tones of voice with each other.
_____ 5. You very frequently find people having fun and interesting conversations.
_____ 6. You can very often hear someone say "thank you" for something, in a genuine way.
_____ 7. People often call each other insulting names.
_____ 8. When people have disagreements, they talk them out calmly in a way that leads to solutions.
_____ 9. When people need to be assertive with each other, they do so tactfully.
_____ 10. People sometimes purposely physically hurt each other.
_____ 11. People try very hard to avoid hurting other people's feelings.
_____ 12. The group ethic is to make sure that no one feels rejected.
_____ 13. When someone has a success, the others feel happy for the person rather than jealous.
_____ 14. People genuinely enjoy spending time with one another.
_____ 15. People are able to "give each other space" without being too dependent.

_____ 16. People spread unkind rumors about one another or say negative things behind their backs.

_____ 17. People have a tolerant attitude toward differences among one another.

_____ 18. People tend to speak to one another respectfully.

_____ 19. People tend to get very upset over very little things.

_____ 20. All in all, people express much more positive feelings toward one another than negative ones.

_____ 21. People encourage people to meet others by introducing them.

_____ 22. When people have problems, they tend not to tell others, out of fear that others will not be supportive.

_____ 23. When someone speaks, someone else often asks follow-up questions to find out more.

_____ 24. When someone makes a bid for emotional connection with another, the response is usually positive.

_____ 25. People seem to compete with each other for attention, in an unpleasant way.

_____ 26. People compliment and congratulate each other when they do something positive.

_____ 27. People often seem irritated with one another.

_____ 28. People are polite to one another.

_____ 29. People are habitually productive enough that there are few conflicts over who should do a certain piece of work.

_____ 30. People often get the feeling that they are genuinely valued by others in this environment.

_____ 31. Arguments never seem to come to any resolution in this environment.

_____ 32. When someone has a problem, others are supportive and helpful.

_____ 33. People often use swear words in speaking to one another.

Appendix 3: Emotional Climate Scale, Form B

Your name: _____

Date:_____

Please rate the following interpersonal environment:

_____

10=Strongly Agree
8= Agree
6=Slightly Agree
5=Neutral
4=Slightly Disagree
2=Disagree
0=Strongly Disagree

_____ 1. People often smile at one another in a friendly way.
_____ 2. People are good listeners with one another.
_____ 3. People often exclude someone from their conversations in a way that's unpleasant for the excluded person.
_____ 4. People often speak to one another in upbeat and positive tones.
_____ 5. People find their conversations thought-provoking, in a positive way.
_____ 6. People often show genuine appreciation for what someone else has done.
_____ 7. People are unpleasantly bossy with one another.
_____ 8. People are able to make joint decisions without getting mad at one another.
_____ 9. People can communicate clearly with one another about their wishes, without being hurtful.
_____ 10. There is a strong precedent against physical violence in this environment.
_____ 11. People tend to form cliques or groups that are very difficult to break into.
_____ 12. People make requests of one another in polite ways.
_____ 13. People feel a frequent need to "one-up" one another or show that they are better than others.

_____ 14. When there are competitions, such as games, people do not get too upset over who wins or loses.

_____ 15. People tend to fear that others will reject them or drop the relationship.

_____ 16. People often laugh with each other in a way that doesn't hurt anyone's feelings.

_____ 17. People give criticism of a hurtful nature.

_____ 18. People frequently insult one another.

_____ 19. People often paraphrase or reflect what the other person has said, to make sure that they understand correctly.

_____ 20. There is a good bit more approval than disapproval in this environment.

_____ 21. People often give pleasant greetings to one another.

_____ 22. If someone is not expert in something, people are helpful and supportive of that person's improving, rather than making that person feel bad about not being expert.

_____ 23. People often raise their voices in anger toward one another.

_____ 24. When people speak, they try to adjust their talking, taking into account the other person's interest in the subject.

_____ 25. There are frequent struggles for who is in control or who is dominant.

_____ 26. People get real enjoyment from their conversations with one another.

_____ 27. People seem to like one another a lot.

_____ 28. The prevailing attitude is one of kindness and caring.

_____ 29. People have expectations of one another that are reasonable, rather than feeling too entitled.

_____ 30. People make each other happy.

_____ 31. People tend to influence each other by threatening harm of others or of oneself.

_____ 32. People often do things with one another that each of them enjoys.

_____ 33. People are considerate not to intrude upon what others are doing when they want time alone.

Appendix 4: Emotional Climate Act Frequency Scale

Your name:_____

Date:_____

Please rate with regard to the following relationship or interpersonal environment:_____

Please rate:

_____ How often you, yourself, say something like each of the following utterances,
or
_____ How often you hear something like each of the following utterances spoken to you?

0=Less than once a month
1=Between once a month and once a week
2= About once a week
3= Two or three times a week
4= Four or five times a week
5=About once a day
6=Two or three times a day
7=Four or five times a day
8=Between five and ten times a day
9=Between ten and twenty times a day
10=Over twenty times a day

_____1. Good morning!
_____2. Thanks for doing that for me!
_____3. I really appreciate what you did.
_____4. Thanks for saying that!
_____5. You did a good job!
_____6. That's interesting!
_____7. Good going!

_____8. I'd be happy to do that for you!

_____9. I'd love to help you in that way!

_____10. I feel good about something I did. Want to hear about it?

_____11. Good point!

_____12. Good job!

_____13. That's really great!

_____14. Wow!

_____15. Hooray!

_____16. I'm so glad it happened like that!

_____17. Sounds good!

_____18. That's beautiful!

_____19. It's good to see you!

_____20. Welcome home!

_____21. Good luck to you!

_____22. I wish you the best on (the thing you're doing).

_____23. Good afternoon!

_____24. Hi!

_____25. I'm glad you're here!

_____26. May I help you with that?

_____27. I'd like to help you with that.

_____28. I'll do that for you!

_____29. That's nice of you to do that for me!

_____30. Congratulations to you!

_____31. You did well on that!

_____32. I hope you have a good day.

_____33. Have a nice day!

_____34. I'll do this job for us!

_____35. Would you like me to show you how I do that?

_____36. Hooray, I'm glad I did this!

_____37. That's OK; don't worry about it.

_____38. I'm glad you told me that!

_____39. Yes, please!

_____40. Good evening!

_____41. I'm glad to see you!

_____42. Tell me more.

_____43. Uh huh . . . (while listening carefully to the other person)

_____44. That's pretty smart!

_____45. Wonderful!

_____46. This is a big help to me.

_____47. It's no problem.

_____48. I can handle it.

_____49. I can take it.

_____50. It's not a big deal. (Discounting the importance of a frustration to oneself, not to the other.)

_____51. How was your day today?

_____52. How are you?

_____53. How have you been doing?

_____54. How have things been going?

_____55. So let me see if I understand you right. You feel that _____.

_____56. So, in other words you're saying _____.

_____57. I'd like to hear more about that!

_____58. I'm curious about that.

_____59. Yes . . . (while listening attentively to the other person)

_____60. Oh? (while listening attentively to the other person)

_____61. I'll go along with what you want on that.

_____62. Here's another option.

_____63. Here's the option I would favor.

_____64. An advantage of this plan is . . .

_____65. A disadvantage of that option is . . .

_____66. Saying or doing funny things, retelling funny things, or laughing when the other person is trying to entertain by being funny - but avoiding sarcasm or making fun of the other person.

_____67. I would love to!

_____68. I'm sorry you had to go through that.

_____69. Unfortunately I can't do it.

_____70. I'd prefer not to.

_____71. No, I'm sorry, I don't want to do that.

_____72. It's very important that you do this.

_____73. Upon thinking about it more, I've decided I was wrong.

_____74. I apologize for doing that.

_____75. I think you're right about that.

_____76. I'm sorry that happened to you.

_____77. I'm sorry I said that.

Appendix 5: Relaxation Script

The ability to relax your body and your mind, whenever you want to, is a skill that is very useful in many different ways. It allows you to calm yourself so that you can think better. It makes it easier to go to sleep. It lets you undo any tension in muscles that would be uncomfortable or painful. It has been found helpful in preventing several physical problems, including headaches and certain types of stomachaches. It gives you practice in controlling your own mood. It allows you to get rid of restlessness. It allows you to better handle and enjoy being by yourself. It is very useful in reducing fearfulness, when you want to do that. It can prepare you for getting good and thoughtful ideas. It helps you in resolving conflicts with other people that come up. It is a skill that is worth working on for a very long time if that's what it takes to master it.

One of the most important ways of relaxing is to notice any tension in your muscles, and to reduce that tension, and let your muscles stop pulling. As you sit or lie down comfortably, it often feels pleasant to let your muscles relax themselves. The more relaxed your muscles are, the more your mind will tend to drift in ways that are calm and peaceful also.

Here is one way that you can practice relaxation of your muscles. You can think about the different muscles of your body, and go through the different muscle groups one by one. You can notice the tension that is already in the muscles, or you can tense those muscles just a little bit. Then you make that tension go away, as totally as possible. If you can notice the difference between full relaxation and even a very small amount of tension in a muscle, you have a very important skill. Because as long as you can notice tension, and even make tension greater, you have the power to make that tension go away. All you have to do to produce relaxation is the opposite of what you do to create tension. When you let off the tension, you let the muscles get very loose and relaxed. You do this for all the muscle groups in the body. You notice what happens when you relax muscles. You feel the difference that happens when you relax. When you've done this enough times, you'll know very well how to tense and relax all the muscles of your body.

You will not have to tense the muscles at all hard, but only very lightly, or maybe not at all, to feel the difference that happens when you relax the muscles.

You might start with gripping your hands into fists, not hard, but very lightly. Even if you do it very lightly, you can feel a tension in the muscles of your forearms and hands. Once you feel that tension, you can let it off, and let your forearms relax and get very loose. Pay attention to the feeling of relaxation, and how it is different from the feeling of tension.

You might next make your upper arms a little tense by trying to make a muscle as though you were going to feel the muscle in your upper arms. You do this by pulling so as to bend your arm at the elbow, but at the same time trying to straighten out your arm. Feel the tension in your upper arm muscles. Then you can let off the tension and let those muscles get loose and relaxed.

You might next make your shoulders a little tense by starting to shrug your shoulders a little, the way people do when they say, "I don't know." Then you relax those shoulder muscles. If someone wants to make their neck muscles tense, they try to pull their head forward, and at the same time pull it back, so that the muscles are pulling against each other. Then when they feel that tension, they can relax those muscles, and let those muscles be very calm.

If someone wants to tense the muscles that are at the side of the face, the jaw muscles, they do it by biting so as to clench the teeth together, while at the same time trying to open the mouth. This produces tension in the jaw muscles, the muscles on the side of the head, and the muscles on the upper part of the neck. Then you can relax those muscles by letting your jaw relax. When you do this usually your jaw will be hanging open just a tiny bit.

If you want to tense the muscles of the upper part of your face, you lift your eyebrows and at the same time try to push your eyebrows down. Then when you feel that tension, ever so slightly, you can let it off.

If you want to tense the muscles of the lower part of your face, you push your lips together a little bit, and pull the corners of your mouth back as though you were smiling, and at the same time you try to purse your lips back as though you were trying to whistle. Then you let all that tension off, and you feel the relaxation of the muscles of the lower part of your face.

Many people find that relaxing the muscles of their face and jaws and neck is just what makes them feel the most calm and peaceful. You might try it if you want to, thinking about the muscles of your jaws, your upper face, your lower face, and your neck.

Some people like to think about their breathing as they are relaxing, and let their muscles get a little more relaxed each time they breathe out. So the rhythm is: Breathe in, relax out. Breathe in, relax out.

Now you might experiment with how to make the muscles tight in your back. If you try to arch your back like you are bending backwards, you can tense the long muscles that run down your back. Then when you feel that tension, you can let it off. If you pull your shoulders back, you can feel tension in the muscles in the upper part of your back, and then let that tension off.

You can also experiment with tensing and relaxing the muscles of your chest and your abdomen, or belly. To tense those of your chest, pull your arms as if you are going to clap your hands together, then relax that tension. To tense the muscles of your abdomen, if you are lying on your back, pretend that you want to sit up, and feel just a little tension in those muscles. Then you can let them off. Or if you are sitting in a chair, you can tense your belly and back muscles by trying to lean forward, while at the same time trying to lean backward. When you feel that tension, let it off, and as always, pay attention to the different degrees of tension and relaxation that you are feeling.

You can make the muscles in your upper legs tense by trying to bend the leg at the knee and trying to straighten it out at the same time. Then you can let off that tension, so that your upper legs are very relaxed. You can tense your lower legs by trying to push your toes down and trying to pull your toes up at the same time. Then you can let off that tension too, so that your lower legs are relaxed.

There are many muscles in the body, including some I didn't mention. It can be fun to experiment with finding out how it is that you make a certain muscle tense. Over time, you will become very much able to tense or relax any muscle in the body any time you want to.

After you go through and actually practice tensing and relaxing your muscles, you can just let your attention go first to one muscle group and then another, seeing if you can make that muscle group any more relaxed and loose and limp than it already is.

You might want to think about your breathing again, and feel the air going in and out, and each time you breathe out, feel some part of your body getting just a little more relaxed than it was before.

The skill of getting your muscles relaxed is one that will be very useful to you, for the rest of your life. It's one that people can gradually improve at over time, simply by noticing what sort of effort tends to tense what muscles, and what sort of relaxation of that effort relaxes those muscles. You will start to find which particular muscles are the most important ones for you.

Relaxing your muscles is only a part of the interesting and pleasant things you can do while you are relaxing.

Another very useful way of relaxing is to practice imagining beautiful and relaxing scenes, nice and pleasant places to be. You may want to think of the following scenes, briefly, when I mention them, and then come back to them later when the tape stops and imagine them more thoroughly. Different scenes are relaxing for different people. How does it feel when you imagine a beautiful sunset? How does it feel to imagine the sound of wind gently blowing among the tree leaves? How about the image of a bunch of beautiful flowers? How about the sight and the sound of a waterfall? How about listening to rain fall on a roof? How about imagining waves rolling in where you are relaxing on a beach? Or the image of how you feel just as you are awakening on a morning where there are no responsibilities you have to carry out? Or the image of sitting in a cool room, with a warm blanket around you, looking at a fire burn in a fireplace? Or what's it like to imagine yourself drinking cool water when you are very thirsty? Or watching snow drifting slowly to the ground? Or can you imagine a rag doll, and imagine that your body is that loose and relaxed? What's it like to imagine watching white clouds drifting by on a day in the spring? Or can you just become conscious of the chair or the bed that is holding you up, and feel yourself being held?

Sometimes the most relaxing images are not just of places, but of people, and people acting kind and gentle and loving and giving with one another. These images let people feel peaceful and relaxed.

You can imagine stories of people's being kind. For example you may want to imagine that someone is searching for something, and someone else in a very calm and kind way helps that person find it. When they find it, the people feel good about each other. If you want you can fill in your own details about where they are, what is being searched for, where they look, and what it looks like when they find it. You can do this in a different way every time if you want, or the same way every time you do it, or sometimes one way and sometimes another. You are in control of your own imagination and you can lead yourself wherever you choose.

Or you may imagine that someone leads someone else on a very interesting and pleasant journey, showing that person something that is very fun or interesting to see. If you want you can imagine your own details, about where the first person takes the second, what sorts of things they see and experience. You can imagine the faces of the first person as that person enjoys what they are doing, and the face of the other person feeling good about giving the other a pleasant experience.

Or you may imagine that someone teaches someone else something that person really wants to know. The teacher is very kind and patient. The teacher wants to let the learner learn at his own pace, and does not rush him. The learner is very grateful to the teacher. The teacher is also grateful to the learner. The teacher and realizes that someone who allows you to teach them something is giving a nice gift, a pleasant memory that the teacher will have for a lifetime. You can fill in your own details of where they are, what is being learned, and how they are learning it.

Or you may imagine that someone helps someone with a job of some sort. As you do it, imagine that the two people feel very good about one another. You can see and hear what they are doing together and what sort of words they are saying to each other, if they are saying anything.

Or you may imagine that people are being kind and loving to each other by playing together. They know in the backs of their minds that the most important thing when they are playing with each other is to be kind and caring with each other. They each take pleasure whenever they can see that they have helped the other feel good. If you want to let a story about this come to your mind, you can imagine where they are and what or how they are playing and what they are saying with each other.

Or you may imagine people showing their love and caring about each other by noticing and commenting on the other person's good acts or accomplishments. You can imagine that people rejoice and feel good when their friends and loved ones have successes. If you want you can imagine exactly what someone is doing and how someone else feels good about it, and how that person lets the other person know his pleasure.

Or you may imagine people sharing things with each other, making it so that there is enough to go around. You can imagine whether they are taking turns with some toy or tool they want to use, or whether they are sharing something to eat or drink, or someone else's attention and time, or something else.

Or, you may imagine one person showing love and caring for another by being a good listener when the other speaks. As one person tells thoughts and feelings, the other very patiently tries to be understanding.

Some people enjoy recalling the things they have done in real life that they are glad they have done. Some people like to think back about the kind things they have done for other people, or the work that they have done to educate themselves and make themselves better or the work they have done to make the world a better place, or the times that they have lived joyously, or the times that they have made good decisions and carried them out. They may want to celebrate the times that they have been honest, or the times that they have been strong and brave.

Some people enjoy thinking about the ways in which they are blessed, and feeling gratitude for those. If they are able to have any material things that make life easier, if they are able to eat and drink so that they do not have to be hungry and thirsty, if they have someone who can take care of them when they need it and be of support to them, if they have friends or loved ones that they can care for and support, they may want to feel gratitude for these blessings.

You can let your mind drift, and think about any stories or images of these things that you want to. You are perfectly free to let your mind drift in any way that you choose. Sometimes people enjoy not choosing, but simply letting the mind drift wherever it wants to go, and observing what happens.

In fact sometimes it's a very pleasant experience just to imagine that your mind is a blank screen, and to simply wait and see what comes on it, and to observe it with interest and curiosity, not trying to control it in any way. You can practice relaxing your muscles, imagining relaxing scenes, thinking of stories of people being kind to each other, or you can simply let your mind drift and see where it takes you. Or you can let your mind drift and not observe it, but simply rest. You can guide your own experience to make it pleasant, relaxing, peaceful, and enjoyable to you. As you do so you have reason to celebrate practicing such an important skill.

Appendix 6: Some Difficult Social Situations, for Practice

You can practice with these situations by brainstorming options, doing the twelve-thought exercise, doing the four-thought exercise, and thinking of advantages and disadvantages of options you have listed. Any of these exercises provide exposure that will help with habituation to these sorts of situations.

1. Someone starts to sit down at lunch. Someone at the table says, "You can't sit here."

2. Your friend tells about a student in one of her classes who started crying in class. You feel a lot of sympathy for the student, and don't like how your friend is talking about her. Your friend says, "Don't you think that's funny?"

3. As you sit down in class, you overhear a kid say to another, "He acted like a real goofball." They are both looking at you.

4. For an activity at school, people are forming into partners. There is an odd number of people, and you find yourself left out.

5. Your friend says to you, "I hate my brother. Wouldn't you just get rid of your brother if you could?" Actually, you get along really well with your brother.

6. Someone in your class is having a party, and you hear people talking about it. But you are not invited to it.

7. You have plans to get together with someone, but just before you leave, you get a text message from the other person that just says, "Cancel – I can't do it."

8. You are trying to plan a get-together with some friends at your house. You are really excited about it. But as the time grows closer, more and more people say they can't come.

9. You did badly on a test. Other people who did well ask you what you got. Part B: You did

well on a test. Other people who did badly ask you what you got.

10. Somebody is getting together with a friend. The first person would like to go sledding. The second person would like to walk around at the mall. Neither of them would enjoy what the other one would most like to do.

11. You are planning a surprise party, and someone tells the guest of honor all about it, so it's no longer a surprise.

12. You have been making lots of contributions to class discussions. The teacher asks a question, and says, "OK, this time anybody but (your name), please tell what you think."

13. You are tying your shoe, and you mess it up and have to start over. Someone notices this and starts joking around, saying things in front of other people, like "You're still working on shoe-tying. How long have you been learning shoe-tying? The last 8 years? Takes a while, doesn't it?" You're being expected to laugh at this.

14. Someone asks, "What's your religion?" You tell them about it. Later they say to someone else, "She has such a weird religion." And the person relays what you had said, as if it's really crazy.

15. You make arrangements to get together with a friend. Not long after, you get a call from another friend, inviting you to come to see a movie that you've been wanting to see for a long time.

16. Someone who is visiting you keeps talking about the things you own, and saying they are not as good at the things she owns.

17. Someone comes over to your house to hang out. The person says, "What do you want to do?" You make suggestions, they don't want to do those things. The person says, "I don't know what to do."

18. You're texting one of your friends. Another person grabs the phone and types in some insulting things and sends it to your friend as if you typed it.

19. A boy tells you he will ask out one of friends. You tell your friend this. The friend tells people, that she doesn't want to go out with the boy. People get mad at you for telling her.

20. You tell a friend that you like a certain boy. A few days later, you find that your friend and the boy you like have become a couple.

21. Your friend is talking about another girl. Your friend says that this girl doesn't know anything. This girl is in one of your classes, and you know that she's actually very knowledgeable.

22. A friend says, "Don't tell anybody, but tonight my friend and I are going to sneak out of the house in the middle of the night and do some gorge-jumping." You tell your parent, who feels obligated to tell your friend's parent. Your friend gets in trouble. The friend is mad at you.

23. You ask someone if she wants to hang out with you the next day. She says, "No way!"

24. You work with younger kids. A younger kid, as soon as you're paired up with him, says, "No I don't want to work with you. I want to work with that person over there." Part B: The kid paired with someone else complains that they want to work with you instead.

25. You have an argument with someone you know. She gets her friends to take her side, and to be against you.

26. You're playing in a basketball game. You are wide open, but when somebody throws the ball to you, you miss. Someone else says, "Don't throw it to her any more; she can't hit it."

27. You are on the phone with someone. The person asks you, "What do you think of Francine? She is so mean." You say, "I guess she can be mean sometimes." You find that Francine is on the line, hearing all you said.

28. You have two friends, and one of them says, "You're my best friend, and I'm yours!" Another friend feels excluded by this.

29. Two friends do a lot of talking, in front of you, about something they're going to do together, that you haven't been invited to, even though you'd like to come.

30. Someone wears ear plugs at a dance, to protect their hearing from the loud music. Someone acts as if this is really funny, and tells friends about it, pulling your hair to the side to show them.

31. You are riding in a friend's car. The speed limit is 55 miles per hour. You watch as the dial on your friend's speedometer passes 55 and rises to 65, and then 75 miles per hour.

32. Someone is having a Valentine's party. Other people are invited, in front of you, but you are not.

33. You have plans to get together with someone. But the person cancels. Then you see the person hanging out with someone else.

34. You are with someone, and you suggest fun things to do. But she just wants to text with other people.

35. You are at a lunch table. A guy comes and says, "My name is Ralph. What are your names?" Nobody says anything, so you introduce him. When he leaves, people at the table say, "He already knew us; you shouldn't have introduced him."

36. You are at another family's house for dinner. You haven't eaten yet, and everyone is standing around talking. Your friend says, "On the count of three, let's sing really loudly, 'We want food!' It would be so funny!"

37. A friend tells you that her parents beat her. You tell her she has to tell somebody, she says "No, no, and don't you tell!" You are scared for your friend.

38. Yolanda is playing a game with her friend, Carmen. Carmen's little sister, Sally, is watching quietly. Sally isn't bothering Yolanda at all. Carmen says, "Go away, Sally. Yolanda doesn't want you here."

39. You are at a dance. Two girls who are not dancing, stand nearby and laugh, and say, "You dance so funny!"

40. You are planning a party for school, with a group of other kids. Someone in the group acts as if every idea you have is stupid and that no one should listen to you.

41. You make friends with someone who is eccentric, but nice. Other people start making fun of you for liking that person.

42. You hit the ball out in a volleyball game, and one of your teammates says, "You're so bad at volleyball."

43. Your friend says, "I'll bet you a dollar that I can beat you in a swimming race across the pool." You win by a lot. When she gets to the other side of the pool, your friend doesn't acknowledge that you won the bet. She never gives you a dollar.

Appendix 7: Some Models of Social Conversation

In working on reducing social anxiety, the "Social Conversation Role Play" is a great way to get more comfortable with talking with people. You can make up both parts of a social conversation. Or, someone else can role-play one of the parts while you make up the other part. It's a good exercise to write these down, or even to simply read examples that someone else has written. As you read the following examples, be aware of

- greeting and parting rituals
- reflections
- telling about your own experience
- facilitations
- follow-up questions
- positive feedback
- avoiding overlong statements, using good turn-taking
- erring on the side of being upbeat rather than pessimistic

Conversation 1: Two neighbors

Two neighbors see each other while one is taking a walk.

1 Hi, how are you today?

2 I'm doing just fine, thanks. How are you?

1 Doing well. What are you up to? Looks like you're getting that lawn cleaned up.

2 Well, I may look like I'm just raking leaves. But what I'm really doing is planning out a play in my mind.

1 A play? Sounds interesting! Tell me more.

2 Well, I'm trying to make up a musical play for people to perform. But instead of writing original songs, I'm using some of the best folk songs that have ever been written, like the Wild Mountain Thyme and The Skye Boat Song and so forth. I'm changing around the words just a little bit for some of them.

1 Sounds like a great idea! Is there a story that goes along with the play?

2 Yes, and that's what I'm working on mainly. Being a musical, I think I should have two young people who meet each other and fall in love and go through troubles but eventually end up

happy with each other, don't you think?

1 Sounds like a great plot for a musical. Who do you think might put on the play?

2 Well, my daughter is in an acting group, and I talked with the director of it about maybe putting it on. I would let them put it on for free, and they could save a lot of money from not having to pay royalties to somebody else for using a famous play.

1 And maybe if it turns out well enough, it will be famous some day too!

2 That would be nice! Thanks for putting that image into my mind! What are you up to, just getting some exercise?

1 Well, I look like I'm just walking, but I'm planning a psychology experiment that I want to do.

2 Oh, that sounds interesting too! Tell me more about it, please.

1 I have a theory that when people take tests, they will do lots better if people use pleasant and cheerful tones of voice after each question that they answer, and that this will encourage them to keep going longer.

2 Sounds like a very important theory. How are you going to test it?

1 I'm going to get a bunch of kids, and give them all some standard tests of reading and math and spelling and so forth. I'm going to divide them into two groups by flipping a coin. Then one group will be tested by somebody who is not really cheerful and enthusiastic, but who acts appropriately anyway. The second group will get tested by someone who is really cheerful and enthusiastic. Then I'll compare how the two groups do.

2 Sounds like a very interesting experiment. Where are the kids going to come from?

1 I work for a school, and the kids in the school will be the ones that are in the experiment. If it works out the way I think it will, all the teachers in my school as well as lots of others will hopefully learn to talk in a more positive way to kids.

2 So if I understand you right, if things work out the way you hope, you'll be able to help lots of kids by helping adults learn to talk with them in positive tones of voice?

1 You understand me just perfectly!

2 Well, good luck on your project!

1 You too! Let me know how the play turns out, please!

2 I'll do that, and you let me know how your experiment turns out, also, please.

1 I'll do that! See you later, neighbor.

2 Nice talking with you!

1 You too!

Conversation 2: On the bus

The two people are sitting by each other on the bus.

1 Mind if I sit by you?

2 Not at all!

1 Great. How has your school day gone today?

2 Good. I went on a field trip today for French class.

1 Oh! Tell me more about it, please!

2 We went to a concert to hear a person who sang educational songs in French.

1 Sounds neat! Was the person a good singer?

2 Pretty good! I enjoyed it, because some songs are rapping, and some songs are slow, and some sounded like rock songs.

1 So, there was a lot of variety in the concert, huh?

2 Yes.

1 I think that learning stuff like languages through songs is a great idea. I study Spanish instead of French, and I have a bunch of recordings of songs in Spanish. Some of them are really good.

2 Cool!

1 Have you ever heard a song called La Golondrina? It's one of my all time favorite songs.

2 No, I've never heard it.

1 It's one of the ones on my Spanish recordings. I'll have to let you hear it some time. Hey, have you ever been to place where people actually speak French?

2 Nope. But I guess there are people who speak French all over, if you can

find them. The guy who did the French songs is from Detroit, and not from France or Canada.

1. Good point. I've been to Canada, but in the English-speaking part. I'd like to go to Montreal some day and hear them speak French everywhere. Would you too?

2 Yes, that would be awesome.

1 Maybe we should plan a trip up there together, once we are able to drive!

2 Sounds great.

1 Well, time for me to get off the bus. Nice talking with you today!

2 You too! Good-bye.

1 Bye!

Conversation 3: Cousins on the phone

A person calls up a cousin, to chat on the phone.

1 Hi ___, this is ____.

2 Hi ____, it's really nice to hear from you!

1 Thanks! I'm glad I caught you in! Am I interrupting you in the middle of anything?

2 Nothing that can't wait. I was just figuring out how to do some recording of music.

1 Cool! Does it take a lot of expensive equipment?

2 It used to, but now, you can do it with some very small equipment, that only costs a few hundred dollars, and make really good recordings from it.

1 So the technology for recording has gotten cheaper along with all sorts of other technology, huh?

2 That's right. I'm recording some songs, and I'm going to put them on the Internet so that anybody who wants to hear them can download them and play them.

1 Are you going to charge money for them, or just put them up for free?

2 Just for free. I don't think I'm quite ready to become rich and famous off my music recordings, but still it's fun to be able to give them away to people.

1 Sounds great! Are these songs you've been composing, or are they

covers of songs other people have written?

2 There are 2 or 3 that I composed, and then there are several instrumental arrangments of folk songs. Have you ever heard the old song called Deep River?

1 Yes! I remember that one! Our grandad used to sing that one, didn't he?

2 Right! You remember that too, that's neat! Well, I played it with the acoustic guitar, and then laid down another track on top of it with the strings from a keyboard. There are several songs like that.

1 That sounds really neat! When you get these onto the Internet, can you please email me the link, so I can listen to them?

2 I would love to. Are you still into ballroom dancing? If so, some of them have a steady enough rhythm that you could use them for ballroom dancing.

1 Great. Yes, I do still do some ballroom dancing. However, with the economic problems lately, I've been having to work a lot more than before.

2 Well, it's great that you have the opportunity to work more. How are you liking it?

1 Pretty well. I'm doing some free lance writing work, editing a book for a publisher. I can do it in my off time. It's a pretty important writer – I'm not allowed to say who it is – but there sure are a lot of errors in the writing. I feel good that I may be able to have a good impact on an important book.

2 Wow, you are doing some important stuff!

1 When it comes out, they may decide to give me credit, in which case I can show everybody the book and show what I did, or they may decide to keep me a ghost writer. We'll see.

2 That will be interesting to find out! I'll be curious to hear what they decide!

1 Well, it's great talking to you. I'll let you get back to your music. Tell the rest of the family hi for me.

2 I'll do that! And thanks so much for calling!

1 Thanks for chatting with me! Bye.

2 Bye!

Conversation 4: At a party

Two people meet at a party; they've never met before.

1 I like that vest you're wearing. It looks very exotic.

2 Thanks. My grandad from Greece gave me this.

1 That must make it a special gift. So part of your ancestry is from Greece, huh?

2 Actually all of it is. My mom and dad are both Greek, and they moved over here before I was born.

1 Did they speak Greek when you were growing up?

2 No, they were into becoming Americanized, and I don't know much Greek at all. My relatives who are still in Greece speak English pretty well, too.

1 Have you had a chance to visit them?

2 I sure have. In fact I went there just last summer. They live near the plains of Marathon.

1 Where the original marathon runner ran, right? Didn't he carry some important message and then fall over dead?

2 Yep, that's what happened to the poor guy, and all the marathons to this day are the same distance as he originally ran.

1 I'm hoping to run a marathon this spring. I've been training for it some. I definitely plan not to fall over dead.

2 That sounds like a very important part of the plan! Where is the race going to be?

1 There's a race in Smithtown, not far from here. It's not a very big one, but that's fine with me, because I'm pretty sure I won't win it anyway. But the course is along very beautiful countryside, and that's why I'm picking that one.

2 That's sounds like a good reason. So there are some scenic places in Smithtown, huh? I've never been there.

1 If you haven't you should think about going. There's a river with lots of rapids and waterfalls, and trails that go beside the river for a long distance. And there are hills and gorges, and some great views.

2 That does sound scenic. Do you like to hike, as well as to run?

1 I do. I got a book last year of 50 hikes in this region, and I've been gradually checking out the places. It's becoming sort of a hobby with me.

2 Sounds like a hobby that can keep you in good shape, huh?

1 If I can get to do it frequently enough, yes. How about you, what sorts of things do you do for fun these days?

2 Well, this gets me back to the subject of Greece, sort of. I've joined a folkdancing group. The great thing about it is that it's just for fun, and not a competition, and we try to make it really easy for people who are just starting up.

1 That sounds like a good way to stay in shape too! Is it just Greek dances?

2 No, it's types of dances from all over the world.

1 How do you learn them? Does somebody know all of them and teach someone else?

2 No, actually what we do is pretty unusual. We have a bunch of dvd's that are really good at teaching these dances. So for the first part of each session, we watch the dvd for a few minutes, and then we practice what we saw.

1 What an interesting way to do that! I'd be curious to try that sometime.

2 Why don't you come along sometime? We're always looking for new people.

1 That would be fun. What's your name? Maybe we can get in touch about it.

2 My name is ___ ___. How about you?

1 My name is ____ ____. I'm glad to have met you!

2 You too! I'll write down my phone number and email address, and maybe we can get in touch and talk some more about this.

1 That would be great. I will look forward to that.

2 Well, nice talking to you.

1 You too! See you later, I hope. Bye.

Conversation 5: Professor and student

A college student visits a professor during the professor's "office hours."

1 Hello, Professor ___. I thought I'd drop by and chat with you a bit, if you don't mind.

2 I don't mind at all; in fact, that's what my office hours are for. Thanks for stopping by.

1 I enjoyed hearing your lecture on the possibility of world government the other day. This is really an important topic, isn't it? It could mean the difference between survival and destruction of the human race, don't you think?

2 I sure do, and I'm glad that you appreciate that point.

1 I was reading about a person named Ludwig Zamenhof, and I was thinking that he would have enjoyed taking part in a discussion of this subject. Are you familiar with him?

2 Oh yes, the inventor of Esperanto, the language he envisioned as a universal second language for all humanity, so that language barriers could be no longer a barrier to peace and unity.

1 Right. I'm curious, how much do you think the fact that people speak all these different languages is a barrier to people's being able to have international law and international cooperation?

2 That's a really good question. I'm glad you've raised it. One could say a lot about it. Some people would argue that language barriers aren't very important any more, because such a large fraction of people in the world speaks English. But in my opinion, the fraction that does speak English is not nearly large enough for English to fulfill the function of a universal second language. And unlike Esperanto, English is a very difficult second language to learn. There are lots of countries with enough of an anti-American outlook that using English as a second language would rub them the wrong way.

1 Good point. And I guess there are some people who would say, we don't need a universal second language because there are good translators around, and because there are good computerized translation programs.

2 That's true that some people argue that way, but there are not very many good translators in the world, and the

computerized translation programs still don't work very well.

1 The computerized translation programs that I've seen on the Internet sure miss the mark in important ways, very often.

2 You've tried those, huh? Sometimes the results can be pretty comical. So to answer your question, I think that language barriers are a very important problem in promoting international understanding and cooperation. I think that with the Internet and phone technology, it is now possible for people to pick up the phone or sit at a computer and communicate with people all over the globe, on scientific matters, giving medical consultations, all sorts of cooperative ventures. The more people do that, the less they feel like going to war with each other. But the language problem is one big reason they don't do that.

1 So it sounds like you agree with Ludwig Zamenhof.

2 I do, and I also think that Zamenhof's solution, which was a second language made up so as to be very easy to learn, with no exceptions to rules, was a very good solution. The big problem is persuading people to go along with it.

1 There was a pretty big movement in Europe to learn Esperanto, before World War II, wasn't there?

2 Yes, and Hitler didn't like the idea of an international language, so he killed all the Esperantists he could get his hands on. Just one of the examples in which the spirit of nationalism opposes internationalism.

1 Well, thanks so much for chatting with me about this.

2 Thanks for coming by, and I'm glad you're interested in this topic. You might think about writing a term paper on it!

1 Great idea, I just might do that! Bye.

2 Bye.

Index

CPSIA information can be obtained
at www.ICGtesting.com
Printed in the USA
JSHW041409300622
27683JS00005B/45